THINKING SOCIOLINGUISTICALLY

THINKING SOCIOLINGUISTICALLY

HOW TO PLAN, CONDUCT, AND PRESENT YOUR RESEARCH PROJECT

PAUL MCPHERRON AND TRUDY SMOKE

BLOOMSBURY ACADEMIC
LONDON • NEW YORK • OXFORD • NEW DELHI • SYDNEY

BLOOMSBURY ACADEMIC
Bloomsbury Publishing Plc
50 Bedford Square, London, WC1B 3DP, UK
1385 Broadway, New York, NY 10018, USA
29 Earlsfort Terrace, Dublin 2, Ireland

BLOOMSBURY, BLOOMSBURY ACADEMIC and the Diana logo are trademarks of Bloomsbury Publishing Plc

First published 2019 by
RED GLOBE PRESS

Reprinted by Bloomsbury Academic

Copyright © Paul McPherron and Trudy Smoke, under exclusive license to Springer Nature Limited 2019

Paul McPherron and Trudy Smoke have asserted their rights under the Copyright, Designs and Patents Act, 1988, to be identified as the authors of this work.

For legal purposes the Acknowledgements on p. ix constitute an extension of this copyright page.

All rights reserved. No part of this publication may be reproduced or transmitted in any form or by any means, electronic or mechanical, including photocopying, recording, or any information storage or retrieval system, without prior permission in writing from the publishers.

Bloomsbury Publishing Plc does not have any control over, or responsibility for, any third-party websites referred to or in this book. All internet addresses given in this book were correct at the time of going to press. The author and publisher regret any inconvenience caused if addresses have changed or sites have ceased to exist, but can accept no responsibility for any such changes.

A catalogue record for this book is available from the British Library.

A catalog record for this book is available from the Library of Congress.

ISBN: PB: 978-1-1376-0597-9
ePDF: 978-1-1376-0598-6
ePub: 978-1-3503-0865-7

To find out more about our authors and books visit www.bloomsbury.com and sign up for our newsletters.

Contents

List of figures vi
List of tables vii
List of researcher to know boxes viii
Acknowledgements ix
Introduction x

Part I Thinking Sociolinguistically   01

1   What is sociolinguistics research?   03
2   Getting started with a sociolinguistic research project   22

Part II Data Collection Methods in Sociolinguistics   39

3   Survey data   41
4   Interviews   59
5   Participant observation   72
6   Linguistic landscape and computer-mediated data sources   90

Part III Data Analysis Methods in Sociolinguistics   107

7   Qualitative data analysis   109
8   Discourse analysis   124
9   Statistical analysis   145
10 Corpus data analysis   165

Part IV Putting It All Together and Finding Your Voice   183

11 Organizing your research paper   185
12 Sounding like a sociolinguist   207

Glossary   220

References   229

Index   240

List of figures

1.1	Sociolinguistic subtopics and connections to other fields	13
1.2	Role of data in sociolinguistics research	21
2.1	Cluster map of example research project *you guys*	26
6.1	Ruschmeyer's survey	103
6.2	Text message collected as part of Ruschmeyer's class project on silence and texting	103
7.1	Trajectory of English name usage from university to professional life	116
9.1	Content of powerlifters' pictures and videos	159
9.2	Content of bodybuilders' captions	159
10.1	Fake news frequencies in COCA	172
10.2	Example concordance of fake news in COCA	172
10.3	Collocates of fake news in COCA	174
10.4	Percentage of male and female uses of uptalk in Sukhnandan corpus	180
10.5	Frequency of uptalk use in the middle of a phrase	180
11.1	Example title page	188
11.2	Writing example 1: Valuable phrases for your introduction	193
11.3	Writing example 2: Valuable phrases for describing your methods	200
11.4	Diagram based on data and figure from Moore & Podesva (2009)	202
11.5	Writing example 3: Useful terms when writing your conclusion	205

List of tables

2.1	Common data sources in sociolinguistic research projects	35
3.1	Examples and evaluation of sampling strategies	47
3.2	Online survey data collection programs	53
7.1	Example research diary topics and questions	112
8.1	Transcription conventions	131
8.2	Key sociolinguistic terms and processes analyzed in DA research	137
8.3	Summary of Almiggabber's data and analysis	143
9.1	Summary of selected quantitative analysis of [r-l]	153
9.2	Ten most frequent bodybuilder hashtags	160
9.3	Ten most frequent powerlifter hashtags	160
9.4	Comparison of bodybuilders and powerlifters on LIWC dimensions	161
9.5	Choosing the right inferential statistical test for your hypothesis and data	164
10.1	Some existing English language corpora available for sociolinguistic research	169
10.2	Three corpus analysis software programs	170
11.1	Lawyer's use of tag questions in first 15 minutes of Jodi Arias trial	202

List of researcher to know boxes

William Labov	10
H. Samy Alim	18
Penelope Eckert	29
Janet Holmes	36
Sali Tagliamonte	48
Barbara Johnstone	62
John Rickford	69
Alexandra Jaffe	84
Elana Shohamy	101
Mary Bucholtz	120
James Paul Gee	125
Rosalyn Negrón	138
Kara Becker	162
Ruth Wodak	178

Acknowledgements

We would like to thank our students at Hunter College and beyond for shaping how we teach Sociolinguistics and bringing in so many thought-provoking examples and questions from their own lives. The writing and exercises in this book all began as classroom activities, discussions, lectures, and projects, and we thank our great students for allowing us to try out much of the book in our classes. In addition, the example student papers that our students have allowed us to share provide useful and meaningful examples of student projects. Thank you to Jessica Balgobin, Amna Khan, Shirley Weng, Jack Kenigsberg, Christy Ruschmeyer, Ally Rosen, Zayneb Almiggabber, April Polubiec, Ryan Sukhnandan, Yan Zeng, and Arianna Chinchilla.

The editors, assistants, and designers at Palgrave have all been remarkably supportive and helpful in producing this book. Thank you in particular to Helen Caunce for your close reading and comments on various drafts and, most importantly, for your flexibility and patience as we worked on those drafts. Thank you to Rosie Maher for your help in everything from the cover design to putting the production pieces together. Moreover, thank you to Paul Stevens, our first contact at Palgrave, for your help in shaping our original book proposal.

We owe a debt of gratitude to Alan Robbins for creating the figures in Chapters 1 and 2, and we thank Mark Davies for allowing us to use screenshots from the Corpus of Contemporary American English in Chapter 9.

Thank you also to a number of our colleagues at Hunter and around the world who have influenced our teaching and supported our work in many different ways. At Hunter, we would like to thank Angela Reyes, Sarah Chinn, Jeff Allred, Barbara Webb, Cristina Alfar, Dennis Paoli, Karen Greenberg, Kate Parry, Harriet Luria, and Deborah Seymour. Further afield, we are indebted to Vaidehi Ramanathan, Julie Menard-Warwick, Tammy Gales, Kyle McIntosh, Patrick Randolph, Linda Hirsch, Sarah Benesch, Len Fox, Harvey Nadler, and Naomi Silverman.

Finally, thank you to our families who have assisted us in the writing of this book with unwavering support (we think). In particular, Trudy thanks Alan Robbins and Paul thanks Jessica, Robbie, Felix, and Rocco – we literally could not have done it without you.

Introduction

Over the years of teaching linguistics, sociolinguistics, and English courses, students have occasionally asked us questions such as "When did you know you were a sociolinguist?" or "How did you become a sociolinguist?" These questions often make us pause and reflect on the fact that we are not sure how or when we chose our career and "became" applied linguists/sociolinguists or even how exactly we ended up in graduate school. Perhaps more importantly, as an introduction to this text, when did we start thinking like them? And why do we feel it is important for students to "think like sociolinguists?"

For Paul, he certainly recognized the differences in speech of classmates and friends in Decatur, Illinois, the Midwestern US city where he was born and attended grades K–12. Growing up, classmates almost all identified as English speakers, but every day he would hear the contrasts between chain-shifting vowels and accent features of Great Lakes English, the *pin/pen* vowel mergers and the lexicon associated with mid-Southern English dialects, and the habitual "be" and other verb conjugations common in the syntax of African American Vernacular English (AAVE). It was not until attending the University of Illinois in the late 1990s, however, that he realized the rich diversity of English speech styles and dialects around which he had grown up. Most importantly, he took a course in which the professor asked students to investigate the debates in Oakland, California, over the teaching of Ebonics, or Black English, by analyzing examples of previous attempts to use AAVE in the classroom in the United States, and to survey fellow college student teachers about their attitudes toward AAVE in the K–12 classroom (Labov, 1972a; Rickford, 1999). At the time, Paul viewed himself as a teacher learning about his students' backgrounds and experiences, but not as someone who could collect data and contribute to an academic discussion. After the project, he began to understand how collecting data and researching helped him work with his students both inside and outside the classroom.

Similar to Paul, Trudy did not know that she wanted to be a sociolinguist and applied linguist as a child, but she did know that she was fascinated with languages and accents, and she knew that languages and accents had power and could cause anger and shame. She remembers listening to her father struggling to pronounce the voiceless dental fricative ө or "th" in words like "theater" and "think." Despite his college degree, he felt shame that he could not pronounce every word perfectly. He spoke Polish and Russian at home and had not learned English until he was six years old, and even then he only spoke it in school. She had grown up knowing about prejudices toward non-English language speakers like her own father, but she never saw herself as a language researcher until she entered a TESOL (Teaching English to Speakers of Other Languages) master's degree program at New York University and studied applied linguistics, advanced English grammar, and linguistics itself. In her classes, she began teaching English as a second language/English-language learner (ESL/ELL) classes and conducting interviews with her students and recording their experiences acquiring a new language and new culture as adults. She quickly realized that, in order to be a good teacher, she also had to be a good sociolinguistic researcher and learn about the language and cultural backgrounds of her students.

Connecting our early discoveries and thoughts about language and society were questions around how language (or code) choices changed with different contexts and communicative functions and how much a person or a group's identity is tied to a language and a way of using language. Further, we each saw early on in our professional lives the important mediating role schools and other powerful institutions in society had on language learning and use. Having taught foreign and domestic students at universities around the world (the United States, China, and Romania) and at universities in urban environments in the United States (New York City and the Bay Area of California) as well as more rural areas (southern Illinois), we have found that our students are already wrestling with similar questions about language, identity, and culture as we did; in other words, our students are often already "thinking sociolinguistically." We start with these brief vignettes about our academic past as both an introduction to ourselves as authors and as examples of our own paths toward "thinking sociolinguistically." The purpose of the following book, then, is to guide students from initial questions and interests in language to the completion of sociolinguistic research projects that draw on established sociolinguistic research methods and offer significant findings in relation to current questions and topics in our field. Inevitably, doing these types of research projects has helped us and our students learn about sociolinguistics, and they have made us better teachers, students, and thinkers through the research process.

Why do sociolinguistic research projects?

Another question that invariably comes up in our classes is "Why should we, as undergraduates, do our own sociolinguistic research projects?" Our main answer to this question is because doing a research project, even a small pilot project, in a classroom can help students apply what they have learned in much more dynamic and meaningful ways than a traditional test or set of homework exercises. Specific to sociolinguistics, we feel that conducting a research project on language in society and related topics helps students learn about their own linguistic backgrounds and that of their communities. In addition, studying language and society pushes students toward a deeper understanding of a number of important political, policy, and education issues, and they will have more informed positions as experts who have conducted their own research on a sociolinguistic topic.

Educators have advocated for many years for more opportunities for undergraduates to take part in research activities. Kuh (2008), in his well-cited analysis of the National Survey of Student Engagement (NSSE), identified undergraduate research as one of 10 high-impact education practices in the United States. Similarly, colleges and universities around the world have come to view research experiences as central to student learning and the undergraduate experience. For example, many universities have created undergraduate research offices or initiatives such as the Office of Undergraduate Research and Creative Endeavors (URACE) at Florida State University. As Lopatto (2010) writes:

> The positive effects of an undergraduate research experience on student learning, attitude, and career choice have passed from anecdote to systematic data. Many educators, particularly in the sciences, have come to see the potential for authentic undergraduate research to be a high-impact educational practice for achieving excellence in liberal education. In the past decade, research on these student experiences has revealed the extensive array of professional and personal benefits. (para. 1)

Of course, a narrow focus on research opportunities in the natural sciences or STEM fields (science, technology, engineering, and mathematics) will limit the opportunities undergraduates have to participate in research, as well as their overall understanding of what counts as research, and we view this book, in part, as expanding more undergraduate research experiences in disciplines outside of the natural sciences and STEM fields.

Many undergraduate research experiences tend to take place outside of classroom learning experiences and involve work on a professor's research project and questions. When we talk with many of our colleagues and students about conducting research, the image often invoked is of a student assistant mixing chemicals in a laboratory and preparing specimens for analysis by the lead investigator. Instead, we hope that this book illustrates the value of making research experiences central to existing courses and teaching topics in all disciplines, but particularly in humanities and social science departments, where linguistics and sociolinguistic topics are typically taught.

Finally, Lopatto (2003) summarizes faculty surveys that identified the many benefits of undergraduate research activities: from awareness and access to literature in the field, to increasing independence and ability to plan and execute research studies, to producing and presenting original and significant results and conclusions in both oral and written communication. In this way, we feel that using research activities in our sociolinguistics classrooms as described in the following chapters helps our students develop as leaders and citizens able to analyze critically competing perspectives and communicate their ideas to both expert and general audiences. As Elrod, Kinzie, and Husic (2010) write:

> Expanding meaningful research experiences to more students is particularly relevant in the face of increasingly frequent conversations about the need for a citizenry that can engage in evidence-based reasoning to deal with this century's complex and global challenges—such as climate change, energy use, water resources, and world health—that involve multidisciplinary perspectives. All students should have a personal experience with the complexity and interrelatedness of the issues facing our global society in order to be competent consumers, communicators, decision makers, teachers, and professionals in this new global century. (para. 12)

With this desire to promote both the professional and personal development of our students, in this book we also draw on the key aspects of student research activities outlined by Elrod, Kinzie, and Husic (2010):

- Challenging students to confront novel ideas
- Engaging students in the collection and analysis of original data
- Emphasizing opportunities for applying research to real contexts or solving real problems
- Increasing the time students dedicate to the project
- Maximizing opportunities for students and faculty to interact and engage in substantive matters
- Being relevant and interesting to students, and influenced by their ideas to maximize engagement and learning
- Providing opportunities for students to receive frequent and meaningful feedback about their work
- Increasing students ownership of the project over time

- Providing an occasion for students to present their work in oral and written formats
- Allowing students to work in teams (para. 17).

In particular, we devote the final chapters of the book to description and activities for helping students write and present the findings of their research projects. We have found that in upper division undergraduate and master's courses, even good writers struggle with organizing, analyzing, and presenting their own work both in writing (primarily through research papers) and in speaking (primarily through poster presentations at the end of the semester).

Overview of the book

Drawing on recent trends in higher education that point toward the importance of introducing research experiences at the undergraduate level, our book is a practical guide for students to the key research methods and approaches in sociolinguistics. It can be used as part of a course in conjunction with a general introductory textbook, or it may be read independently by students interested in an introduction to sociolinguistic research methods. The book is not designed to offer an in-depth introduction to all aspects of the field of sociolinguistics, though we survey major parts of the field in Chapter 1. Also, many introductory textbooks in linguistics and sociolinguistics offer short research exercises or food-for-thought questions for students about their research interests, but in the following chapters we focus exclusively on guiding students through the process of planning and executing their own projects from beginning to end. In short, the goal of the book is to guide student explorations and applications of course material by helping students view themselves as sociolinguistic researchers in their own learning contexts.

The book's content is geared toward undergraduate and graduate students enrolled in courses on sociolinguistics, linguistics, education, or related topics, and practicing language teachers who are interested in learning more about sociolinguistic research and conducting their own research projects may also find the book useful. The book may also be a good starting point for graduate and undergraduate language and linguistics instructors who want to add a research aspect to one or more of their courses, or school administrators and education researchers who wish to apply sociolinguistic concepts and research methods in order to understand better their own teaching, learning, and research contexts.

Our approach in our courses and in the book is based on student-led explorations and applications of sociolinguistics course material through summaries of research studies coupled with practice activities, exercises, and discussion questions. In each chapter, we introduce key sociolinguistic researchers through "Researcher to Know" boxes, and chapter activities encourage readers to complete small and large-scale investigations into their own communities, leading eventually to a plan for students to complete their own larger sociolinguistic studies.

The book has twelve chapters divided into four main sections. In Part I: "Thinking Sociolinguistically," Chapter 1 offers a brief review of the major fields and research methods in sociolinguistics, and Chapter 2 offers suggestions, guidance, and examples about how students can start their own projects. Next, Part II: "Data Collection Methods in Sociolinguistics" contains four chapters surveying key methods for collecting data in response to sociolinguistic research questions. In Chapter 3, we focus on techniques related to collecting survey data, including strategies for sampling a targeted population and tips for designing reliable and valid survey items. In Chapter 4, we summarize aspects of conducting an effective interview, from finding participants to preparing interview questions, to effective listening and response tips. In Chapter 5, we describe the ethnographic technique of participant observation and how students can complete smaller observation studies in comparison with published accounts, but still address basic sociolinguistic questions about language and community from the existing literature. The final chapter in Part II, Chapter 6, compares the similarities and differences in two new sociolinguistic data sources, linguistic landscapes and computer-mediated data sources. Examples in Chapter 6 come from published reports and student work that reveal exciting new digital and online sources of data, as well as how students complete a sociolinguistic study by walking around their neighborhoods and systematically recording the language used in signs and other public spaces.

In Part III: "Data Analysis Methods in Sociolinguistics," we offer chapters that focus on data analysis techniques that allow researchers to respond to their research questions and draw conclusions based on their collected data. Chapter 7 offers an overview of qualitative data analysis and presents ways to organize, code, and interpret qualitative data, often leading to a thematic data analysis. In Chapter 8, we focus on one qualitative analysis method—in particular, discourse analysis—and we describe techniques for creating transcripts, coding spoken interactions, and analyzing a variety of discourse contexts. Next, Chapter 9 covers statistical and quantitative methods in sociolinguistic data analysis. We look at how sociolinguists use descriptive and inferential statistics to answer their research questions, and point to data analysis programs and software as well as further guides that sociolinguists use when taking a quantitative approach. Finally, in Chapter 10, we survey the relatively new use of corpus analysis in sociolinguistics research and summarize popular existing corpora used in research studies. We also offer tips on constructing and analyzing a new corpus of texts. In Parts II and III, we focus much of the discussion on examples from both published research studies in leading sociolinguistics journals as well as previous student projects from our classrooms. In this way, we present the diversity of research methods and questions explored in the field and illustrate how students can connect their research questions and projects to the wider field of sociolinguistics.

Finally, we feel a central part of helping students "think" sociolinguistically is helping them to read and write sociolinguistically, and in Part IV: "Putting It All Together and Finding Your Voice," we draw on many published and student examples presented earlier in the book to offer tips and examples about how to guide students through the writing conventions of sociolinguistics and academic discourse in general. In Chapter 11, we focus on the major sections of a research paper and offer models for language students to use in organizing their research papers. Then, in Chapter 12, we describe sentence-level style choices that students have when writing, as well as offer some final thoughts on thinking and sounding like a sociolinguist. We have found that many students struggle with how to present their findings in an academic voice, and in Chapters 11 and 12 we take a step-by-step approach to demystifying the common moves and language used in research writing and presenting through analysis and examples from published articles as well as student papers.

By writing this book, we hope to summarize and share the research activities that we have found so useful, as well as to provide a space for instructors and students to create their own projects and activities. Different from a traditional introduction to a field of study or research methods, our goal from the first chapter is to help readers "think like researchers," or, more importantly to our course goals, to "think sociolinguistically." The book comes out of our teaching an undergraduate sociolinguistic elective course for linguistics majors at our university, and the examples, published studies, and student papers we cite throughout this text can all be classified as sociolinguistic studies. At the same time, both co-authors come from sociolinguistics, applied linguistics, and TESOL backgrounds, and we feel that much of the book could be applied to doing student research projects in all three fields as well as other social science disciplines that study language and society, such as sociology, anthropology, and psychology.

Part I

Thinking Sociolinguistically

1 What is sociolinguistics research?

> **CHAPTER OVERVIEW**
>
> - Introduction
> - What Do Sociolinguists Research?
>   - Languages in Communities
>   - Language Variation
>   - Languages in Interaction
>   - Connections to Other Fields: Sociolinguistics, Education, and Social Justice
> - How Do Sociolinguists Research? Qualitative, Quantitative, and Mixed Methods
>   - The Quantitative Tradition
>   - The Qualitative Tradition
>   - Mixed Methods
> - Final Thoughts

Introduction

The field of sociolinguistics is broad, diverse, and touches on aspects of our daily lives. For example, Wardhaugh and Fuller (2015) offer the following definition of our field:

> Sociolinguistics is the study of our everyday lives—how language works in our casual conversations and the media we are exposed to, and the presence of societal norms, policies, and laws which address language. (p. 1)

Drawing on a similar description of sociolinguistics as an investigation of everyday interaction, Bell (2014) describes sociolinguists as "professional eavesdroppers—not on what people say, but on how they are saying it" (p. 1). He describes sociolinguistics in almost poetic terms: "It [sociolinguistics] is about language as social fact and as identity bearer; language as interaction, as communication, as a bridge between self and other; language as expresser; language as delight" (p. 1). Further, the *Journal of Sociolinguistics* describes the diversity and range of sociolinguistic topics in their mission statement about the types of research they publish:

> The Journal is hospitable to linguistic analyses ranging from the micro to the macro, from the quantitative study of phonological variables to discourse analysis of texts . . . Data in published articles represent a wide range of languages, regions and situations - from Arabic to Mongolian, from Sweden to Tokyo, from genetic counseling sessions to asylum interviews. (*Journal of Sociolinguistics*, 2018)

As a general definition of the field, it is clear sociolinguistics has the everyday use of language and its connection to norms, institutions, and identity in a wide variety of contexts at its heart. As we often say to our students on the first day of class, "Sociolinguistics is less about language itself and more about what we do with language."

We do not want to repeat here the in-depth summaries of the field of sociolinguistics found in other introductory texts, but we feel that it is important in this opening chapter of our book on doing research projects to "clear the ground" a bit and offer a summary of what sociolinguists study and how they study it. We then move on to connect how responses to those *what* and *how* questions can help guide student researchers as they get started working on their own research projects.

EXERCISE 1.1: Sociolinguistic topics in your own life and speech communities

We all participate as members of many speech communities and communities of practice that influence how we use language in a variety of contexts, from English name choices with a foreign English professor in China to the language we choose for praying or performing other religious ceremonies and acts. Consider the speech communities that you are a member of or that exist in your neighborhood, area, town, city, state, or nation, and discuss the following questions with a partner:

1. What do you consider your first language or languages?
2. What languages have you learned as a second or additional languages? Include when and where you have learned languages. Was their support (both institutionally and at home) for you to learn additional languages? Please describe.
3. Describe your abilities in the different languages you speak. Consider the four traditional channels of communication (speech, hearing, listening, and writing). Do you ever "code-switch," or move between different languages and dialects within a conversation? Describe when you code switch or why you do not do so.
4. Are there geographical or regional differences in the languages and dialects used in your area? Please describe.

5. What are some specific features that identify the regions, social groups, or ethnic/racial groups that may influence your language use? For example, *hella* marks speakers from northern California, as it is used as an adjective meaning "a lot of something" *(hella games left to play)* or an adverb that means "very" *(hella cool)*.
6. What aspects of your speech or the language used in communities in your area would you be interested in researching and learning more about?

What do sociolinguists research?

We start here with our summary of what sociolinguists study. As noted above, sociolinguists, in particular variationists, tend to research primarily how we might say something, and do not focus necessarily on the content of a conversation or particular linguistic utterance. In examining the "how" of language use, sociolinguists have at times started with a focus on what has been termed a speech community or a group of people who participate in "a set of shared norms" regarding language usage (Labov, 1972b, p. 120). In this way, not all speakers in a speech community will speak the same, but they all agree on the social meanings of particular pronunciation features or vocabulary usage. Milroy (1987) offers the following example:

> All New York speakers from the highest to lowest status are said to constitute a single speech community because, for example, they agree in viewing presence of post vocalic [r] as prestigious . . . Southern British English speakers cannot be said to belong to the same speech community as New Yorkers, since they do not attach the same social meanings to, for example [r]: on the contrary, the highest prestige accent in Southern England (RP) is non-rhotic. (p. 13).

Thus, one of the first answers to the question "What do sociolinguistics study?" is speech communities and the inherent variation within and between speech communities.

In addition, it is also important to include a discussion of how sociolinguists define language, dialect, and variety. For example, introductory sociolinguistics textbooks such as Wardhaugh and Fuller (2015) and Mesthrie, Swann, Deumert, and Leap (2009) offer introductory sections entitled "Language or Dialect?" and "A Language as a Social Construct," in which they note the ease in which language users typically can name the language or languages they speak (e.g., "I speak Korean"). Alternatively, sociolinguists and linguists focus on and point out differences in language definitions due to political, cultural, and historical considerations. Examples include changes in the status of Scandinavian languages after Norwegian independence as well as the new differentiation of Serbo-Croatian into three independent languages in what was formerly Yugoslavia: Serbian, Croatian, and Bosnian.

Taking a slightly different tack in defining language, Bell (2014) introduces the *what* of sociolinguistic research by defining the four aspects of language for sociolinguists: (1) language is social, meaning the context of where language is used is central to studying its use; (2) language is dialogue, meaning that even when someone is speaking to him- or herself, language use is always shaped by other interlocutors, both present and absent; (3) language is profusion, meaning that language is defined by variation and change; and (4) language is ideology, meaning that language is often not so much about content as about the social meanings and indexes that utterances represent (p. 4).

Finally, the section headings of two popular sociolinguistic readers, Coupland and Jaworski (2009) in *The New Sociolinguistics Reader* (NSR) and Meyerhoff and Schleef (2010) in *The Routledge Sociolinguistics Reader* (RSR), illustrate the ways sociolinguists define and divide the *what* of language study in the names of their subsections listed here:

- Language and Variation (NSR); Variation and Change (RSR)
- Language, Gender, and Sexuality (NSR); Gender (RSR)
- Style, Stylization, and Identity (NSR); Identities, Style, and Politeness (RSR)
- Language Attitudes, Ideologies, and Stances (NSR); Perceptions and Language Attitudes (RSR)
- Multilingualism, Code-Switching, and Diglossia (NSR); Multilingualism and Language Contact (RSR)
- Language, Culture, and Interaction (NSR); Social Class, Networks, and Communities of Practice (RSR).

Drawing on the above brief survey of how prominent publications, textbooks, and journals define sociolinguistics and what we study, we place the different subfields and research topics in sociolinguistics into three broad categories in order help novice researchers map the field of sociolinguistics, define their research interests, and become critical readers of sociolinguistic studies. The three categories we use are (1) languages in communities, (2) language variation; and (3) languages in interaction. The categories are by no means exclusive, with most studies falling into two or more areas of study, but we use them here when referring to different published studies and student work throughout the book. Exercises 1.1 and 1.2 offer further introductions to sociolinguistic topics and what sociolinguists study.

Languages in communities

We include in this area of studies in sociolinguistics the many and divergent studies that have taken macro, or "top-down," looks at languages and communities as a whole and attempted to document how languages operate in society and how languages and language use have shifted over time and from generation to generation. Influential in the 1950s and 1960s, when sociolinguistics was still a relatively young field, what we call languages in communities studies are illustrated by writings on diglossia by Ferguson (1959) and Fishman (1966); studies of language maintenance, shift, and death (Fishman, 1991, 2001) and ethnolinguistic vitality (Giles, Bourhis, & Taylor, 1977); studies of regional dialectology (Kurath & McDavid, 1960; Orton & Wright, 1974); and the many studies of pidgins, creoles, and new languages such as World Englishes (Mühlhausler, 1991; Kachru, 1986, 1992). These studies have primarily drawn on a functionalist or a functional-structuralist perspective by focusing on the community or society as a whole, mapping who uses a particular language or dialect, and analyzing how a part of society such as language contributes to maintaining the overall whole. For example, in studies of the shift and loss of particular languages, sociolinguists such as Joshua Fishman have investigated how the status and role of languages in society has changed over time. These and other studies in this area of sociolinguistics attempt to tie the languages spoken to the needs and histories of communities in contact.

By examining and comparing over time what languages have been used in particular settings and by whom, languages in communities researchers can define which languages are more prestigious and dominant (and therefore vigorous and well maintained) and which languages have served few functions in a society (and therefore show signs of going extinct, or "dying"). Functions can include institutionally supported functions such as education, religion, media, and law, but functions can also include the use of language among friends, family, and in other face-to-face or online communication, or in writing, literature, and creative work. Many students in sociolinguistics find studying language shift and maintenance relevant because they may have experience as a speaker of a "threatened" language or are a member of a community or family associated with that language. In addition, as discussed and illustrated in the next chapters, many students in sociolinguistics courses have completed projects examining the language shift or more broadly the sociolinguistic profile and use of languages among a particular linguistic or speech community, including the use of World Englishes and the creation and status of creoles and pidgins. These projects often draw on research into education policy (Alim & Smitherman, 2012; Rickford, 1999; Shin, 2012) and linguistic human rights (Phillipson, 1992, 2009; Skutnabb-Kangas, 2000).

Language variation

Coming after the initial studies of regional dialectology and the drawing of dialect and isogloss maps, variationist sociolinguistics, or what we are calling language variation studies, have been central to sociolinguistics, particularly in the United States, from the 1960s onward. The central figure in variationist sociolinguistics—at least the first "wave" of variationist research studies (Eckert, 2012)—has been William Labov. In his early studies of Martha's Vineyard (Labov, 1963) and New York City (Labov, 1966), Labov moved the focus of sociolinguistics from primarily looking at regional differences and macro studies of diglossia to analyzing the systematic variation within particular groups, what he termed "structured heterogeneity." For Labov, the community (or speech community) has typically always been conceptually and analytically prior to the individual, and the basic unit of analysis was the linguistic variable or language feature that distinguished members of different speech communities. In other words, the linguistic system that an individual uses is representative of the social groups of which he or she is a member. As Eckert (2012) describes, in this view of language, "speakers emerged as human tokens—bundles of demographic characteristics" (p. 88). For example, in his classic department store study, Labov illustrates how the use of postvocalic [r] functioned as a marker of upper middle-class speech and how the lower middle class tend to hypercorrect in more careful speech tasks (Labov, 1972b).

As described in more detail in the following chapters, these studies use survey, interview, and quantitative methods in examining preexisting categories of class, race, ethnicity, and gender. In addition to Labov's work on New York, Philadelphia, and New England speech, other important variationist work using these methods includes studies of social class in Norwich, England, and Glasgow, Scotland (Macaulay, 1977; Trudgill, 1974) and studies of multilingual speech communities such as Barbara Horvath's work on Australian English and changes in the Sydney dialect (Horvath, 1985).

Eckert (2012) describes these early variationist studies by Labov and others as focusing on the big picture of sound change and structured heterogeneity, but she and others argue that sociolinguistics should also examine language variation using ethnographic research methods and "participant-designed categories and configurations" instead of or in combination with the surveys and preexisting demographic categories associated with the first wave of variation studies (Eckert, n.d., para. 2). In this way, language variation studies such as Milroy (1987), Rickford (1986), and Eckert (1989) have revealed how the social agency and networks of particular groups of speakers affect the use of vernacular and standard dialects just as much or more than particular categories of interest to the researcher.

Further, recent work on language variation has focused on how speakers use linguistic variables to perform particular social identities. For example, Cutler (1999) examined how a white, upper-class, New York teenage boy uses African American Vernacular English (AAVE) to index toughness and an urban identity, and Zhang (2008) studied how young and cosmopolitan elites in Beijing avoid particular speech variables associated with a Beijing dialect of Mandarin Chinese. In this work, we can see how language variation studies may focus on the speech community as a whole or may analyze the style choices of individual speakers or small groups within a larger speech community. In other words, the *what* of sociolinguistics can consider questions such as "What are the linguistic variables associated with upper-class speech in Tokyo?" or questions more like "How do Japanese speakers use formal and informal linguistic variables to position themselves as rebellious or cosmopolitan in different contexts?"

Students new to sociolinguistics often find studies of language variation insightful and relevant to their daily lives, as variation and style choices are part of everyone's everyday experience of using language. In doing language variation projects, students often confirm that, despite claims to the contrary, English is not becoming more homogenous. Instead, regional, ethnic, and social differences in usage persist, but the student projects often point out that speakers will often consciously draw on language differences rather than be defined by them. At the same time, many variation projects require extensive data collection and advanced quantitative analysis that most students in introductory sociolinguistics courses do not have. For that reason, many instructors have organized classes around the completion of one research topic in which every student in the course collects data in relation to the same linguistic variable or language feature. For example, Kiesling (2004) collected data as a classroom project on the use and spread of the term "dude" among different speaker and addressee pairs, and Tagliamonte and Hudson (1999) and Tagliamonte and D'Arcy (2004, 2007) analyzed data collected by a series of undergraduate sociolinguistics students that track the usage across grammatical contexts, gender, and age of the quotative "be like." We use these class project studies as examples throughout the next chapters, but our students have typically completed projects individually or as students working with one partner.

> **RESEARCHER TO KNOW: William Labov**
>
> Professor of Linguistics at the University of Pennsylvania, where he is director of the Linguistics Laboratory, William Labov is considered the founder of variationist sociolinguistics. One of the most influential thinkers in the field, Professor Labov received his PhD from Columbia University in 1964, and his dissertation, published as *The Social Motivation of Sound Change*, became a model for doing variationist sociolinguistic research. His study involved an analysis of speech patterns, most particularly the shift and the social reasons for the shift in the pronunciation of the diphthongs /ai/ and /au/ in Martha's Vineyard, a seaside community off the coast of Massachusetts. Labov's study relied on questionnaires, readings, interviews, and observations in casual and more formal situations. He, in many ways, set the stage for the types of studies conducted by Kara Becker, Mary Bucholtz, Penelope Eckert, Scott Kiesling, Robert Podesva, Sali Tagliamonte, and many other sociolinguists we discuss in this book. His 1966 study of New York City speakers, published as *The Social Stratification of English in New York City*, was replicated by Kara Becker and is discussed in Chapter 4. His research on changes in rhoticity, or the pronunciation of /r/ in words like *floor* and *fourth*, has been replicated both by professional sociolinguistics as well as by students who conduct and analyze short interview studies as part of their research projects. Moreover, although in semiretirement, Labov continues to do research more than 50 years after his early studies. Labov's seminal work on language in regional America and on the Northern Cities Vowel Shift led to his 2005 book *Atlas of North American English*, an overview of pronunciation patterns of major regional dialects spoken in the United States and Canada. In addition to his many awards and honorary doctorates, he won the Guggenheim Humanities Award in Linguistics in 1970 and 1987.

Languages in interaction

A third category that we use for organizing the *what* of sociolinguists' study is what we call languages in interaction studies. Work that falls in this category is not as concerned with a broad, "top-down" view of languages and speech communities; instead, these studies share a broad interest in analyzing how participants use language to construct, maintain, interact, and shape local communities and identities, often by focusing on observations of speakers (or just one participant) in naturally occurring settings that have not been constructed by the researcher. In these studies, the roles of speakers and the linguistic variation or language choices of speakers are not decided before beginning to collect and analyze data. Instead, participant roles and their relationships to their communities are examined as negotiated and rearticulated practices that are shaped through interaction and participation in speech communities and in interaction with others. These studies tend to draw on qualitative, ethnographic, and "bottom-up" research methods in which the researcher is a participant observer in a local community. These studies are also often longitudinal and triangulated in that the researcher is involved in a community over a period of time and collects a variety of types of data, from observation notes to recorded dialogues, to interviews with participants. Or, as is the case with some discourse analysis and conversational analysis studies, the focus is less on a particular community or participant and more on a conversational style, language ideology, or innovative linguistic practice.

Some of the earlier work on languages in interaction investigated the notion of communicative competence—Dell Hymes's counter to Chomsky's notion of linguistic competence—that he defined as the grammatical, pragmatic, discourse, and strategic competence "that enables members of a community to conduct and interpret speech" (Hymes, 1972, p. 52). In this way, early studies in what has sometimes been called "interactional sociolinguistics" have investigated silence in Western Apache language and culture (Basso, 1970, 1990), dialect use in Norway (Blom & Gumperz, 1972), and German-Hungarian code-switching in eastern Austria (Gal, 1979). More recent studies of languages in interaction have investigated the linguistic resources or repertoires that New York City Latinos draw on in conversation to create a shared Latino identity (Negrón, 2014) and how speakers use family dogs to mediate interpersonal interaction by speaking "as, to, or about" them (Tannen, 2004). As this work starts from the belief that languages are not only grammatical judgments and lexicons but also flexible products of social interaction, many studies of language in interaction have direct connections for language learning and classrooms or draw on data collected in classrooms or educational settings. For example, Shirley Brice Heath's influential study of literacy practices in rural white and African American communities in South Carolina (Heath, 1983) or James Paul Gee's extensive work on situated learning and social discourses both in and out of schools (Gee, 2015, 2017).

In analyzing how languages are used in small-scale interactions, one key aspect that many studies share is a focus on how social meaning is assigned to certain linguistic forms and varieties. For example, in Taiwan, Liao (2008) illustrated how, in small group interactions before 2000, speaking Mandarin with a Taiwanese accent was understood within a local context as indexing a strong Taiwanese identity, whereas speaking standard Mandarin was assumed to correspond with a Mainlander identity (i.e., a person who supports close ties and eventual unification with mainland China). After the election of 2000, in which the pro-independence party in Taiwan came to power, features of different varieties of Mandarin were not just linguistic resources used in small-scale interactions between two or more Taiwanese speakers, but the relationships between linguistic forms and meanings became rationalized and intentional choices made by different political parties depending on whether one supported the reunification with China. According to Liao (2008), the Taiwanese and standard Mandarin accent features before 2000 were illustrative of what Silverstein (2003) would call *first-order indexicality*, or the basic differences in speech between two social groups, what variationists would term *social variation* or *indicators*. The accent features post-2000 illustrate more overt linguistic choices and what Silverstein (2003) would term *second-order indexicality*, or indexes between linguistic form and social meaning that have become noticed, appropriated, and intentionally used, that is, the way Taiwanese media and party propaganda use particular accent features to further status and political intentions.

Drawing on the study of social meaning and indexicalities, we can group many sociolinguistic studies that examine a wide variety of concepts in society, from code-switching (Myers-Scotton, 1993; Li & Milroy, 1995) to power and politics (Fairclough, 2001, 2006), to gender (Holmes, 1995, 2006; Tannen, 1994), to social justice (Piller, 2016), to language ideologies (Irvine & Gal, 2000). Further, a recent movement toward what has been termed a translingual approach to discourse and interaction has questioned whether languages exist at all outside of ideological and political belief structures (Canagarajah, 2013; Blommaert, 2005; Pennycook, 2006). Many students find doing work related to language in interaction and studies of beliefs and indexicalities very interesting because they can collect data from their own experiences and speech communities, and they can easily use interviews or participant observation approaches to collect the data.

Connections to other fields: sociolinguistics, education, and social justice

As we hope is clear from the brief summary of *what* sociolinguists study, topics in the field are far ranging and connect with many other fields and disciplines, and this interdisciplinary basis for sociolinguistic research has been very appealing to researchers since the beginnings of the field (Bright, 1966). Although perhaps there has never been a uniform agreement on goals or methods (Hazen, 2014), sociolinguists from William Labov onward have pointed out that sociolinguistics is not simply an "applied" version of more theoretical fields of study (Labov, 1972b). In other words, sociolinguists have stressed that sociolinguistics does not function as a "'service discipline' to fill out empirical detail in an effort to validate pre-existing generalisations" (Coupland, 2003, p. 465). Rather, in discussing ways sociolinguists have addressed theories and incorporated concepts from other fields, Coupland (2003) writes that sociolinguistics must keep its "own familiar priorities— being accountable to language data in social environments, pursuing issues of social value in language variation, and critiquing the linguistic and discursive bases of social inequality" (p. 466). As a way to summarize the connections to other fields and to organize the subfields as we have generally constructed them above, we find it useful to arrange the various fields and topics that comprise sociolinguistics into a chart that can visually show some of the fields' influences and connections (see Figure 1.1).

As should be clear from the diagram and our summary above, most sociolinguistic studies strive to offer "real-world" connections and address pressing needs in communities around the world. Examples such as Alim (2009), Baugh (2015), Piller (2016), Rickford (1999), and Skutnabb-Kangas (2000) are just a few that connect their data and research findings to questions of social justice and linguistic human rights. In class, our students are often drawn to studies that investigate social issues and tensions related to linguistic practices, and we draw on these papers and the above subtopics and connections to other fields when discussing example sociolinguistic studies throughout the book.

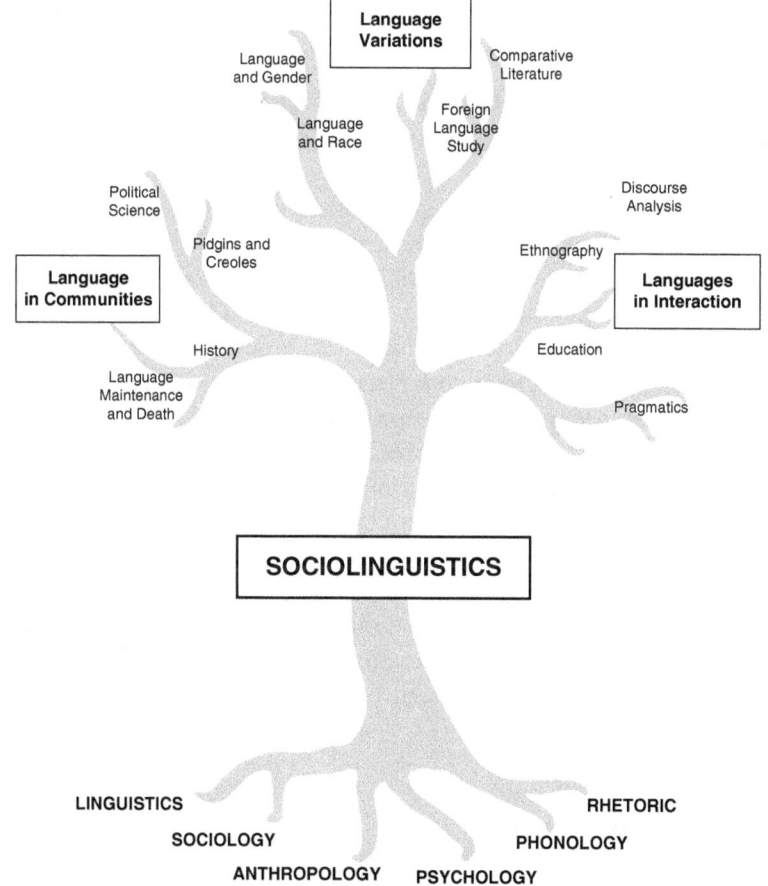

Figure 1.1 Sociolinguistic sub-topics and connections to other fields

> **EXERCISE 1.2: What types of sociolinguistic research are you interested in?**
>
> What topics in sociolinguistics are the most interesting for you to read about? In other words, what types of data, theories, and studies are you most interested in? Rate the topics listed here according to the following scale:
>
> ++ very interested   + interested   √ somewhat interested   x not interested
>
> ___ Regional language variation
> ___ English as an International Language (EIL)
> ___ Code-switching or code-meshing
> ___ Language ideologies
> ___ Multilingualism
> ___ Language and education
> ___ Sign languages
> ___ Social language variations
> ___ Language and gender
> ___ Language maintenance
> ___ Creoles and pidgins
> ___ Language shift over time
> ___ Language policy and planning
> ___ Conversation analysis
> ___ Language and power structures
> ___ Class-based language variation
>
> Other topics (include ranking):
>
> ___ _____   ___ _____
> ___ _____   ___ _____

How do sociolinguists research? Qualitative, quantitative, and mixed methods

Now that we have summarized the *what* of sociolinguistic research, next the chapter previews some basics of sociolinguistic data collection and analysis methods and connects them to specific tips for getting started with your own research project. As Coupland (2003) noted above, a core tenet of sociolinguistic research is working with "language data in social environments"; thus, sociolinguistic studies and research projects are typically empirical in that they are based on observed, measured, or collected data from actual speakers and in a specific context. They are not typically entirely theoretical or a review of a theoretical model or argument. Sociolinguistic studies also typically begin with specific research questions, a population or behavior to be studied, and a clear method and justification to collect data about the proposed research question and population. Part II of the book provides more explicit detail about particular research methods for collecting data, but as a further introduction to the field of sociolinguistics, this section provides a brief overview of the *how* of sociolinguistic research by detailing the two main empirical research traditions in sociolinguistics–quantitative and qualitative research.

The quantitative tradition

To start, the qualitative/quantitative distinction is not an absolute contrast; rather, these two methods are simply different starting points for recording and analyzing observations of our social world. In the quantitative tradition, aspects of the social world (for sociolinguistics this is typically linguistic variables and variation) are equated with numbers in order to statistically compare and analyze variation across individuals and groups. For quantitative researchers, a major problem with understanding the social world is the impossibility of collecting data and examining all participants related to a particular research question. Dörnyei (2007) writes that the quantitative solution to this problem is to collect a large enough sample of the feature or aspect under study "in which the idiosyncratic differences associated with the particular individuals are ironed out by the sample size and therefore the pooled results largely reflect the commonalities that exist in the data" (p. 27). In collecting enough data to provide a valid and reliable response to a researcher's questions, quantitative research is typically deductive in that the collected data tests a researcher's hypothesis, and the conclusions of the project then support or provide further questions for a more general theoretical framework. This process, also known as the "hypothetico-deductive approach" (Riazi, 2016, p. 85), is central to the scientific method and based on the belief that reality can be fixed and observed objectively without the subjective interpretation of the researcher.

Data collection in the quantitative tradition thus involves obtaining enough instances or examples of a particular aspect of language use—from the use of *be like* to introduce reported speech (Tagliamonte & D'Arcy, 2004) to the number of English-dominant bilingual Spanish and English speakers in Miami under the age of 10 (Porcel, 2006). Typical data collection methods include experiments and quasi-experiments in which researchers collect responses to linguistic input through a matched guise technique, an identification task, or a discrimination task (Drager, 2014). These types of experiments are particularly useful in identifying bias and how linguistic and social variables affect listener perception. Other data collection methods include surveys and questionnaires using a variety of question types, from closed questions to Likert-scale items to open-ended questions (Schleef, 2014).

Hazen (2014) notes that the distinction between quantitative and qualitative research is not as polemic or "quarrelsome" as in the past because sociolinguists, just as in other fields in the humanities and social sciences, have quantitative and qualitative research data collection methods available to use, and researchers understand that in quantitative research projects they must define aspects of the research qualitatively in order to assess numerically. Nunan (1992), however, writes that the distinction between quantitative and qualitative research methods has persisted among researchers because "the two approaches represent different ways of thinking about and understanding the world around us" (p. 10). As the characteristics of quantitative research listed above make clear, researchers approaching sociolinguistic problems and questions from these two traditions may not share the same understanding of "truth" or agree on whether universal laws and generalizability are possible. Nunan (1992) further outlines important questions to consider as one begins to read and research in a field such as sociolinguistics with its diverse and varied research traditions:

> In developing one's own philosophy on research, it is important to determine how the notion "truth" relates to research. What is truth? (Even more basically, do we accept that there is such a thing as "truth"?) What is evidence? Can we ever prove anything? What evidence would compel us to accept the truth of an assertion or proposition? These are questions which need to be borne in mind constantly as one reads and evaluates research. (p. 10)

We would add that these are important questions to bear in mind as you begin to develop your own research interests and assess how you would like to approach a particular sociolinguistic problem and research question. As the next sections point out, this does not mean adopting only a quantitative or qualitative approach, but making informed decisions about what data you will collect and how.

The qualitative tradition

Unlike the deductive hypothesis-testing approach that is typical of quantitative research, qualitative research is defined by the centrality of collecting data in a specific context before making any generalizations or comparisons to a larger population or theory. As Berg (2009) writes, qualitative researchers are interested in "how humans arrange themselves and their settings and how inhabitants of these settings make sense of their surroundings through symbols, rituals, social structures, social roles, and so forth" (p. 8). As alluded to in the above summary of studies of languages in interaction, qualitative researchers in sociolinguistics typically view language choices and linguistic variation as inherently social, changing, and indexed to different orders of meaning. From a qualitative research perspective, reality and meaning are inherently social, multiple, and subjective. These assumptions derive in part from the early work on qualitative research methods in sociology and anthropology that advocated a symbolic interactionist perspective as defined by Blumer (1986):

> Symbolic interactionism . . . does not regard meaning as emanating from the intrinsic makeup of the thing, nor does it see meaning as arising through psychological elements between people. The meaning of a thing for a person grows out of the ways in which other persons act toward the person with regard to the thing. Their actions operate to define the thing for the person; thus, symbolic interactionism sees meanings as social products formed through activities of people interacting. (p. 4)

In taking a symbolic interactionist position, Creswell (2013) points out that qualitative researchers place a value on positioning themselves and their own perspectives in their research—what other researchers have called a reflexive stance in which researchers openly point out their backgrounds and biases as part of their data analysis and findings.

The reflexive and subjective stance forefronted by qualitative researchers is related to the focus on emic perspectives and thick description in many qualitative studies. An emic perspective privileges the view from participants and not outside researchers and theories. For example, in studies such as Eckert (1989) and Moore and Podesva (2009), ethnographers want to know and document the terms used by different social groups at a high school to describe themselves. In this way, researchers should address questions that are important in the lives of their participants and build their understandings of language and culture based on the specific data examples and contexts in which they work. One of the main ways qualitative researchers document these emic perspectives is through thick description in which researchers collect multiple sources of information related to their research context and questions, from historical documents to participant interviews, to recorded interactions. Thick description typically takes time and involves a researcher living or working closely within a community for many months and years. Another way to illustrate thick description is that enough details from the participants and context must be collected that "readers can put themselves in the shoes of the described cases and see and feel the experiences" (Riazi, 2016, p. 323).

Typical data collection methods in the qualitative tradition focus include interviews and participant observation of place or group members in relation to the researcher's questions or topics of interest, for example, a high school in Michigan (Eckert, 1989), rural families in South Carolina (Heath, 1983), or businesses in Corsica (Jaffe, 1999). Researchers analyze their data for themes in order to describe how individuals and groups establish norms for behavior. Researchers also may collect other public or personal documents in order to analyze and describe the meaning of a particular experience or interaction. In addition, qualitative researchers often look for comparisons between one or more cases (e.g., an event such as a workplace meeting; or an individual case such as two students in the same school system) in order to provide a holistic and complete view on the research question, which can lead to more valid generalizable themes and cross-case comparisons. Of course, not all qualitative research is strictly focused on emic perspectives and building themes from the bottom up. Some studies we examine incorporate etic or top-down perspectives associated with quantitative approaches, but it is important to note as an introduction to qualitative research methods the distinction between deductive research that focuses on testing hypotheses and the more inductive approach, favored by many qualitative researchers, that involves building theories and answering research questions only after thoroughly analyzing collected data.

> **RESEARCHER TO KNOW: H. Samy Alim**
>
> Similar to many sociolinguists, H. Samy Alim comes from a linguistics background, but his research spans multiple subtopics and methods in sociolinguistics, from language and race studies to political science and educational policy studies. Alim is a professor in educational linguistics at Stanford University and holds appointments in anthropology and linguistics. In his research, Alim pairs linguistic analysis with ethnographic studies of youth and education. For example in his co-authored book with Geneva Smitherman (2012), *Articulate While Black*, Alim and Smitherman closely analyze the speaking styles of former US president Barack Obama, in particular his use of AAVE and his ability to code-switch when speaking to different communities and even in the same speech. The authors connect an analysis of Obama's speech styles to a discussion of language policy and pedagogical activities. In particular, our students are often impressed by Alim's own use of AAVE in writing this book and in other work. In addition to advocating for African American culture and language, Alim's own academic work opens up new forms for communicating academic knowledge. As Alim writes in a chapter from his 2009 co-edited book on global hip-hop cultures, entitled *Global Linguistic Flows: Hip Hop Cultures, Youth Identities, and the Politics of Language*, "In order to keep it real with our students, we need to recognize that the full body of available research on language, its structure, its use, and its role in constructing identities and mediating intergroup relations, is not produced solely for the consumption of scholars. Rather, this knowledge can be used to develop pedagogies that create high levels of metalinguistic awareness through reflexive ethnographic and sociolinguistic analyses of speech" (2009, p. 227).

Mixed methods

From the above survey, it is clear that sociolinguists have a variety of approaches to draw on when completing research studies, and current trends in research methods value drawing on multiple approaches and data collection methods. As Miles and Huberman (1994) note:

> Quantitative and qualitative inquiry can support and inform each other. Narratives and variable-driven analyses need to interpenetrate and inform each other. Realists, idealists, and critical theorists can do better by incorporating other ideas than by remaining pure. Think of it as hybrid vigour. (p. 310)

Further, Dörnyei (2007) notes that in applied linguistics and sociolinguistics, mixed-methods perspectives can combine micro- and macro-analyses and offer the types of data triangulation researchers seek. Next, we summarize the three general approaches to mixed-methods data collection presented in Dörnyei (2007).

1. *Quantitative → Qualitative:* In this format, a survey or quantitative measurement or task is analyzed before interviews, observations, or other qualitative methods of data collection are conducted. Researchers may vary this method to emphasize the interviews or qualitative data collection by using the survey/quantitative data as pilot data that can be used to inform interview questions or thematic coding of data. Or researchers can use the qualitative data only for follow-up confirmation of key findings from the quantitative analysis.

2. *Qualitative → Quantitative:* In the reverse of the above format, researchers can use qualitative data as the basis for an experiment, survey, or other quantitative research study. Or researchers use a follow-up survey that can confirm key findings and themes from the qualitative data collection.

3. *Quantitative + Qualitative:* Instead of a sequential design, many studies benefit from a "concurrent design" in which two or more data collection methods are used at the same time, and neither type of data influences the collection of the other. Results from all data collection methods are analyzed and reported on together.

As an example of the power of mixed-methods research designs, Paul McPherron (one of the co-authors of this text) has worked on a mixed-methods project examining English learning in Chinese university classrooms. In one part of the study regarding the use of English among university graduates in China in their professional lives, McPherron first sent out an online survey to over 100 participants in order to analyze general themes in the professional use of English in Chinese workplaces, including what skills were most often used (writing, reading, speaking, and listening), what tasks were completed in what languages (office meetings, email, etc.), and what languages were used during informal office conversations, including whether English names used at university were used, changed, or discarded. After collecting and analyzing the survey results, McPherron was able to conduct interviews and workplace observations that focused on key themes and questions that came out of the initial survey (see McPherron, 2016, for a write-up of this research study).

In addition to relying on mixed methods in examining English teaching in Chinese universities, McPherron's project with students and teachers at one university in southern China over a 10-year span from 2004 to 2014, as detailed in McPherron (2017), is an example of a longitudinal research study, another popular but complicated research model that sociolinguists can draw on for addressing their research questions. Menard (2002) defines longitudinal research as data collected at two or more times and drawn from the same or comparable participants. This is in contrast to synchronic or cross-sectional research that looks at a research question or phenomenon at one particular point in time. Students in semester-long sociolinguistic or applied linguistic courses typically only complete cross-sectional research studies because of the limits of time, but in the following chapters we discuss reasons for completing longitudinal studies, as well as offer examples of key longitudinal studies that draw on quantitative, qualitative, and mixed methods in their research design. Use Exercise 1.3 to further think about the difference in research methods in sociolinguistics.

> **EXERCISE 1.3: Comparing qualitative and quantitative research methods**
>
> Compare the quantitative and qualitative methods and analysis described above and in other sociolinguistic studies you have read. What are some strengths and weaknesses of each? Which do you prefer to read? Which type of research would you prefer to conduct?

Final thoughts

As should be clear from the discussion above—and is further illustrated throughout the following chapters—sociolinguistics is very much a data-driven field in which researchers use the data they have collected to make inferences and draw conclusions about their research questions and topics. There are certainly published papers and books that are more theoretical and offer commentary on language and language-related issues, but overall, published work in sociolinguistics—be it qualitative, quantitative, or mixed-methods—involves collecting, analyzing, and reporting on data that were collected by the researcher. As we discuss throughout the next chapters, researchers must make many decisions throughout the research process to ensure the reliability and validity of their data collection and analysis methods, and then they must make choices in how to write, discuss, and present their conclusions based on their data. Regardless of what type of project a student completes, however, data are as central to the research process as sociolinguistics, as illustrated in Figure 1.2.

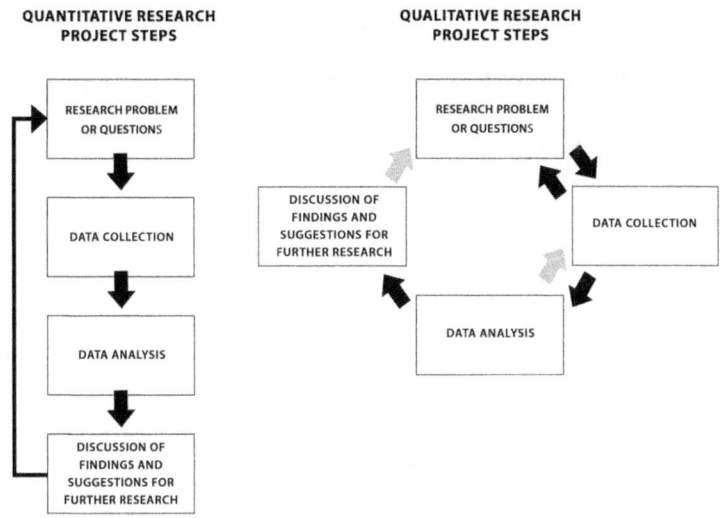

FIGURE 1.2   ROLE OF DATA IN SOCIOLINGUISTICS RESEARCH

As illustrated by Figure 1.2, researchers must make many decisions throughout the research process—from defining their research question to deciding where and how to collect data, to choosing the appropriate methods for analysis of their data. As we illustrate and discuss throughout the next chapters, the process is in many way iterative, with data collection often reshaping research questions in qualitative studies and findings, leading to new questions in both qualitative and quantitative studies. Student research projects completed as part of coursework will certainly not be as extensive or include as many data and analyses as the example studies described in this chapter and the rest of the book, but the thought processes and decisions students must make in order to complete even a small or pilot project are similar to those of a larger study. In addition, student projects can also connect to patterns, findings, and bigger questions found in published research in sociolinguistics. These similarities and connections to the larger field of sociolinguistics are why doing these student research projects is so valuable and exciting to our students.

2 Getting started with a sociolinguistic research project

> **CHAPTER OVERVIEW**
>
> - What to Do First: Getting Started with a Sociolinguistic Research Project
>   - Defining Your Topic: The Research Problem and Context
>   - Locating Previous Research
>   - Formulating Your Research Question
> - What Counts as Data and How to Collect Data
> - Final Thoughts: Research Is Messy

What to do first: getting started with a sociolinguistic research project

Few researchers start a research project thinking that they want to do it according to any one category or subtopic of sociolinguistics. More commonly, researchers start by considering a problem (e.g., a lack of knowledge about a particular linguistic practice) or a context (e.g., a group of speakers that exhibit some unique or interesting linguistic practice and shared style). They then think about what exact question they want to answer and what data they need to collect in order to address their research question. Researchers also consider their own orientations and biases in constructing the research study.

As researchers begin to put together the key aspects of their research topic, they will find that their research interest aligns with one or more of the three categories of research, and this can then be a basis for exploring the previous studies and coming up with more specific research questions and data collection methods. For example, if a researcher is interested more in a macro, or top-down, perspective on a particular linguistic practice or language, the research study may fit more with a languages-in-communities research perspective and draw on policy documents, demographic data, and other documents that illustrate the history and use of a particular language in a particular community. If the researcher is interested more in how individual and group language practices are representative of the social groups that people belong to, and the ways language reflects class, gender, and racial differences, he or she may adopt a language-variation research perspective and conduct a variationist sociolinguistic study. Finally, sociolinguistic researchers who start off with questions that look at language as it is used, whether by groups or individuals, as a means of indexing identity may adopt a languages-in-interaction research perspective that analyzes how speakers use language to construct, maintain, interact, and shape local communities and identities. Regardless of which orientation your research project eventually falls under, we see the following three steps as essential in getting started with your research project: (1) defining your topic, (2) locating previous research, and (3) formulating your research question(s).

Defining your topic: the research problem and context

The first step in doing research is to decide on a problem: something that interests you, about which you can gather data. Creswell (2013) writes that the research problem is not necessarily a "problem" per se, but rather the "need for the study" or the "rationale for the need for the study" (p. 130). Your research problem can come from everyday life experiences. In fact, students sometimes take sociolinguistics because they have questions about language, such as these:

- Where do people pronounce the words *talk* like *tawk*, *far* like *fah*, *water* like *warter*, or *dancing* like *dancin*?
- Why do people pronounce *ask* as *aks* and are censured for it?
- Why do court officials need to be told not to use *honey* to refer to women attorneys?
- Why are people who speak in certain dialects or switch from one language to another criticized instead of admired for their language ability?

You probably have had your own experiences with the ways people use language to judge and evaluate individuals, and these can become the basis for your research question. For example, students have told us about applying for jobs in expensive stores or high-end offices where they were given passages to read to make sure their speech patterns matched a "higher register" of speaking or to ensure that they had the "correct" accent. A student in our class told the other students that she lost her job as a receptionist in a doctor's office when she mistakenly said "had went" instead of "had gone."

Even though the student never made the same mistake again, she did wonder why some people are harshly judged by their use of language and some are not. In other words, why does language hold so much power? Thinking and reading about these kinds of issues may give you a sense of what you want to research, and as you will learn through completing a research study, doing research is a process, and it usually starts with a question or a problem.

As an introduction to this discussion, consider this short narrative about how the co-author Paul McPherron defined and began to research a "problem" in his classrooms when teaching in China. On his first day at a university in southern China, McPherron had a very interesting but also confusing discussion with students in each of his advanced English classes about their use and choice of names in his class. For example, he began the class by attempting to pronounce the student names from the roster he was given which only contained the students' names as Chinese characters (*han zi*). He wanted to write in the *pin yin* spellings (roman script used to write Chinese characters) for each student and begin learning their names. At first students entertained McPherron by helping him pronounce and spell their names, but many students began telling him that they wanted to use their English names, such as John or Joe or Susan. McPherron was hesitant to use these names as he felt his students were only picking them to appease the *lao wei* ("foreign") teacher, but he also wanted to call the students what they wanted to be called. Then, some students asked to be called by what Paul considered to be novel or new names he had never heard before, such as Moon or Blueman or Ice. By the time a student asked McPherron to call him "Sayyousayme" after the Lionel Richie song with the same name, he decided that more was going on in the classroom than simply students aligning their English use to the expectations of the foreign teacher, but he did wonder if the students were somehow laughing at him or English norms for name choice and uses.

From these initial experiences and discussions with his students, McPherron first looked to find literature and research studies that may have addressed the choice of English names among Chinese or foreign English language students. Aside from a few studies or side discussions of the choice of English names among immigrant students in the United Kingdom and the United States (Edwards, 2006), McPherron only found general interest newspaper articles on the English names of students studying English as a foreign language (Langfitt, 2015). From this existing literature in both academic and general interest sources, McPherron developed a research project that investigated how his students chose their English names, why they often chose such creative names, and how their name choices both indexed and resisted naming conventions in English speaking cultures. He went on to look at how students used their names in the university English classroom (McPherron, 2009) and in their professional lives after graduating (McPherron, 2016). Unlike previous discussion in the literature on English name choices, McPherron did not find examples of ignorance or resistance to naming conventions by his students. Instead, he found students employing creative processes of choosing and using English names inside and outside English classrooms in order to display unique personalities and differentiate themselves from other students and coworkers. The names also created spaces in which students could move between multiple language standards and identities and have fun in a new language. These findings began with the initial discussions between McPherron and his students and led to his search for previous literature on the topic before moving on to specific research questions and data collection.

Often the original problem or topic is very broad such as the basic questions: "Why do my students keep picking such creative English names?" and "Should I do anything about these nontraditional names?" Over the years, students in our courses have begun with a variety of general problems or topic questions, such as these:

- How does gender affect language production?
- How has slang changed among teenagers, and what are the most recent popular terms and phrases by university students?
- Do teachers prefer a particular dialect to another?
- How do people's language patterns change over the course of their lifetimes?
- How and when do people who speak more than one language or dialect use their languages or dialects?
- Why is one person's accent considered charming and another's disdained?
- Should someone need to use the "standard" variety of a language to be considered educated or employable?
- What are the differences between a person's online writing and in-person speech?

Although all of these are areas of study in sociolinguistics, they are also big questions and topics, and your professors are likely to tell you to narrow down your proposal into something more focused and doable over the period of a semester.

How do you narrow down your problem in your proposal? The first step is to ask yourself what it is that you really want to know. Begin by breaking down your general question into a list of smaller related issues.

There are a few good strategies for doing this. One is to brainstorm with a classmate. Another is to create a cluster map with your big research question in the center and some smaller issues relating to it in circles around the central point. With both strategies, you are trying to refine the general question into more focused and specific problems that you can research.

In Figure 2.1, we illustrate this process. Let's say you are interested in the big issue of changes in terms of address. After listing several different expressions or words you have heard, you start to narrow down to one. Perhaps you have noticed that your friends and people in your school use *you guys* to refer both to mixed sex, single sex, and even all-female groups. In doing this, you have narrowed your research problem to the use of one particular usage and something that you should be able to research in one term. Next is to think about where you can find the data you need to collect in order to do your analysis.

You will often need to write out your research topic for approval by your teacher. For example, examine the following topic proposal written by the same student for her project examining *you guys*:

> For my research paper, I propose to investigate the use of "you guys" as a second person plural by college-age students. My participants will be male and female

FIGURE 2.1 CLUSTER MAP OF EXAMPLE RESEARCH PROJECT "YOU GUYS"

students in my school and neighborhood. I will listen to individuals in my neighborhood and in my school for one week and notice when the phrase is used and by whom it is used. I will also conduct an anonymous survey where participants need to enter gender and age and answer 5 questions about their use of "you guys." My hypothesis is that both males and females use "you guys" when speaking to more than one person regardless of the sex of the members of the group. I will look at Scott Kiesling's "Dude" to help me develop my method and survey questions.

The description above includes the topic of research, the methodology to be used to collect data, the hypothesis, and an example of prior research that will inform the study. This proposal seems to fit best in language variation, a category where we may use observational data and surveys to get a better understanding of the ways in which a particular linguistic form works to perform one's social identity.

Locating previous research

In the examples above, the researchers began with a question about language use or about a particular context that they wanted to know more about. In addition to narrowing down the topic into something that can be researched, both McPherron and our student searched for previous literature on their topic in order to understand what has already been studied and reported. This process of locating and reading previous research on your topic is essential when beginning a project as well as when you eventually write and present your research findings. Many students, however, do not know where to start in order to search for previous studies, and the following section offers some guidelines for surveying the previous literature on your topic.

The first place you will likely look for previous studies is through an internet search of scholarly databases. Of course, you can also start by putting your topic or related search words into a general internet search engine, and you may find a variety of articles and information from both academic and general interest sources. Examining how a wider audience addresses your topic may be important at some point in developing your research, but we suggest starting early with searches of academic databases, where you can search peer-reviewed, and in particular blind-refereed, journals and books that have been organized around particular topic areas. A university librarian can help with accessing databases available through your local library. Here is a partial list of commonly used databases in sociolinguistics:

- Linguistics and Language Behavior Abstracts (LLBA)
- Modern Language Association (MLA)

- Education Resources Information Center (ERIC)
- JSTOR (journal storage)
- Google Scholar.

When searching in these databases, it helps to take time to choose your search words carefully in order to ensure you find articles on your topic. It may help to consult with a librarian to ensure that you have organized your keywords in the best way for the particular database and used all possible variations of a keyword. In addition, most databases will allow you to use a truncation symbol such as the asterisk (*) in order pick up variations on a word. For example, using the asterisk at the end of *speech** would pick up variations such as *speak* or *spoke*, as well as *speech*. We also recommend using the keywords listed for articles you have already read as search words in databases. Keywords are terms chosen in order to group the article with articles on similar topics.

In addition to general searches of databases, you can use the bibliography or references sections from articles and books you have already read on your topic as a way to find more sources. Or you may want to find all of the work done by a particular author, as researchers often write and present on a particular topic more than once, and an author's previous work may relate to your topic as well as lead you to related literature as cited in earlier work. We also recommend simply reading through recent and archived volumes of influential journals in sociolinguistics and related fields in order to understand topics that have been addressed, the methods used to collect data in relation to the research question, and the general findings and consensus on key issues in sociolinguistics. Even if the articles you read do not address your topic of interest specifically, you may learn about an important data collection or analysis method that you will use and cite in your final project, and more generally, it is important to stay abreast of current work in the field. Here is a partial list of well-known journals in sociolinguistics that are good places to start a search:

- *Journal of Sociolinguistics*
- *Language and Society*
- *Applied Linguistics*
- *Journal of Language, Identity, and Education*
- *American Speech*
- *Language Variation and Change.*

In summary, your investigation into previous research on a topic for your class project should provide you with a better understanding of where your study can fit into the existing literature and what gaps or unanswered questions your study could address (see Exercise 2.2). The notion of "addressing a gap" in previous literature or, at minimum, following up on previous work through your new collection of data will be an important way for you to frame your study when the time comes to write and present your results.

> **RESEARCHER TO KNOW: Penelope Eckert**
>
> Penny Eckert is an influential sociolinguist whose work spans the multiple "waves" of linguistic variation research. She began her career in sociolinguistics when she completed her PhD at Columbia University under the direction of William Labov. She is perhaps most famous for drawing on ethnographic research techniques when studying the language variation of teenage groups at a Detroit area high school, published in various papers and in the 1989 book *Jocks and Burnouts: Social Identity in the High School*. As illustrated throughout our book chapters, she is also known for her work on language and gender, her work drawing on a communities-of-practice (COP) framework, and her belief that language variation is best examined as part of a speaker's identity and stylistic choices. In this way, she theorizes the indexical relationship between language choices and identity. For example, in her 2012 article "Three Waves of Variation Study: The Emergence of Meaning in the Study of Sociolinguistic Variation," she writes, "It has become clear that patterns of variation do not simply unfold from the speaker's structural position in a system of production, but are part of the active—stylistic—production of social differentiation" (p. 98).

Formulating your research question

After defining the topic or problem to be studied and looking into previous studies of the topic, most researchers and research textbooks note that the next step in a research project is to write clear, researchable questions that will guide the research design and collection of data. In quantitative or variationist research, this has typically involved defining the linguistic variable or pattern that is to be studied and hypothesizing about the role of social factors that may influence the language variation pattern under examination. Or the question may be directly testing a particular concept or hypothesis that others have already investigated. For example, Labov's early studies of NYC speech focused on if, when, and where r-sounds were produced in casual to formal speaking contexts or on the patterns of vowels in different speech communities.

As illustrated in Figure 1.2 in Chapter 1, the initial statement of a research question in quantitative research studies tends to remain fixed or at least continue to drive the research design and data collection. Alternatively, qualitative research studies can be more exploratory and driven by the context and data collected. In this way, researchers may write and revise their research questions as patterns in their data emerge, and the focus of the study may shift based on their analysis. Despite this, we still recommend student researchers who are collecting qualitative data to generate one or more research questions at the beginning of a project even if these questions change over the course of a project.

In writing research questions, Dörnyei (2007) writes what may seem obvious at first glance: "In general, good research questions need to address interesting issues" (p. 73). Of course, we may think all of our interests and questions are "interesting," but what Dörnyei (2007) and others who write about research design are pointing out is that in deciding what to research, we need to be able to explain *why* this topic is worth exploring and have a concise response to the inevitable friend, relative, or coworker who asks, "So what?" Part of this response can be based on performing a comprehensive search and reading of the existing literature, as McPherron did before starting his project on English names. This is why in all of our classes we require a bibliography of previous research as part of the initial research process, and we recommend that in formulating your research question, you also construct a bibliography as detailed as the one in Exercise 2.1.

In addition to writing "interesting" research questions, you should also try to move from the broad topic that you may have defined when stating the problem to more refined and targeted questions that your specific data will respond to. It may help to think about the larger question and context that your study may contribute to, and then write subordinate questions that your particular study will address. For example, to return to McPherron's study of English names, he had initially identified a larger research question that addressed all English language teaching at the university where he taught in China, which he named China Southern University:

What are the responses of English language learners to teaching reforms and internationalization efforts at China Southern University?

Based on this larger question but wanting to investigate the particulars of the English names in his courses, he wrote the following two research questions for his 2009 study of English names in the classroom:

What English names do students choose? How do they pick the names? And why do they tend to pick original and creative names?

What do student name choices reveal about student investment, resistance, and compliance with English culture and pedagogical norms? How do foreign and local teachers influence and react to student name choices?

Both of these questions were based on findings and analyses in previous studies on English names, and they each could be answered through the interviews and journals that McPherron planned to collect.

In addition to ensuring that the research questions are narrow, some other considerations to keep in mind as you write your research questions are these:

- Can you define all of the concepts?
- What would constitute evidence to answer your questions?
    - Interviews—of whom and on what?
    - Observations—and of what specifically?
- Do you have access to the kinds of evidence you need?
- What are the assumptions underlying the question?

Finally, as you generate your research questions, it may be useful to consider the changes in sociolinguistic research and research questions over the past 40 years. As summarized in Hazen (2014), technology and data collection methods have changed the types of data we can collect as well as the questions we can answer. Perhaps just as important, there has been a noticeable shift in our understandings and beliefs about identity and language that is reflected in sociolinguistic research questions, as revealed in the following examples from Hazen (2014):

1970 research question: How do women speak differently from men?

2010 research question: How does this speaker in this local context construct gender through language? (p. 17)

Thus, as you write your research questions and begin to outline your research design, it may be useful to consider not only what has been written and published about your potential topic but also how it has been studied and the underlying assumptions in how you are asking your questions.

> **EXERCISE 2.1: Topic selection, locating previous research, and initial research questions**
>
> Respond to the following questions in as much detail as needed to explain a proposed research topic and research questions.
>
> 1. Describe the speech community(s), social group(s), person, context, domain, activity, policy, region, and so on that you are interested in studying. Briefly explain why you are interested in this group/setting/interaction/language practice.
> 2. What are some specific language features or topics (anything from sound variation to pragmatics, to language shift/maintenance, to code-switching, to educational policy, etc.) that you are interested in looking into?
> 3. Briefly brainstorm some sources of data that you may use and how you will obtain the data.
> 4. Find and list at least 10 articles, books, or book chapters related to your topic. Provide each source's full academic citation, and write at least a three-sentence summary of each source that includes a line about how you expect the piece to relate to your own research topic (e.g., "I plan to use the same survey methods and adapt the questions to address my research topic").
> 5. In one or two questions, write down what you hope to discover by doing this project. Write this down as research questions. For example: How do Chinese international students decide whether to use their Chinese first or last name or an English name in classes or with non-Chinese speaking colleagues? If they use an English name, how did they choose their name?
> 6. Briefly describe any potential problems or difficulties you envision you may have in collecting, analyzing, and/or writing up the data for your project.

What counts as data and how to collect data

Once you have clearly outlined your research topic and narrowed your study to specific questions that you can investigate within the confines of your class schedule, you will need to decide what types of data you plan to collect, and create a research design or plan for collecting and analyzing the data. As we discussed above, you may want to choose a qualitative, quantitative, or mixed-methods design based on your research questions and ability to collect various types of data. In a term or short class, our students typically create a type of mixed-methods design that integrates interviews and observations with surveys or focused questionnaires related to the research topic. In Table 2.1, we summarize the main sources of data used in sociolinguistic research and used by our students. In the table, we include both quantitative and qualitative data and a short description of how the data are typically collected by our students.

Data source	Description	How collected	Example studies	Research fields associated with this data source
Interviews	Can involve one-on-one or group settings in which a researcher asks for responses to a set of questions or passages	Generally recorded in audio or video form; may strictly involve preset questions (a more directive interview typical of language variation studies) or may allow for different follow-up questions based on responses (a more nondirective interview typical of case study research)	Alim (2009); Menard-Warwick (2005, 2008); Chand (2011); Labov (1972a, 1972b, 2005); Pope, Meyerhoff & Ladd (2007)	Language variation; languages in interaction; linguistic anthropology; contact linguistics; language and identity
Surveys	A method of collecting written and spoken information from a large number of people; typically focused on a particular topic or related topics such as attitudes about linguistic variables	Can be conducted outside of class, by email, on the phone, or as a method of self-reporting; may involve asking a number of people to complete an activity (e.g., coding a map) or offer responses to a short video or audio recording	Preston (1996, 1998); Rubin (1992); Yuasa (2010)	Language variation; language attitudes; language ideologies; language policy and planning; dialectology; contact linguistics
Questionnaires	A type of survey that contains a written list of questions that typically contain fixed or limited response options and can be analyzed using statistical data analysis procedures	Often given to larger groups of individuals to build a data set for analysis	Clark & Schleef (2010); Fuller (2003, 2005)	Language variation; language attitudes; language ideologies; language and gender; dialectology; contact linguistics

Method	Description	Details	References	Related areas
Observations	This method involves a long commitment and repeated participation in a group's activities (e.g., meetings and activities of an Asian American student group) or observation of a particular social context (e.g., a Polish bakery)	Sometimes years long and involve an enormous amount of data collection; usually a combination of general observation notes, interviews, and surveys; undergraduate projects are typically shorter, pilot observation studies or a reanalysis of previously collected observation data	Eckert (1989); Blommaert (2005); Cameron (2001); Johnstone (2009a); Jaffe (2009).	Language in communities; languages in interaction; linguistic anthropology; language and power; language and identity.
Visual media	Includes photos, art work, or any visual representation that illustrates language use and social context	Some studies use existing collections of images or photos (e.g., Getty images or business websites); others document linguistic practices through researcher-taken photos (e.g., photos of business signs in a particular neighborhood)	Sayer (2010); Shohamy, Ben-Rafael, & Barni (2010); Hansen & Machin (2008)	Discourse analysis; linguistic landscapes; language attitudes; language ideologies; language and identity
Audio and video recordings	Any recording of interviews or naturally occurring speech and dialogue; can include conversations with members of a particular speech community under study or any recording that documents the language feature, practice, or topic under study	Researchers must always get permission before making a recording; researchers transcribe the recordings to analyze for particular linguistic features and themes	Baugh (2015); Reyes (2005); Bucholtz (1999)	Discourse analysis; corpus linguistics; conversation analysis; linguistic anthropology; languages in interaction; language variation; code-switching; pragmatics

Documents and other extant data	Includes a variety of existing sources that may already be organized or will be organized and curated by the researcher including documents such as interview transcripts, media articles, online posts (e.g., Twitter comments), or newspaper articles	Research question defines what types of documents are collected; important to clearly define why certain documents are or are not included in the document collection to be used for analysis	Deumert & Lexander (2013); Grundmann & Scott (2012); KhosraviNik (2010); Tagliamonte & Roberts (2005)	Discourse analysis; corpus linguistics; language and identity; language and gender; language and power
Extant data from a previous study	Reanalysis or reinterpretation of studies that have already taken place; using the data and analysis of a previous research project allows researchers to offer different conclusions or support alternative theories	Data from any type of study could be used for reanalysis or reinterpretation; conversation analysis studies that reanalyze existing transcripts or corpus studies that reanalyze a previously compiled corpus are common examples	Auer (1998); Cameron (2011)	Variety of topics depending on original research project

Table 2.1 Common data sources in sociolinguistic research projects

Table 2.1 reveals the variety of data sources available to you for work on your sociolinguistic research project. Later chapters and sections delve into more detail, and provide examples about best practices for data collection and analysis (e.g., how to design valid questionnaires, tips for effective interviewing, best practices for sampling and coding your data, etc.). For now, you should have a good understanding of the major subfields of sociolinguistic research studies, some of the main sources of data, and a good idea of what you might want to study in your own research project.

> **RESEARCHER TO KNOW: Janet Holmes**
>
> Janet Holmes is Emeritus Professor in Linguistics at Victoria University of Wellington in New Zealand. Her research interests and writings have covered many topics in sociolinguistics, but she is well known for her work on language and gender and workplace discourse. She is presently involved in an ongoing study of language in the workplace that focuses on intercultural differences in communication involving humor, politeness, small talk, and leadership. Holmes continues to publish the popular textbook written with Nick Wilson, *An Introduction to Sociolinguistics*, 5th ed. (2017), as well as many articles including most recently "Discourse in the Workplace" found in Tannen, Hamilton, and Schiffrin's (2015) *The Handbook of Discourse Analysis*.

> **EXERCISE 2.2: Examining a recent research article**
>
> Find a recent sociolinguistic study that is related to a topic you hope to research. Answer the following questions based on that article:
>
> 1. Identify the main research topic and the question that article addresses and investigates.
> 2. Is the article responding to any gaps in the field or responding to previous studies? In what ways?
> 3. What types of data are collected and how? Do you categorize this study as primarily qualitative, quantitative, or mixed methods?
> 4. Briefly state the conclusions or findings of the study.
> 5. Would you be able to replicate this study or use part of the study in your own research project? Explain with reference to the article.

Final thoughts: research is messy

When novice researchers are taught about research methods, they are usually only ever exposed to "ideal" research designs, where all avenues of validity, reliability, generalizability, and ethicality have been carefully contemplated and accounted for. When beginning their data collection, however, things may not go according to these perfect plans; they cannot get the representative sample they were hoping for, participants drop out from their longitudinal study, an institution decides not to grant them access to their planned research context, working within a vulnerable community proves more difficult than expected, or they struggle to maintain a positivist, objective stance in an area of research in which they have invested considerable personal and emotional energy. (Rose & McKinley, 2017, p. 3)

Now that we have surveyed the major fields and research methods of sociolinguistics in Chapter 1 and have pointed you toward the basic steps to take in narrowing your topic and finding your research question in Chapter 2, we can move on to more specific examples and discussions of the major data collection and analysis methods in sociolinguistics that you will draw on in your research project. As a final thought in ending Part I of our book, Rose and McKinley (2017) make an important point in that published research studies and presentations typically present an idealistic view of the research process that assumes that most researchers knew exactly what they were doing as they completed their project, that the researchers never experienced any problems in their data collections, and that overall their data can be confidently analyzed to answer their research questions and come to specific conclusions. In the same way, presentations of research methods in textbooks such as this one tend to present the methods of collection and analysis in their "ideal" state, outside of the messiness of actual practice in the field or research setting.

We cannot avoid a bit of generalization when presenting the methods in the next chapters, and when we use examples from published work, we will be analyzing the finished product so that one could forget that the data collection and analysis for the researcher was not as clear or polished as earlier in the research process. As we read, summarize, and comment on both published and student research studies, we hope to avoid the portrayal of research as a simple linear practice that is not messy and full of false starts and anomalies. In the end, sociolinguistics research is studying the role of language in society, and for that reason alone, we should expect that our research projects will never be simple or straightforward.

Part II
Data Collection Methods in Sociolinguistics

3 Survey data

CHAPTER OVERVIEW

- Introduction: What Are Surveys in Sociolinguistics Research?
- Preparing to Collect Survey Data
  - Strategies for Survey Sampling
  - Types of Survey Items
  - Issues of Survey and Item Design
  - Issues of Reliability and Validity
  - Online Survey Data Collection Programs
- Use of Surveys in Published Research
- Use of Surveys in Student Research
- Steps for Collecting Data through Surveys

Introduction: what are surveys in sociolinguistics research?

Surveys are common data collection tools in many areas of social science research, from sociology to education, to linguistics. In sociolinguistics, they are particularly useful in languages in communities research studies because they often are completed quickly either in person or online, allowing researchers the ability to reach a large number of participants. As discussed in Chapter 2, sociolinguists generally consider surveys to include research methods that survey and describe the characteristics of a population or community through the collection of data from a sample of that group. They may vary in size and scope, from a large census study conducted by a government to a smaller survey of a particular group of interest investigated by one researcher.

Perhaps just as important as being quick and easy to distribute, surveys collect data that Dörnyei (2007) describes as "readily processible" (p. 102); that is, researchers and students can easily analyze the collected data through descriptive and inferential statistics as well as qualitative data analysis methods. Most collection tools can easily transfer data into statistical analysis programs such as Statistical Package for the Social Sciences (SPSS), saving time and providing a reliable place to store and manage the data. At the same time, despite the ability to obtain and analyze data quickly, researchers must think carefully about a number of questions before distributing a survey, in order to be able to interpret the results and draw reliable conclusions. For example, writing good questions is not simple, and a researcher must take time in constructing questions, piloting them with a small group of respondents, and then editing and refining as needed before distributing to a wider group of participants. As a colleague of ours often tells students in relation to survey questions, "You put garbage in, you'll get garbage back!" Further, researchers must think carefully about whom they choose as the targeted population for the survey and how they will ensure that they receive enough responses.

Survey research is typically quantitative, but it differs from experimental research designs in that the researcher is not attempting to affect the participants or alter the context. In fact, as Jaeger (1988) writes, "The more intrusive the survey, the lower the chances that it will accurately reflect real conditions" (quoted in Nunan, 1992, p. 140). Thus, in planning a survey research project, students will need to think through many aspects of survey design and implementation before distributing their survey and analyzing the results. The sections of this chapter summarize these aspects of preparing and distributing a survey research project and the many decisions researchers make in constructing their survey, writing questions, and finding participants.

Preparing to collect survey data

When designing a survey study, researchers should first think about the best type of survey to use for addressing their research questions. Questionnaire surveys are by far the most popular type of survey used in sociolinguistics and many other social science fields. In a questionnaire study, the main instrument of data collection is the questionnaire, which is composed of a number of items that elicit the beliefs, opinions, language usage, or any other construct addressed by the study's research questions. A questionnaire can include many different types of items and is different from an interview survey in that participants generally choose from a fixed or closed set of responses.

We discuss interviews in Chapter 4, but some researchers may use a type of structured interview protocol in a similar way to questionnaires in that they ask participants the same set of questions in the same order and do not diverge into other topics, only recording how participants respond. In this way, the researchers can more easily compare participant responses which they cannot do in a less-structured interview, and they can perform similar statistical analyses as with questionnaires. Of course, the data for interview surveys are typically obtained in person, and that can make it difficult for one researcher to collect data from many participants. Interview surveys, however, can be a useful tool for students because they may have easy access to their participants if they are members of the same community, and student researchers or their participants may not have access to the online tools typically used in questionnaire surveys.

Census versus sample surveys

In addition to comparisons between questionnaires and interviews, surveys can be categorized as either a census survey or a sample survey. A census survey includes collecting data from the entire population of a country, nation, or region. For that reason, students would only conduct sample surveys for a class project in which they collect data on a representative sample of the population from a larger group. Census surveys are considered very reliable because they have measured every member of a nation or territory, and researchers do not have to worry about sampling errors of misrepresentations in the data. Although students will not collect census survey data, many government census results are available through a country or territory's office of data and statistics. If the research questions are appropriate and the students have access to the data, it may be possible for students to use and analyze existing census data as part of a course research project or use the census data as part of the data analyzed and compared for a project.

Longitudinal versus cross-sectional surveys

A further comparison can be made between survey projects that are longitudinal—surveying the same participants at different points over an extended period of time—and survey projects that are cross-sectional surveys—taking "snapshots" of a sample of participants at one point of time. Similar to census studies, longitudinal studies require much more time than is usually possible for a term-length research project, so most students perform cross-sectional survey projects if they are using surveys to collect data. Longitudinal studies, however, do not necessarily mean that data collection is continuous during the time the researcher is collecting data. For example, a researcher could administer the survey to participants at four different points over a four-year period in order to see how responses change, and the researcher may not collect other data between each data collection period. In this way, it is possible that students could use a longitudinal survey design in a term-length course by surveying the same participants that they had already used in a previous course or project that was started before the class started. As an alternative, students could also use the survey from an existing, published survey project and collect new data with similar participants as were used in the published study, adding a longitudinal aspect to their project, although in this case the students would be comparing their results to an earlier study and not actually completing a longitudinal research project. Finally, instructors may be part of existing longitudinal survey studies, and they could have students collect data from surveys of their existing research participants; in this way the students would gain experience in longitudinal research design. In the end, however, most students will design cross-sectional research studies in which they collect data once from a sample of participants, and the next section discusses sampling strategies.

Strategies for survey sampling

There is no one method that works for all research projects, but it is useful to consider the places and people you already know or have access to, especially in the limited time of a semester-based course. In fact, you may want to start early on in the course developing relationships and contacting possible participants. In this way, you are already performing what is called nonprobability or purposeful sampling by targeting specific participants who meet specific criteria you are looking to explore. The corollary to nonprobability sampling is probability sampling that is defined by the fact that every participant has an equal and random chance of being selected. Importantly, probability sampling allows researchers more confidence to make generalizations from a smaller sample size to the larger population being studied by using descriptive and inferential statistics to measure the reliability and validity of responses. Deciding on a sampling strategy is very important to ensuring a survey study's validity—generally defined as the credibility or measure of trustworthiness of the reported findings and conclusions. Throughout the book, we discuss issues related to both validity and its related term, reliability—generally defined as the consistency and replicability of a study and its data collection instruments—as they pertain to different data collection and analysis techniques.

Next in this chapter, we offer short summaries of different probability and nonprobability sampling strategies that can work in term-length student research projects, and discuss the pros and cons of each strategy.

Probability sampling

Four common probability sampling procedures include: (1) simple random, (2) systemic, (3) stratified, and (4) cluster. In a simple random sampling design, the researcher selects participants at random by assigning a number to each possible participant and then randomly selecting numbers until enough participants have been chosen. Survey data collection software programs can perform this task, or if the sample size is smaller, students can simply use slips of paper with the numbers of all participants and then pick the required number of participants. A systematic sampling strategy is similar to simple random, but some sort of system is used, such as picking 1 out every 10 participants, instead of a completely random selection. A stratified sampling design first divides participants according to a particular feature of the participants in order to ensure that responses are obtained for a valid comparison. For example, participants could be divided between male and female or graduate and undergraduate students, and then the researcher could choose randomly from each group. A final possible probability sample is cluster sampling, in which a researcher randomly selects a particular subgroup or unit from a larger population or grouping that is being studied. Then, the researcher randomly selects participants from the subgroup. For example, a researcher may want to study how male high school students in a city use a particular innovative pronunciation feature. It is too unwieldy to survey all male high school students, but a researcher could randomly pick one high school and survey all male students there, then extrapolate to the larger region.

Nonprobability

Nonprobability or purposeful sampling is more common in qualitative research designs and student survey projects because the selection of participants is not entirely random, and there is no intention to generalize to a larger population based on statistical methods. In this type of sampling, the participants are chosen because the researcher feels they are particularly informative, representative, or revealing in relation to the research questions. For example, a researcher may ask a participant to find other colleagues or friends who share a particular background such as growing up in a particular neighborhood. This type of sampling is known as snowball or chain sampling and is particularly useful when you are building your research questions around group practices. Two other ways to think about selecting and finding participants that have been useful for our students are convenience sampling and maximum variation sampling. Convenience sampling is what it sounds like: researchers use the participants that they have access to and build their research questions and conclusions around the characteristics of the participants they find who are willing to participate. This is often the way our students end up selecting participants during a semester-long course. They may be able to limit their sample to the ethnic or linguistic group that they wish to study, but then they use whomever they can find to complete their survey or interviews. This is the same case when the focus is on observing a place. Students may only be able to gain access to one site that represents the neighborhood or community group they wish to focus on, and therefore this site becomes the locus of their research project. Maximum variation is also similar to how it sounds in that it involves choosing participants that offer very different perspectives, backgrounds, or examples based on the research questions. In this way the researcher can point out the similarities and differences in the participants and draw conclusions based on the different characteristics.

An alternative way some survey studies use to find participants is to randomly "cold" call, or request participation either in person or online. In this method, researchers may find addresses or contact information through public records such as a telephone book or student directory and can then contact everyone on the list or those who fit some predetermined criteria they are examining. In this way, the researcher can still attempt to focus on characteristics such as age, neighborhood, sex, or ethnicity, and can cast a wide net to find as many participants as possible. At the same time, without any personal connection to a study, participants may be skeptical of the motives, and the researcher may not be able to ensure enough participants to draw reliable conclusions about some categories he or she wishes to examine.

For many students, even if they try for a probability sampling strategy, they end up using some combination of snowball and convenience sampling in order to have enough responses to complete the research project during the term of the course. We feel that this type of sampling is fine because nonprobability sampling is still used in many published survey studies and certainly used in qualitative research studies. In addition, we feel that students can learn from adapting their research design and conclusions based on the realties that they confront when collecting data. Table 3.1 summarizes the pros and cons of different sampling strategies that are often used in student qualitative and quantitative language variation projects.

Type of sampling	Pros and cons
Random or systematic	Able to collect data quickly with the possibility of high response rates on surveys; lack of control of who participates as well as ability to know more in-depth background information
Snowball or chain	Able to connect to with a wider potential pool of participants and sites; may be limited to initial participants' group of contacts and limit your image of the entire group
Convenience	Uses all available participants or sites that researcher has access to; efficient and quick but may limit the depth and reliability of the study's findings

Stratified or cluster	Allows for built-in comparisons of two different sites and diverse perspectives of participants; may be time-consuming, and sites may be difficult to find or participants may be clearly different in some or all characteristics to be examined

TABLE 3.1 EXAMPLES AND EVALUATION OF SAMPLING STRATEGIES
Source: Based on Miles and Huberman (1994) and Creswell (2013)

Types of survey items

Once you have decided on the type of survey you will design and your sampling strategy for selecting participants, the next thing you should do is perhaps the most important: write your survey items or questions. When developing your survey, you can draw on a number of established item formats from previous studies to create closed or open questions for your survey, that is, questions or stems with fixed responses or those that require participants to respond in their own words.

One of the most popular ratings scales used by our students is the Likert rating scale. Likert scales are considered closed questions because participants must choose from a selected range of responses. Likert scale items ask participants to agree or disagree with a statement according to a phrase or number linked to a phrase. For example, our student Jessica Balgobin used the following Likert scale question about language and identity in Indo-Caribbean communities:

Not speaking my mother tongue weakens my connection to my ethnic group.
Strongly Agree   Agree   Neutral   Disagree   Strongly Disagree

As a further example of a Likert scale design, consider question 22 from the questionnaire used in Morris (2014) that surveyed student beliefs and uses of Welsh in schools (p. 72):

22. The following statements are about the work which is being done to promote Welsh. Say how much you agree or disagree with each one (1 = Strongly Disagree, 7 = Strongly Agree)

- Private companies should do more to offer a bilingual service.
- More jobs should be filled by Welsh-speakers only, in order to offer bilingual service.
- Councils should do something to ensure that people who don't speak Welsh do not move into areas where the language is strong.

> **Other commonly used closed items on questionnaires**
>
> - True/False items:
>
>   "Do you consider yourself part of the South Asian community?" (from Balgobin's survey)
>
> - Semantic differential questions:
>
>   "I think studying Arabic is . . ."
>   Useless _____ Useful
>
> - Multiple choice items (from Schleef, 2014, p. 47):
>
>   Based on the recording you've just heard, this person gives the impression of being (check all that apply):
>   ☐ Reliable
>   ☐ Educated
>   ☐ Friendly
>   ☐ Other (please specify)
>
> - Rank order items (from Nunan, 1992, p. 144):
>
>   Rank the following from 1 to 4 in order of preference.
>   "I learn best by studying . . ."
>   ☐ with the whole class.
>   ☐ in small groups.
>   ☐ in pairs.
>   ☐ independently.

In addition to closed questions, many researchers include a few open-ended questions on questionnaires in order to allow for a larger variety of responses. Examples include (1) sentence completion: "The thing I like most about my accent is . . ."; (2) short-answer questions about a specific aspect of the study: "What qualities of a person's accent make it good or correct?"; or (3) clarification questions that follow up on a closed question: "If you do not feel AAVE is a correct way of speaking, why?"

> **RESEARCHER TO KNOW: Sali Tagliamonte**
>
> Sociolinguist Sali A. Tagliamonte, a professor in the Department of Linguistics at the University of Toronto, earned her PhD from the University of Ottawa. Her research has been in variationist sociolinguistics, especially in language changes made by young people. Tagliamonte and D'Arcy (2009) is one of her research projects that helps students understand language variation studies. The study concerns changes in quotative use from the more traditional *say/said* to *be like*, as in "She was like, 'That's your best answer?'" Of particular interest to students, Tagliamonte and D'Arcy's (2005) analysis relied on data gathered in interviews

conducted by second-year university students. Tagliamonte and Roberts (2005) is another good example for students of her work on language change, in this case on intensifiers like *very*, *really*, and *so*. The data for the analysis was gathered from the transcripts of *Friends*, a long-running TV program, and supports the claims that media language reflects change in language and that television data can provide useful data for sociolinguistic study.

Issues of survey and item design

In addition to selecting the types of questions or items you will use in your survey, you will also need to consider aspects of item and survey design in order to ensure reliability and the overall quality of the data you collect. First, remember that many items on a questionnaire are not actually questions, but statements or lists that ask participants to react or select a number from a rating scale. Next, when writing your questions or survey items, you should consider the types of content your questions will address. Dillman (1978) summarizes five types of questions on surveys: behavior, beliefs, knowledge, attitudes, and attributes (p. 80). Dörnyei (2007) condenses this list to three types: factual, behavioral, and attitudinal (p. 102). Either way, it is important first to focus your question or questions on specific content areas in order to avoid vague questions that can open themselves to multiple interpretations. Further, Dörnyei (2007) cautions that researchers need to remember that survey questions should not have right or wrong answers and should not be designed to evaluate a respondent's knowledge or skills. You should let your research questions guide you in considering the types of content your questions will cover.

After determining the content of the questions, researchers need to consider the format of the questions. In general, it is important to aim for short, simple items of around 20 words, and the survey should ideally take 30 minutes or less, if possible. In addition, you should consider the following tips about writing good items:

- Include negatively and positively worded items, but avoid negatively worded questions; for example, instead of writing, "I don't enjoy learning English," we can write "Learning English is a burden for me" (Dörnyei, 2007, p. 109);
- Avoid loaded terms and phrases that imply the correct answer: "Compile a list of adjectives and adverbs and test how different people react to them" (Rasinger, 2010, p. 63);
- Avoid technical vocabulary, ambiguous terms, and biased questions or questions that respondents may not have sufficient knowledge or experience to answer;

- Avoid double-barreled questions, that is, questions that ask two or more questions in one item but offer or expect only one response. For example, "Do you always do your homework thoroughly and to the best of your ability?

See Exercise 3.1 for practice writing survey questions.

Finally, in constructing your survey, it is important to remember to pay attention to aspects of quality layout and design as well as to consider how the survey will be distributed and to whom. There are at least four main ways to distribute a survey, including (1) direct administration of the survey by the researcher or a research assistant; (2) telephone surveys; (3) computer-based surveys, including email, online programs, or the use of social media; and (4) mail surveys. Many of our students have used survey functions on Facebook, Survey Monkey, or Instagram to pilot a survey and contact possible participants. These programs are useful for piloting and acceptable in our courses, as the time frame is limited; however, we caution students that conducting a larger research study of a particular language or community may not be possible online due to the limited potential audience for online programs and other potential cultural problems.

Issues of reliability and validity

Broadly, the term *reliability* in survey research refers to the internal consistency of the questionnaire results and the replicability of the research process by another researcher. For example, items on a questionnaire that measure a particular construct should be internally reliable in that if you give the same questions to the same participant—either using the same questionnaire on a different day or as different questions within the same survey—you will always get the same response from that participant. Externally, in a reliable study, a second researcher should be able to examine the collected data, come to the same conclusions, and if possible conduct the same data collection procedures, but with new participants, and find similar results.

In shorter research projects, reliability may be a difficult aspect of the survey design to control as there is often little chance for multiple administrations of the survey or collaborations with outside researchers to examine the procedures or evaluations made by the student researcher. For example, in Becker (2009), she ensures the reliability of her results by having two other researchers transcribe and code her data for presence or absence of the syllable coda /r/. She and her coders agreed on 90 percent of the instance of either /r/, revealing a high level of reliability. Students may not have the time to ask colleagues to evaluate or replicate their procedures, but they can try to have multiple items in their survey address the same theme and then compare the participants' responses to ensure that they are consistent and can be used in the findings. The survey in Morris (2014) is an example of this type of reliability in that he asked four or five questions about the same theme and then used a statistical measurement of the respondents' responses to reveal if the responses in each theme were reliable indicators for the entire theme. Thus, for example, Morris (2014) had to drop two of the themes from his analysis because the scores within each participant's survey fluctuated too much to be considered reliable. We discuss the statistics used in computing reliability measures in Chapter 8, but regardless of your use of any statistical tool for measuring reliability, we encourage students to address in some fashion how they will work to ensure that their survey procedures will be reliable. Often, this is through multiple administrations of the survey or multiple items in the survey addressing the same theme.

In terms of validity and the ability to generalize your findings from one survey to a broader population, one key aspect of data collection is response rate and recruiting enough participants to take your survey. The general rule is that the larger the number of participants, the more likely the differences you see between groups or variables are actually there, and the more valid your conclusion will be. Of course, sample size or response rate may be difficult to increase in the short period of time that you have to finish a course project, and as previously mentioned, your class research project can serve as a pilot survey that can then be expanded to recruit a larger sample size. And regardless of your strategy for recruiting participants, the best plan is to be persistent and to continue asking for participation through multiple channels.

Tips to increase survey sample size

- Advertise and recruit participants through a variety of sources. If you have primarily recruited friends through social media, consider putting up flyers around your college or asking participants to recruit further participants as in a snowball sampling strategy.
- Target particular populations of participants with demographics that you need to include for analysis. For example, gearing your recruitment strategies to increase the participation of women or speakers of particular languages.
- If your questionnaire is small enough, consider administering it as an interview as well as a questionnaire. This may be particularly important in recruiting participants who do not have access to or facility with online survey tools.

Online survey data collection programs

As a final section introducing what to do in preparing to complete a survey research project, in Table 3.2, we summarize and comment on three of the most popular and useful programs for collecting survey data used by students. As with all technologies, programmers are constantly creating new software that may replace the programs listed here, and improvements and changes are often made to these existing programs. We recommend that you speak with your instructor as well as survey recently published articles in order learn of new online and computer software tools for collecting survey data.

Program	Website	Description/feature
Facebook Surveys	http://survey-app.co	▪ Easy and simple way to embed survey questions into a Facebook page or site. ▪ Limited question options, security, and privacy. ▪ Ability for students to get quick responses and data, which may work for a course project. ▪ Data with this tool would likely not be published in a sociolinguistics journal article.
Survey Monkey	https://www.surveymonkey.com	▪ Offers a variety of customizable survey, data visualization, and data analysis tools. ▪ Can send surveys, track participants, and offer reminders to participate. ▪ Security and password features can limit access to a restricted number of participants. ▪ Limited free package may work for small, student projects. ▪ Most researchers will need to buy an expanded package in order to access more features.

Qualtrics	https://www.qualtrics.com/survey-software	<ul><li>Similar to SurveyMonkey.</li><li>Offers a survey builder and survey library that guides beginners through creating a survey.</li><li>Offers a tool to display survey results, graphically and statistically, and export data to analysis packages such as Excel or SPSS.</li><li>Many universities and libraries offer student access to paid packages though institutional accounts.</li></ul>

TABLE 3.2 ONLINE SURVEY DATA COLLECTION PROGRAMS

EXERCISE 3.1: Asking questions of your survey questions

- Rank the following survey questions according to the scale: 1 = Well-constructed question; include as is in a survey; 3 = Question needs work; include in survey after edits; 5 = Throw out this question, and never speak of it again.
- Discuss with a partner the reason for your scores and what makes certain survey questions better or worse than others.

  1. Someone else's lack of ability to speak my mother tongue makes me feel more legitimate in my identity. (Strongly Agree, Agree, Neutral, Disagree, Strongly Disagree)
  2. Do you always pay attention and take notes in class? (Yes or No)
  3. We should not require all students, beginning in second grade, to study a foreign language. (Strongly Agree, Agree, Neutral, Disagree, Strongly Disagree)
  4. "I think code-switching is . . ."

     Important ____ ____ ____ ____ Not Important
  5. Rank the following from 1 to 4 in order of preference.

     "I prefer to text with . . ."
     - Professors
     - Relatives
     - Parents
     - Friends
  6. Write your own poorly worded question. Compare your question with a partner's.

Use of surveys in published research

In this section of the chapter, we profile one sociolinguistic study, Kiesling (2004), which uses different types of surveys and sampling strategies and provides a good example of survey research for course projects. Kiesling (2004) analyzed the meanings and uses of the term *dude* among undergraduate students in the United States in order to examine how the use of *dude* expanded throughout the 1980s, from primarily an address term to include uses as a discourse marker, exclamation, and agreement marker. Kiesling (2004) is a language variation study that focuses on one linguistic variable, and many students use the design of one or both of the surveys in the study to either replicate his study of *dude* or investigate another common discourse marker or phrase used among their peer groups.

In the first study reported in Kiesling (2004), students in an undergraduate sociolinguistics class recorded the first 20 times they heard someone say the term *dude* over a three-day period. The students wrote down the entire sentence or context in which the term was used, including the gender and ethnicity of the interlocutors, their relationships, and the context or situation. The class then compiled all of these examples into what they labeled the *Dude Corpus* (DC), a 519-token collection of all of the student-recorded examples of the use of *dude* that then became a central data source in the paper. The second survey used a self-report questionnaire, which students distributed to friends and family members, that asked about the respondent's use of the term (how often and with whom). For example, the survey contained the following question using a Likert scale of 1 to 5 (1 = Not likely at all, will never use it with someone like this; 5 = Very likely, use it all the time with people like this).

2. What kind of person are you likely to use it to address?

The person is your	The person is also a man	The person is also a woman
Girlfriend/boyfriend	1 2 3 4 5 n/a	1 2 3 4 5 n/a
Close friend	1 2 3 4 5 n/a	1 2 3 4 5 n/a
Acquaintance	1 2 3 4 5 n/a	1 2 3 4 5 n/a
Stranger	1 2 3 4 5 n/a	1 2 3 4 5 n/a
Sibling	1 2 3 4 5 n/a	1 2 3 4 5 n/a
Parent	1 2 3 4 5 n/a	1 2 3 4 5 n/a
Boss	1 2 3 4 5 n/a	1 2 3 4 5 n/a
Professor	1 2 3 4 5 n/a	1 2 3 4 5 n/a

The survey also asked respondents about their perception of *dude* users with questions such as "What kind of person do you think uses it frequently?" (p. 301).

Overall, through the surveys, Kiesling (2004) found the use of the term *dude* had expanded both in terms of who uses it and how it is used. Male speakers continued to be the dominant users of the term, particularly when speaking among male–male pairs, but women did use the term frequently, often when speaking to other women and men who were their close friends. Perhaps just as revealing as who was using *dude*, Kiesling (2004) also collected and analyzed recordings the author made with fraternity members, and summarized the variety of discourse functions *dude* performs in those recordings, including (1) discourse structure marking, (2) exclamation, (3) confrontational stance attenuator, (4) affiliation and connection, and (5) agreement. Kiesling (2004) provides extended examples of each type of use, including its use as a discourse marker indicating cool solidarity, as in the following example in which a fraternity brother, Speed, is making a claim for whom to elect to a position in the fraternity:

Speed: Ritchie. I like Ritchie 'cause he's smart, and he probably (writes really good) too, so let him do it, dude.

In sum, the survey data in combination with the recorded observations and conversations with fraternity members provide a macro- and micro-perspective on the use of *dude* among young adults and university students and allow Kiesling (2004) to make comments on both the linguistic and sociocultural ways *dude* is used. He concludes that *dude* "carries indexicalities of both solidarity (camaraderie) and distance (nonintimacy) and can be deployed to create both of these kinds of stance, separately or together . . . what I call cool solidarity" (p. 286). As an example research study using a survey research design, we recommend students read the entire study and pay particular attention to mixed-methods data collection. Students should note the snowball sampling techniques used to find participants for the surveys as well as the simple but effective use of Likert scale questions on the questionnaires, both data collection techniques that are easily replicated in term-length research projects.

Use of surveys in student research

As we discussed in the Introduction, we plan to introduce student work throughout the chapters as a way to personalize the data collection and analysis methods as well as provide examples of the types of work that are possible in class-based research projects. We provide the full research paper of all student examples in supplemental materials located on the book's website.

In this section, we present a project written in a sociolinguistics course by Jessica Balgobin, entitled "Language and Identity in Indo-Caribbean Communities."

For her project, Balgobin was interested in examining the linguistic and cultural beliefs and differences between what she refers to as Continental South Asians and Indo-Caribbeans. She explains in the introduction to her paper:

> I myself descend from Indian indentured servants; most of my great great-grandparents, and some of my great-grandparents were born and lived in pre-partition India before being uprooted by the British to work in Guyana, where my entire family was born and raised. I don't know where in India my ancestors originate . . . As I got older, I started to question my Indian roots more and more; I wanted to know more about where my ancestors came from. I resented things like the fact that I couldn't speak Hindi, which, in my mind, could help me connect better to the South Asian community as a whole. The majority of my Indo-Guyanese family, however, wasn't particularly interested in fitting in and didn't preoccupy themselves with labeling themselves Indian. "We are not Indian!" I've heard this time and time again, and I wanted to know how exactly we could be anything else if not Indian. (p. 3)

In order to investigate why her family and friends from Guyana and other Indo-Caribbean communities appeared not to identify strongly with Indian languages and culture, Balgobin designed a survey that she gave to both South Asian and Indo-Caribbean participants. She writes, "I wanted to understand how and if this presence [knowledge of South Asian languages] serves as a connection to Indian roots and influences how Indo-Caribbeans self-identify . . . I also wanted to know how continental South Asians viewed Indo-Caribbeans" (p. 4). In addition to the survey, she interviewed one Pakistani and one Indo-Guyanese participant in order to further investigate South Asian identity and language attitudes and compare these with the survey results. She summarized her methods in the following paragraph:

> I surveyed twenty people: ten continental South Asians and ten Indo-Caribbeans, all from my family or groups of my friends. The age range in my sample varied from teens to twenties, forties to fifties, and seventies. For my Indo-Caribbean sample, most of my participants were Indo-Guyanese who either spoke both Creolese and English or English alone.

Balgobin's survey consisted of four yes/no questions and six Likert scale questions asking participants to rank their responses from "strongly agree" to "strongly disagree." In addition to the earlier example, we provide examples of each type of question below.

1. If you are Indo-Caribbean (of Indian descent from Guyana, Trinidad, Jamaica, Suriname, Barbados, etc.), do you consider yourself to be part of the South Asian community?

    Yes   No

6. Speaking my mother tongue determines my ability to identify with my ethnic group:

   Strongly Agree   Agree   Neutral   Disagree   Strongly Disagree

The questions were effective for Balgobin's project because they were clear and simple, and the questionnaire was not too long. In addition, the questions were directly related to her research question, and she was easily able to compare survey responses with her interview data. Balgobin presented her findings as a series of graphs representing the survey and themes that emerged from the interviews.

In addition to her clear survey and mixed-methods approach to the research questions, what most impressed us about Balgobin's project was her final analysis and movement from a small student survey project to a larger generalization. She writes:

> I posit that Indo-Caribbeans because of the lack of knowledge of South Asian languages find it difficult and feel a disconnect from the South Asian community. Hindi is still very much present throughout Indo-Caribbean culture, but that doesn't change the fact that the language is not spoken everyday by Indo-Caribbeans; most Indo-Caribbeans cannot understand it on a broad scale. The lack of linguistic ability along with the superiority and rejection of Indo-Caribbean South Asian identity by continental South Asians prevents Indo-Caribbeans from fully feeling comfortable as members of the South Asian community. There seems to exist a typical, acceptable way to be South Asian, and speaking Hindi/Urdu is one huge requirement to fit in. (p. 12)

Of course, Balgobin's sample size is small, and she could have expanded the survey to add more questions to increase the reliability of her responses, but we offer her paper as an example of a small pilot survey study that students can accomplish in a short amount of time that still connects to important questions in sociolinguistics as well as a student's own life experiences.

Steps for collecting data through surveys

As a final section in the chapter, we summarize the various methods described above through a series of steps. We do not think you need to follow each step in the same order, and not all steps will relate to every survey project. We offer the following steps at the end of each data collection chapter not as an explicit guide to follow one by one, but more as suggestions and steps to consider as you put together your survey project.

1. Decide on your project and survey objectives, that is, what you want to learn and why.
2. Review existing literature on your topic as well as on previous survey methods used to explore similar topics. You may find a previous survey that you can adapt or reuse or a sampling technique that works well with your participants.
3. Determine whom you will survey. Identify the group you will survey, how many participants you hope to have, and how you will reach them (i.e., your sampling procedures).
4. Design your survey. Will you use a questionnaire or interviews? What programs will you use to help collect and analyze the data? Pilot your survey items or, at the least, have a second reader review your items, checking for bias and unclear questions.
5. Collect responses from participants. You may need to revise your collection procedures or tweak the items on the questionnaire as necessary. Be sure to throw out any items that were not well constructed, and work to ensure reliability during your data collections.
6. Analyze your data and write up your findings. We discuss this in more depth, as it relates to survey research, in Parts III and IV of the book.

Further reading on survey data collection methods

For further reading about survey data collection techniques, we recommend the following texts:

Dillman, D. A., Smyth, J. D., & Christian, L. M. (2014). *Internet, phone, mail, and mixed-mode surveys: The tailored design method*, 4th ed. Malden, MA: Wiley-Blackwell.

Dörnyei, Z., & Csizér, K. (2012). How to design and analyze surveys in SLA research. In A. Mackey & S. Gass (eds.), *Research methods in second language acquisition: A practical guide* (pp. 74–94). Malden, MA: Wiley-Blackwell.

Fowler, F. J., Jr. (2013). *Survey research methods*, 5th ed. Thousand Oaks, CA: Sage.

Nardi, P. (2014). *Doing survey research*, 3rd ed. New York, NY: Routledge.

Schleef, E. (2014). Written surveys and questionnaires in sociolinguistics. In J. Holmes & K. Hazen (eds.), *Research methods in sociolinguistics: A practical introduction* (pp. 42–58). Malden, MA: Wiley-Blackwell.

4 Interviews

> **CHAPTER OVERVIEW**
>
> - Introduction: What Are Interviews in Sociolinguistics Research?
> - Preparing to Collect Interview Data
>   - Learning to Listen
>   - Developing Questions
>   - Selecting Participants
> - Use of Interviews in Published Research
> - Use of Interviews in Student Research
> - Steps for Collecting Data through Interviews

Introduction: what are interviews in sociolinguistics research?

One of the most frequently used fieldwork methods for collecting data on social and cultural uses of language is the interview. Many sociolinguistic research projects, especially qualitative research projects, involve conducting interviews. From confirming the results of participant observation, to introducing a researcher to a site or speech community, to understanding the use of a specific variable, interviews are an essential tool that almost all sociolinguist researchers will use at some point in their work. It is important to note as well that interviews are useful in quantitative research as part of survey data collection or as a follow-up to an existing survey.

The length and number of participants of interviews vary based on the project, from a small number of questions to many questions, and from one meeting to several meetings over the course of many years. Most sociolinguists conduct one-on-one interviews in order to prevent the speech of interviewees being biased by those around them, but some research topics that seek to understand community opinions, beliefs, and opinions may be suited for a focus group interview format in which a researcher interviews multiple participants in one session. Focus groups can also be an efficient way to collect responses if time is limited, as it is in many student projects. Researchers should just be aware of the potential bias and limits on confidentiality that exist when conducting focus group interviews.

Regardless of whether you are conducting individual or focus group interviews, the overall goal of sociolinguistic interviews is to create a comfortable environment so that people's natural language patterns emerge and researchers can document participants' true feelings and unselfconscious speech patterns. As Hoffman (2014) writes in paraphrasing William Labov, "We would like our participants to pay more attention to what they are saying and be less conscious of the way they are saying it" (p. 33). However, the researcher generally records or videos the interaction in order to transcribe it at a later time, and this recording can make participants uneasy. Thus, the researcher needs to do everything possible to make participants feel at ease. One way the interviewer can assist this is by asking a few icebreaker questions like "How are you doing today?" or "Did you have any problem finding the room?" and so on. For example, in an interview that Trudy Smoke (one of the authors of this text) conducted at a participant's home about attitudes toward immigration in the neighborhood, she asked a question about a plant growing on the windowsill, and the speaker told her about it and clearly began to relax. In most situations after a few minutes, participants begin to forget the recording device and start to speak in a more natural way.

There are three basic formats for interviews: structured, semi-structured, or open. In the structured format, every person interviewed is asked exactly the same questions; in semi-structured interviews, the set of questions functions as a guide and may involve changes in topics and follow-up questions; and in open interviews, the approach is closer to an evolving conversation. We suggest that in most student studies, the structured or semi-structured approach works best because these interviews allow you to control the topic, and make analysis and writing up a report of your project easier. The next sections of this chapter further discusses these three basic formats as well as other key aspects of interviewing as part of a student research project.

Preparing to collect interview data

As stated above, the goal of helping participants to pay more attention to what they are saying and not how they are saying it is true of all sociolinguistic interviews. Achieving this goal requires practice and attention to your interviewing skills, and to guide you in developing these skills, we focus on three key aspects of interviewing: (1) learning to listen, (2) developing questions, and (3) selecting participants.

Learning to listen

Listening may not seem like a skill that a researcher would need to practice, but novice researchers quickly recognize that conducting an interview is much more than simply having a conversation. To start, interviews are, at least on the surface, fundamentally one-sided in that the interviewer typically initiates the discussion, focuses on key research topics, and then controls the interpretation of the interview transcript. This power dynamic is perhaps unavoidable, but we have found that a basic way to put your interviewees at ease as well as reduce the power differential between you and the interviewee is to be a good listener, and this will take practice. Perhaps the best way to practice is simply to do many interviews, but you will not want to use up all of your potential participants. Exercise 4.1 below gives you a chance to practice your interview skills and especially your listening skills. After this, you can practice by piloting your interview questions before actually collecting interviews with your participants for your research, and we encourage you to do even short 5- to 10-minute practice interviews with classmates and friends in order to practice your listening skills. You can record these interviews and then replay them to see how well you listened and where you may have interrupted your interviewees or not provided a comfortable context for them to present their ideas. And if your study is focused on particular language variables, you need to make sure that you have collected data that will enable you to access the best ways to elicit your participants' accents or language choices.

EXERCISE 4.1: Practice Interview - Listening

1. Conduct a short 5- to 10-minute interview with a classmate or a friend, recording it on your phone or other recording device. When you play back your interview, you will be focusing mostly on yourself as a listener. Notice whether you interrupted or filled in when there were gaps. How often did you backchannel with expressions such as "Mmm" or "Yes" or "No way," for example? What effect did your responses seem to have on the interviewee? How did you handle quiet moments? It is also useful to video the interview if you have the technology available. Then you can notice your own and your participant's body language.
2. Some good topics for a short semi-structured interview might be asking about a person's favorite music, a favorite food, a favorite sport or athlete, a problem registering for classes in your school, or a movie that the person loved or disliked and why. These are topics that are not too personal and are good for a first practice experience. Write out three questions, and start the interview with the first one. If the interview seems nonproductive, move to another question. Notice how you feel when there are silences and how long it takes you or your participant to fill in the quiet space.
3. After listening to the interview several times, focusing on yourself as a listener, write a reflection on yourself. What were your best moments? How can you improve as an interviewer?

Further, as you practice your interview skills, be attentive to the following list of best practices adapted from Richards (2003, p. 54):

- Listen carefully, both through your ears and through your nonverbal cues such as eye contact and head nods.
- Offer supportive backchannel responses and feedback through filler words such as "hmmm," "uh-huh," and "yes."
- Respond to the emotional content or responses by your interviewees with nods and filler words.
- Avoid adding your own opinions, and instead listen and observe your interviewee.
- As much as possible, let the interview take its own shape, and let the interviewee move the discussion more than you lead it.

You should also try to conduct the interview in a quiet space so you will be able to hear the interviewee and the interviewee can hear you. This is important as you listen to and transcribe your interview. Outside noises can make it difficult to hear the participant, especially when you are listening for particular linguistic features in the person's speech. Outside noise is also distracting. You also want to make sure that your interviewee hears what you say. In William Labov's study on patterns in New York City speech, the interviewer asked a question about whether the interviewee believed in "fate." The interviewee responded by talking about his "faith" and how important it was to him. The interviewer spelled out the word "fate" to explain the question; the interviewee revised his answer, and the interview continued (Labov, 1966, 2005).

RESEARCHER TO KNOW: Barbara Johnstone

Barbara Johnstone is a professor of rhetoric and linguistics in the Department of English at Carnegie Mellon University in Pittsburgh, Pennsylvania. Her research is in discourse studies—an intersectional area of study that includes rhetoric, linguistics, and critical theory—and she uses sociolinguistic interviews in many of her research projects. Her research has focused on many areas of the world, from the Middle East to her own city of Pittsburgh, where she has conducted interview studies focusing on "Pittsburghese," a local language and dialect. She is interested in how linguistic resources such as the use of Pittsburghese are used to index particular local identities, and in Johnstone (2013), *Speaking Pittsburghese: The Story of a Dialect*, she describes her study and findings of Pittsburghese. Johnstone is also known for *Discourse Analysis*, 3rd ed. (2018), a book designed to teach discourse analysis research methods and used by many universities.

Developing questions

In order to provide a coherent structure for your interview, you need to vary your questioning strategies and topics to move from opening statements ("Could you talk about your experience as ... ?") to probing questions ("I'd like to hear more about why you didn't like working on that project ... ?") to interview structure comments ("Let's move on to talk about your current neighborhood"). These are all ways to structure your questions as you ask them, but before you are in the interview, you will want to decide on an overall format for your interview: structured, semi-structured, or open. In our experience, few interviews are truly open, and few interviews are completely structured. Instead, most sociolinguistic interviews start with a list of questions that the interviewer uses to guide the interview, but a skilled interviewer allows space for the interviewee to move the conversation in new directions. As Richards (2009) writes, a semi-structured interview is not simply a combination of an open and structured interview with questions becoming more open as the interview goes on:

> A semi-structured interview, then, is one where the interviewer has a clear picture of the topics that need to be covered (and perhaps even a preferred order for these) but is prepared to allow the interview to develop in unexpected directions where these open up important new areas. (p. 186)

We have found that leading successful semi-structured interviews does take practice, and you often will become better with each interview as you develop more familiarity with your questions and start to narrow the key ideas that you hear in multiple interviews.

Although semi-structured interviews are much more prevalent, there are times when a structured or open interview structure may be the most appropriate. For example, a structured interview may take the place of a survey if it is easier to interview participants about the survey questions because any other type of survey distribution will lead to low response rates. In these cases, the questions will need to be exactly the same for statistical comparison. For student researchers, a structured interview approach may be useful because it can be used to focus quickly on a few key questions that can be easily analyzed and reported.

On the opposite side, an open interview may begin with a few topics proposed by the interviewer, but the aim of the interview is to let the interviewee, in dialogue with the interviewer, examine any idea or topic that comes out of their discussion. Open interviews may be difficult for novice researchers to analyze, and they may take much longer than structured or semi-structured to complete. One of their main values, however, is that they do typically provide many examples of natural speech in order to see where participants use a particular sociolinguistic variable. When conducting open interviews, you should still determine what topics you want to discuss during the interview, as well as practice good listening and follow-up questioning techniques. In terms of possible topics, many researchers prefer asking about familiar and comfortable topics that will induce extended narratives and less self-conscious speech. See Exercise 4.2 for practice developing interview structure. For example, Becker (2009) revisited the location of William Labov's foundational work in variationist sociolinguistics on the Lower East Side (LES) of Manhattan in New York City. She wanted to connect the role of place and meaning by examining one feature of New York City English, non-rhoticity, or r-less speech. To do this, in her interviews, she simply told her participants that she was interested in discussing the Lower East Side neighborhood, and she listened for how often, when, and where the r-less speech occurred. Becker (2009) describes her reasons and methods for finding her participants as part of her profile of the history of the LES:

> I set out to identify white-ethnic residents who were born, raised, and still live on the same block where I live in the neighborhood. I was interested in talking with these residents as they are a demographically dwindling group, and I sensed that those who had remained on the block amidst great change were staunchly attached to the neighborhood. I spent time at a community center on the block, where I first met a few of the interviewees, who then introduced me to their siblings and children. (p. 640)

The data that Becker collected from these open interviews were then compared to other data sources, including the reading of a short passage and list of words in order to perform her quantitative analysis, in which she found 3,000 words with a syllable-code /r/.

EXERCISE 4.2: Deciding on an interview structure

Think about the following questions in relation to your project, and talk with a classmate about them. Then make a list of answers.

1. What is the main goal of your project? What do you want to learn?
2. What is the main goal of the interview(s)?
3. Who will be your participants? How will you find them?
4. What do you need to tell your participants before the interview? They will want to know why they are being interviewed. You should be prepared to explain something about your project without giving details about the specific variable you are listening for.
5. Where will you interview them?

6. Which structure—structured, semi-structured, or open—seems best for your project and interviews? Why?
7. What is your first question?
8. What is your follow-up question?

In terms of writing and developing your questions, for language variation and languages in interaction research projects, researchers recommend avoiding asking about politics, religion, or very personal issues, as interviewees may speak in a more rehearsed or formal style if they are echoing opinions that they have heard elsewhere (though this may be interesting for a more discourse analysis–based study, a subject we discuss further in Chapter 8). Topics such as food, music, sports, or work may be productive in creating a relaxing atmosphere and producing more natural speech patterns, whether you are listening for a variable such as rhoticity, code-mixing or code-switching, or tag questions as examples of the types of research for which interviews have been used.

At the same time, many languages in communities research projects investigate attitudes and opinions about particular language practices or policies and cannot completely avoid political or contentious topics. In these interviews, it is important to establish trust with the participants and the community beforehand, and it helps if you are not meeting the interviewees for the first time during the interview. In addition, interviewers will need to be attentive as the interview is proceeding, and be able to move away from a topic if the interviewee is upset. Over the course of an interview or through multiple meetings, it may be possible to circle back to earlier questions that the interviewee avoided, but interviewers will need to develop sensitivity as to when and how to do that. Overall, interviewers need to understand that interviewing is a social practice, and each interview will develop in its own way. The key skill for interviewees to develop, particularly in open and semi-structured interviews, is the ability to guide the interactions without overly prescribing where the discussions go.

Selecting participants

In thinking about how to build trust and develop good questions for an interview, a last point in preparing for an interview project should be made about connecting with a community and selecting interview participants. Many students will already have participants in mind when beginning a research project, but if your researcher question does not involve a community where the researcher is already a member, it will be important to think through how access to the community and participants can be gained. Depending on how much time you have to make connections in a community, you may find that you have difficulty getting the right balance of participants to participate in your interviews, and you will have to either change your research questions or analysis based on the background of your participants. For example, our student Rebecca Galpern conducted an interview survey study about attitudes toward Yiddish among member of an Orthodox Jewish community in Brooklyn, New York. She wrote in her paper that she had difficulty contacting men to interview because of the conservative social customs of Hasidic men and the tendency to avoid speaking with unfamiliar women. She writes this about her first attempts to collect interview participants:

> I avoided approaching men in the neighborhood, rendering all Boro Park respondents women. This posed a problem for my research since women have starkly different views on and capabilities in English than men do (Abraham, 1999). However, I was able to collect surveys from several men, such as Rabbis and former Hassidim whom I have had previous contact with.

Thus, in preparing for interview studies, student researchers will want to think deeply about the participants and how they will find them. In doing this, they should also do some preliminary research into the history of the community, its demographics, changes, and previous sociolinguistic studies.

Use of interviews in published research

In most cases, students will choose a semi-structured or open interview format in order to allow participants to pay more attention to the content of what they are saying about a specific topic, rather than to how they are speaking, and we offer two examples of semi-structured interviews from published reports as examples that students can use for their own interview study design.

In Chand (2011), the researcher wanted to better understand the role among elites of Hindi, the national language of India, as to whether it functioned as a unifying language across classes and age groups "under the banner of a shared Indian identity" (p. 6). Specifically, she asked the following research questions:

1. Are Indian elites unified in their language practices and/or ideologies?
2. What role do these elites see for Hindi in their own lives and in India—does this population see cultural value, modern national identity, and/or a historical precedent for personally valuing and/or using Hindi?

In addressing these questions, Chand's primary source of data was 35 sociolinguistic interviews with residents from upper-class, elite south New Delhi communities. She conducted the interviews primarily in English, occasionally code-mixing/code-switching to Hindi. She describes the methods she used in recording the interviews in the follow description:

> Thirty-five sociolinguistic interviews were conducted from 2007–9. While primarily conducted in (Indian) English, Hindi was used for terms with no direct translation, and stylistically exploited through code-mixes/codeswitches. Most participants (aged 18–87, spanning three generations) were aware of my interest in language as part of their experiences; however, their perspectives on language were presented within the context of informal life-history interviews lasting 45–135 minutes. (p. 16)

What makes the interviews semi-structured is that Chand told her interviewees that she wanted them to talk about a specific topic. She made it clear to her interviewees that she was interested in language as part of their experiences, but that she wanted to hear "their perspectives on language ... within the context of informal life-history interviews lasting 45–135 minutes. They, thus, reflect individualized musings on the role of Hindi within their lives, histories, and aspirations" (pp. 16–17). The interviews took place in south New Delhi, in the interviewees' homes, in an area where Chand had family members and that she knew well, making it easier for her to get participants.

When analyzing the data, Chand (2011) first offers an extensive discussion of the language policies and histories of local and foreign language in India and the little attention given to elite perspectives on language use. This sociolinguistic profile functions as part of the main data and provides needed context for the researcher when she thematically presents her analysis of the interviews according to the following three themes: Hindi insecurity, Hindi in the education setting, and Hindi in friendship and home settings. Thus, student researchers can use Chand (2011) as a good example of semi-structured interview methods as well as an example of how to move from the larger setting when planning an interview to then discussing the data and pointing to future work. In addition, it was clear that the researcher did extensive investigations into the role of Hindi, English, and other languages and language communities in India before developing her research and interview questions. See Exercise 4.3 for further discussion of Chand's research methods.

EXERCISE 4.3: How would you have approached Chand's research topic?

Imagine that you are developing a method for answering Chand's two research questions and you want to use interviews. Discuss the following questions with a partner, or write responses on your own to share with a group.
- What types of participants do you think would be most useful to interview?
- With a partner, decide on three questions you would ask your participants.

> - Find Chand's article on the *Journal of Sociolinguistics* website. The article was published in 2011, vol. 15(1). You will find excerpts from her interviews. What did Chand learn from her interviews? What information does she provide about her interviewees? What parts of the excerpts does she italicize? Why those parts?
> - What aspects of Chand's overall research design and writing would you replicate if you were conducting a research project using interviews? What things would you change or alter?

Different from the languages in communities research questions in Chand (2011), Yuasa (2010) used interviews in a language variation study to examine the vocal quality known as creaky voice or vocal fry in young, educated American and Japanese speakers. Creaky voice is produced by slow vibrations in the vocal cords that do not contribute to differences in phonemes in English (i.e., using creaky voice does not change the meaning of a word or produce minimal pairs). In the past, it has been associated with masculine and authoritative speech, but more female English speakers, particularly young speakers, have been using creaky voice, and Yuasa (2010) was interested in the use of creaky voice and its sociocultural meanings.

Yuasa's methodology involved analyzing for creaky voice interviews with 12 American English and 11 Japanese speakers and comparing the use of creaky voice in the interviews with the results of a survey about attitudes toward creaky voice conducted with 175 American college students in California and Iowa. For the interviews, the female participants spoke only with female researchers, but the male participants spoke with either male or female researchers. The interviews were conducted in a lounge or living room, not in a lab, in order to relax the participants and encourage natural conversation. The conversations averaged 10 minutes in length, and individuals were instructed "to talk only about food, a topic judged to be emotionally non-provocative but interesting enough for everyone to participate" (p. 322). The researcher wanted participants to speak naturally, but participants knew they were being recorded, and the individuals even consented to wearing a microphone to pick up their speech patterns. After the interviews were transcribed, Yuasa listened to each interview for creaky voice and, when she found an instance, used the phonological analysis software Praat 4.1 to examine the waveforms and spectrograms to confirm the presence of creaky voice. In total, she reported that American females used creaky voice more than twice as often as male English speakers and the Japanese speakers.

Yuasa (2010) did not find a particular context where her participants used creaky voice more often, such as a particular topic or place in the phrase. For the survey, she used an example of creaky voice as an audio prompt for respondents to rank on a scale in terms of how formal the voice sounds and how educated the speaker is. Overall, she argues that creaky voice is not used by female American English speakers to sound authoritative or masculine, but she reveals that its use is associated with educated, urban, and upwardly mobile women, and in that way, despite the negative portrayal of the voice feature in some recent popular media, the feature will likely increasingly be used among young American women. For students, Yuasa (2010) is a good example of a mixed-methods data collection design in which an interview study and analysis informs the survey questions and analysis. In addition, students could read more carefully about how Yuasa set up her open interview format as a good example for language variation interview procedures.

> **RESEARCHER TO KNOW: John Rickford**
>
> John Rickford is the J. E. Wallace Sterling Professor of Linguistics and the Humanities at Stanford University. He is a sociolinguist who specializes in language and race, language and ethnicity, language and social class, and style. He has published widely on pidgins, creoles, and African American English, and often uses interviews as his primary data source. Rickford's 2000 book *Spoken Soul: The Story of Black English*, which he co-authored with his son Russell J. Rickford, won the American Book Award. His 2016 book, edited with H. Samy Alim, Faculty Director for Diversity in the Arts at Stanford, and Arnetha F. Ball, Associate Professor of Education at Stanford, entitled *Raciolinguistics: How Language Shapes Our Ideas about Race*, introduces a new field of study, theorizing and closely analyzing the relationship of race and language. The volume examines contested racial and ethnic issues worldwide and from a wide range of perspectives.

Use of interviews in student research

Building on Yuasa (2010) and wishing to examine vocal fry in her own speech communities, our student Amna Khan conducted a study on vocal fry among Punjabi, Urdu, and Hindi speakers in the United States. She borrowed the open interview technique and food topic of Yuasa (2010), and she recorded six bilingual speakers, three men and three women, of South Asian descent. All spoke English and Punjabi, Urdu, or Hindi. In the study, Khan analyzed when and how often the participants exhibited vocal fry during casual discussions in their two languages. In order to switch between the languages, Khan initiated her interviews in English with questions such as "What is your favorite food?" She then switched to the participants' native or first language to ask further follow-up questions about other food-related topics. Khan recorded and then transcribed the interviews, which each lasted about 8 minutes. For additional data, Khan also conducted a brief survey of the participants' attitudes toward creaky voice. At the end of the open interview about food, Khan would play a short video from YouTube of the actress Zooey Deschanel discussing her work, in which she uses creaky voice. Participants were then asked three short questions on a survey about their impression of vocal fry and its use by men and women.

Kahn's findings were similar to those of Yuasa (2010) in that she showed that female participants used vocal fry more than male participants and that creaky voice occurred more frequently when using English than the speaker's native language. In particular, she observed the prevalence of creaky voice with the word *yeah* among her female participants. Khan interpreted this as a marker of hesitancy and nonaggressiveness on the part of the female speakers. Using research that you read and discuss in class is a good way for students to develop their own research questions, build on strategies used by published researchers, and learn to use analytic tools used in those research studies.

Steps for collecting data through interviews

When we look at the variety of ways in which interviews have been used across a wide number of studies, we can see how important it is that students conducting sociolinguistics studies practice and build interviewing skills and how useful this practice will be when developing research proposals and doing data collection. Here is a list of some of the key steps and tips we mention in the chapter that you need to consider as you prepare for an interview study:

1. Decide on the topic and number of participants for the interviews, for example, one-on-one interviews or focus groups.

2. Obtain consent, and in most cases signed consent, from your participants. Assure participants that their information will be totally confidential. In writing up your findings, do not use real names. Use pseudonyms or initials so participants' identity is protected.

3. Develop your interview questions and decide on a question format, for example, structured, semi-structured, or open ended.

4. Make sure you have a quiet, comfortable space that you can use for the entire time of the interview.

5. Check your phone or recording technology to make sure that everything is charged and ready to go, so you do not have to interrupt the interview. Test everything before the interview.

6. Begin with an icebreaker, a question designed to help relax the interviewee.

7. Listen to the participant(s) and let the conversation move in the direction they take it. Don't jump in with your own stories.

8. Don't interrupt the participant with your own ideas, but do backchannel with nods and *hmm*'s in order to make it clear that you are listening.

9. Steer away from personal or embarrassing moments for the participants.

10. If possible, bring a bottle of water for the participants.

Further reading on interview data collection methods

For further reading about interview data collection techniques, we recommend the following texts:

Feagin, C. (2002). Entering the community: Fieldwork. In J. K. Chamber, P. Trudgill, & N. Schilling-Estes (eds.), *The handbook of language variation and change* (pp. 20–39). Oxford, UK: Blackwell.

Hoffman, M. (2014). Sociolinguistic interviews. In J. Holmes & K. Hazen (eds.), *Research methods in sociolinguistics: A practical guide* (pp. 25–41). Malden, MA: Wiley.

Richards, K. (2009). Interviews. In J. Heigham & R. A. Croker (eds.), *Qualitative research in applied linguistics* (pp. 182–99). London, UK: Palgrave Macmillan.

Roulston, K. (2012). Interviews in qualitative research. In C. A. Chapelle (ed.), *The Encyclopedia of Applied Linguistics*. doi:10.1002/9781405198431.wbeal0572.

5 Participant observation

> **CHAPTER OVERVIEW**
>
> - Introduction: What Are Participant Observation Data Sources?
> - Preparing to Collect Participant Observation Data
>   - Taking Notes
>   - Interviews, Artifacts, and Other Data Sources
> - Use of Participant Observation Data in Published Research
> - Use of Participant Observation Data in Student Research
> - Steps for Doing Participant Observation Research

Introduction: what are participant observation data sources?

If we look at the two terms *participant* and *observation*, we get a good sense of what this type of research entails. By including the word *participant*, the research implies that the researcher is not simply an outside "observer," but is in some way a part of or participant in the group, culture, or society being researched. Participant observation is often used in languages in interaction studies that are "bottom up" in their analysis of observations of speakers in naturally occurring settings and contexts that have not been constructed by the researcher. Participant observation is a tool in ethnographic research in which the researcher records and analyzes the interactions of a group, culture, or society over time. The intent of these studies is to better understand authentic language in use, or as we say in Chapter 1, "how participants use language to construct, maintain, interact, and shape local communities and identities." The researcher in a participant observation research project is to some degree both an insider (emic perspective) and an outsider (etic perspective) in the sense that the researcher is part of the group being studied but is also looking at it from an outside, or meta, perspective. In these ways, the data collected in such a study are varied and complex.

Alexandra Jaffe describes the method as "a way of capturing the *dynamic, multilayered*, and *shifting* nature of context" (2014, p. 215). She further points out that participant observation can focus on (1) one group of individuals in different contexts (e.g., home, school, or with friends);

(2) a particular context with different participants (e.g., a courtroom, a bar, or a public park); or (3) a particular linguistic practice or genre in different contexts with different participants (e.g., greetings at a local bakery vs. greetings at a school). Jaffe's own study of bilingualism in Corsica took place initially over months, and eventually years, during which time she recognized how individuals chose to study the Corsican language primarily for cultural reasons, but this action also had political implications in a predominantly French-speaking country. Judging from the amount of time and the findings in a study such as Jaffe's, we can see that participant observation research is deep, expansive, and often longitudinal in scope. As a typical data collection method conducted when doing ethnography, participant observation researchers spend months and sometimes years with a group.

Participant observation studies entail rich descriptions because of the interactions of the researcher and the participants. They rely on extensive note taking and researcher observations and may be paired with other data collection methods such as conducting interviews (see Chapter 4), surveys (see Chapter 3), and linguistic landscape analysis (see Chapter 6), among others. One common way to describe participant observation research is that researchers are "hanging out" with participants or in a context, but they take the time to record, video, sketch maps, and keep careful field notes documenting conversations, observations, and events as they conduct their study. As a result, these studies produce massive amounts of data. Although the analysis of the data collected is generally qualitative, some of the data gathered lends itself to quantitative tools, enabling triangulation, the ability to validate data through multiple sources.

We recognize that in a typical one-semester sociolinguistics class, students are not able to do the kind of in-depth study that participant observation research usually entails, but students can develop studies that are meaningful and intellectually satisfying. Students can do smaller focused studies of their own communities, sports groups, family occasions, school clubs, or social media groups, for example. These types of studies necessarily involve shorter periods of time for data gathering but still present the opportunity to both participate in and observe an ongoing community in action in order to develop a deeper understanding and enable rich descriptions and analysis—the kind of inside/outside aspects that make participant observation such a good learning experience. The focus of the studies will vary, but we have found that students are often interested in such sociolinguistic issues as code-switching, style or register shifting, use of slang or jargon, use of discourse markers, and gender or class power relations, among others. The next sections detail some key aspects of this data collection method that students can do in these shorter participant observation studies. See Exercise 5.1 for more thoughts on finding your research topic.

> **EXERCISE 5.1: Preparing to do a participant observation project**
>
> Take some notes on the following questions and topics, and discuss with a partner.
>
> 1. What sociolinguistic variable or language practice do you want to know more about through a participant observation project? Here is a preliminary list for you to think about and add to: code-switching; use of "like"; use of tag questions; use of "be like" as a quotative; use of hedges such as "sorta," "kinda," "I think," and "like"; differences in formality between professors in different disciplines.
> 2. What are some groups that you are a part of and attend regularly? What steps do you need to take to get permission to record and/or take notes or observe one of these groups?
> 3. What articles have you read that will help you refine your research question and approach? What research have you read that you would like to replicate using your own participants?

Preparing to collect participant observation data

As previewed above, data collection in participant observation research studies typically requires doing fieldwork, or observing language use and interaction firsthand. Unlike quantitative research designs that typically follow clearly defined steps and procedures, fieldwork in participant observation may lead in different directions as researchers find new angles and perspectives on their research question. Even if your project changes over the course of data collection, participant observation research begins—where all sociolinguistic studies do –with deciding on a research problem or question and then making a plan to collect data to answer your research question. For example, our students in the past have examined questions such as "When and how often does code-switching take place in a meeting of the [language] group in my school?"; "How many times do members of my class say 'like'?"; or "Is the use of 'like' gendered?"

Your research questions will lead you to determine what group or community of practice will best answer the questions, and you will need to decide what places or participants will allow you access to gather the data in response to your questions. You need to obtain permission from the group in order to take field notes and potentially take pictures and recordings. This may involve contacting a gatekeeper such as a head teacher, business owner, or parent, or someone who has the authority to give you permission to participate in some way and record the activities of the group. To get sufficient data for your study, you need to observe your group or context as much as possible and take as many different types of notes as possible in order to reliably answer your research question.

Taking notes

Taking notes during your observations is the central data you will collect in a participant observation research project, and the main goal that directs your note taking should be thick description. Heigham and Croker (2009) define thick description as

> the rich, vivid descriptions and interpretations that researchers create as they collect data. It encompasses the circumstances, meanings, intentions, strategies, and motivations that characterize the participants, research setting, and events. Thick description helps researchers paint a meticulous picture for the reader. (p. 322)

Often students may not know where to start taking notes, and the idea of thick description does set the bar quite high. In shorter projects, we recommend that students focus on example instances of the linguistic feature they are researching and record who uses it and when (e.g., when discussing what topics, between what interlocutor, time of day, etc.).

Or if the focus is more on the context or group communication patterns, it may help to start with a list of categories and write notes about each category each time you visit your participants. Richards (2003) recommends the following four categories for notes that we have found useful for students to use in short sociolinguistics projects: setting, systems, people, and behavior. We expand on these categories by adding some specific activities and topics to look for:

- *Setting:* Describe the physical space and objects around the participants. This may involve drawing a map of where participants and furniture are located or move, describing the languages or topics overheard on media (e.g., TV, signs, radio, or public announcements), or what people are wearing.
- *Systems:* Look for systems or patterns among the language used or other categories. What appear to be the linguistic conventions or norms? What indicates differences in formal/informal, male/female, or class styles? What happens if someone breaks a norm or linguistic rule among the participants?
- *People:* Who are the main actors or participants in the context? What are the relationships between participants? How are relationships and feelings expressed and maintained through interactions?
- *Behavior:* Document the common routines, interactions, and processes in daily or special events.

As you begin to take your notes and become familiar with your context and participants, you can start to memo, or take notes on, your notes or recordings. You can listen to the recordings and look closely at your notes, paying attention to the patterns or elements that you are interested in knowing more about. Here are some categories and questions you can ask about your notes and recordings as you read them for the first time:

- *Open-ended notes:* What are your overall impressions of the interaction or passage in your notes? What are your initial thoughts on how this interaction works or why a participant spoke in a certain way? What do you not know about this interaction and want to find out through further observations and interviews?
- *Closed category notes:* Go through your notes or recordings, and mark each instance that fits a particular preset category of interest, such as code-switching, use of nonstandard dialect feature, or discussion of a particular topic. After noting each occurrence, examine the linguistic context and any other aspect of the example that is worth further observation and analysis.

Eventually, you will transcribe the recordings and look more closely at all of your notes during data analysis, but this initial memoing, or taking notes on your notes, can help you focus on specific variables or features that you plan to analyze and which you can look for during your next visits to your site.

Interviews, artifacts, and other data sources

As mentioned above, observation notes and recordings can be paired with other data sources from the observation site in order to provide further information in response to the research questions. Interviews with participants the researcher has met through participant observation in particular can be a useful addition during data collection. In participant observation studies, interviews typically occur after initial observations and note taking as a way to gain further insight and evidence to support analysis of research questions. An interview may take place, however, early in a study as an entry into a community and a way to understand the relationships between participants. In this way, an initial interview with a key community member or gatekeeper can help the researcher focus on aspects of a community for observation.

In a participant observation study, researchers should be careful to select interviewees who they feel represent the community well and can provide meaningful insight into the research question and context. In participant observation research, interview participants will likely come from the observation site, and the researcher will already know the participants well. Interviews will typically be open ended or semi-structured, but researchers should have clear questions or topics that they would like to discuss in order to ensure that the interviews provide needed insight. Researchers may also find it useful to bring transcripts from recorded conversations or excerpts from their notes to the interview. They can ask participants for their perspective on how or why a particular interaction took place.

In addition to interviews, the following artifacts and other data sources may also provide valuable information for participant observation researchers:

- Online videos and materials
- Textbooks and other materials used in classrooms for instruction
- Classroom work and projects, including language tests that demonstrate proficiency and language usage
- Photos or personal documents from participants.

Collecting these various types of data assists with triangulation of data sources, which is important to most research projects but particularly relevant in participant observation research as it avoids the bias that can come from any one source, including the researcher's own bias.

Now that we have reviewed some basics for preparing to conduct a participant observation project, complete Exercise 5.2 to gain firsthand experience using these methods.

EXERCISE 5.2: Observation exercise

Conduct a practice observation of a particular social setting (e.g., a café, the student bookstore, a grocery store, or an exercise gym). Choose a place that you have easy access to and where you will be able to overhear conversations and language interactions. Complete the following tasks:

1. Observe the chosen site at least twice, for an hour each time.
2. Take notes about the people and how they interact. Write down information about how people are dressed, how long they stay, who sits with whom, how the store or restaurant is organized, and any other details that are important in describing the place to another person. Try to take notes on the four aspects of setting, systems, people, and behavior. Be sure to note any aspects of interactions or language use that appear to be outliers, as well as what appear to be some rules for interaction.
3. Interview at least two people at the site. Tell them that you are doing a class project and you are interested in learning about the place. Store clerks or wait staff would be good people to ask first as they may be the

most friendly. Ask questions about why they work or come there, what they like about the site, and so on. (Provide the date and times of your observations/interviews in your reflection.)
4. Review your notes and perform an initial coding and/or memoing about them, offering initial analysis and asking questions about outlier data.
5. Prepare a 5–7 minute summary about your social setting, to share with partners. Include information on what sociolinguistic aspects of the social setting you would be interested in exploring in more detail and how you would go about conducting further research on your setting.

Use of participant observation data in published research

It is instructive to look at participant observational research to understand the complexities of gathering, interpreting, and analyzing a rich data set. For example, consider the lengths of time the following researchers spent gathering data:

- Penelope Eckert did field work for two years in a high school in Detroit, Michigan, to research the dynamics of high school behavior and identity and how these were reflected in linguistic choices (Eckert, 1989).
- Shirley Brice Heath spent nine years gathering data comparing the language practices in two South Carolina communities to understand the role that environment and family practices play in language development (Heath, 1983).
- Benjamin Bailey collected data in both Providence, Rhode Island, and the Dominican Republic over the course of one year to explore how a group of Dominican Americans uses language to make sense of their social identities (Bailey, 2000).
- Alexandra Jaffe studied the language shifts between the use of Corsican and French in French-dominated Corsica for close to 30 years (Jaffe, 1999, 2007).

We recommend that students read these participant observation studies and others as a way to learn about the complexity and power of participant observation analysis, and in the following sections, we summarize in depth two further studies, Reyes (2005) and Sierra (2016), as examples of data collection techniques in different settings.

Reyes (2005) worked closely with an Asian American youth group in Pennsylvania over a four-year period, collecting data to establish the role that African American slang played in identity formation. To gather and analyze data, the researcher worked as a volunteer and coordinator of a teen video-making project at the Asian Arts Initiative near Philadelphia, Pennsylvania. She studied the interactions of Asian immigrant youths from countries such as Cambodia, Laos, Thailand, Vietnam, and the Philippines in order to examine how the use of language variables and other social behaviors helped to construct their identities. Her focus in the article was on the relationship between class stratification and the role that the appropriation of African American slang plays for these teenagers. In this way, Reyes (2005) draws on both foundational works such as the study of social stratification in Labov (1966) and research on the appropriation of African American slang by whites in Cutler (1999). As Reyes (2005) writes, she is exploring "how processes of racialization, appropriation and authentication are integral in examining the ways in which speakers actively construct their identities through discursively constituted links between linguistic styles and categories of persons" (p. 511). Specifically, the study focuses on two African American slang terms: *aite* ('all right') and *na mean* ('do you know what I mean'). The following is an excerpt of a conversation between four teens in the study: three females, Macy, Anh, and Van; and one male, Will. See Table 8.1 in Chapter 8 on p. 130–131 for list of transcription conventions.

1	Macy:	say na mean (.)
2	Will:	[come on
3	Van:	[I can't talk slang
4	Macy:	you can't?
5	Will:	what's slang
6	Anh:	[slang
7	Macy:	[slang
8	Will:	oh what's slang oh- oh sla::ng
9	Van:	except if I'm really mad
10	Will:	[na mean (.) na mean
11	Macy:	[hmm hmm hmm the ghettoness comes out
12	Van:	heh heh yes heh heh (p. 517)

After the above exchange, Reyes meets separately with Van to understand how Van interprets her use of African American slang and its relationship to her identity. Van explains that she uses slang when she wants to sound "scary" or "mean,". Reyes interprets this to suggest that Van is embarrassed about her racialization of the slang as belonging to African Americans and particularly those living in South Philadelphia. Van's connection of place, class, and race further distinguishes differences between Van and Will, who live in middle-class neighborhoods, and Macy and Anh, who live in South Philadelphia. For student researchers, it is important to note that Reyes was able to make this in-depth analysis through her connection of the recorded interaction with a personal interview with Van, a nice example of triangulation and the mixed data collection methods of participant observation.

In another excerpt, Reyes (2005) presented a discussion about a script that has two fictional characters, Moi and Hoa. The interlocutors in the discussion are four teens, Jill, Enoy, Cindy, and Rod; and one adult, Didi, who is working with the teens as a scriptwriting artist.

```
26  Didi:   okay so he—so Hoa says [she's—she's kind of cute? And then—
27  Jill:   [<writing> still watching
28  Didi:   —yeah still wa—
29  Enoy:   nobody (gonna) use the word cute, it like i-I she look kinda
30          aite.
31  Didi:   yeah, but what word will you use
32  Enoy:   she look kinda aite
33  Jill:   <writing> she (.) look (.) kinda (.) aite (.) I can't spell (?)
34  Cindy: [hmmm hmm
35  Enoy:  [hm m hmm
36  Jill:   that's all right (they're not gonna like this)
37  Rod:    <pointing to the word look that Jill wrote> erase this
38  Jill:   <writing> still (walking)
39  Rod:    she's kinda aite
40  Didi:   she's [kinda what? (1.1) <leaning in to read what Jill wrote>—
41  Jill:         [she look kinda aite
42  Didi:   —aite.
43  Enoy:  [aite
44  Jill:  [aite
45  Didi:   oh [I ge(hh)t i(hh)t heh heh.
46  Jill:      [heh heh
47  Cindy:[heh heh
48  Jill:   <pointing to her left with thumb, palm facing her and fingers
49          closed> they'll know what we're talking about heh heh (p. 522)
```

Reyes (2005) pointed out how "slang is established as the legitimate language" and that "an in-group of teens against which Didi is positioned is constituted. Didi is further removed from this group of teens when she displays that she does not know the word *aite* and the teens do not facilitate her comprehension" (p. 522). She continued her analysis by looking closely at lines 48 and 49 and at the use of the pronominal indexicals "they" and "we" as well as Jill's gesture seeing how they "further solidify a distinct boundary between the adult out-group and the youth in-group" (pp. 522–23). Reyes (2005) stated that the "'we' indexes a group that includes only the teens in the immediate interaction and not the adult, while 'they' indexes a group that includes only the other teens, and no adults. Thus, both 'they' and 'we' constitute two groups that consist of only teens, while adults are excluded from the indexical field" (p. 523).

In this participant observation study, Reyes analyzed transcripts of the interactions among group members and her interviews with individuals, as well as her thick description of the group interactions. The analysis helped to show the function and purpose of the slang terms for this group of teens as well as to reaffirm the Labovian theory that language use indexes class and community status. As is often the case, the data collected in Reyes's participant observation research study is vast and rich, and we discuss analysis methods such as discourse analysis in more depth in Part III. What is important to note here is that while she was collecting the data, Reyes continued to refine and focus her observations based on what she was seeing in particular aspects of the data collected—in this case, to focus on two particular phrases used by the participants and to examine closely several conversations among the participants. Analysis in participant observation research usually relies on qualitative methods, as Reyes's did, but it may also involve quantitative methods in order to quantify both how and why a group uses language and behaviors to establish its identity, culture, and norms, and to triangulate findings. See Exercise 5.3 for more in-depth question on Reyes' topic and research methods.

EXERCISE 5.3: How would you analyze Reyes's data?

Consider the following questions and topic about Reyes (2005).

1. Look at the two discussions from the Reyes article, and notice the brief interview Reyes had with one of the participants. If you were to meet with another of the participants in the group, which one would you choose to meet with? What question(s) would you ask? What might help you understand the role of the use of slang for that person?
2. Next, find Reyes's article on the *Journal of Sociolinguistics* website. The article was published in 2005, vol. 9. What is Reyes's research question? How does she let her readers know the context of the study and why it is important and necessary?

Recently, participant observation research has begun to look closely at the effect of the internet and media—TV shows, video games, blogs, texting, or other social media—on our identity construction and on how we index ourselves as part of a community. For example, Sierra (2016) explores the role of intertextuality in her examination of the appropriation of texts from the video games a group of friends play. Intertextuality refers to the back and forth of old and new texts in our conversations and dialogues. To examine this notion in the context of a participant observation research study, Sierra acted on her observation that her group of friends had developed a speech community that shared textual references and language with video games that they had been playing as a group for some time.

After getting permission from her friends, she recorded everyday conversations with her "nerd" friends and herself over a period of three months, sometimes in a shared house and sometimes in restaurants. She explained that her "participation in these conversations had distinct advantages, such as allowing [her] to know as much as possible about the conversational setting and the participants' relationships with each other" (p. 223). One of the games the group played is *Papers, Please*, a video game that "focuses on the psychological toll of working as an immigration officer in the fictional dystopian country of Arstotzka" (p. 223). The main task involves role-play among a cast of characters inspecting documents at a checkpoint location. One of the conversations that Sierra (2016) recorded came from three game participants: two women, Sylvia and Lana, and one man, Fred:

Sylvia: We have been paid by `Arsto:tzka`..
Fred: [hahaha You [received some cre:dits for processing [the language.
Lana: [haha   [haha   [hahahahaha
Sylvia: [hahaha   hahaha
Fred: You're lucky you drew [this jo:b in the `la:bor lottery.' (p. 227)

Lana and Fred are using a "Borat" voice, a voice based on a fictitious character in the 2006 comedy film *Borat*. The comment about being paid by 'Arsto:tzka' is an implicit comparison between the work setting, in this case an academic department in a college, of the participants and the bureaucratic government in the video game. The statement about "drawing the job" in the labor lottery directly refers to how in Papers the players may be assigned roles as border control agents or in the labor lottery, which players seem to prefer. As players overlap their own life experiences, they use the situations and characters of the video game "while still anchoring the talk in the real-life frame of money and work." Changing the voice and register of two of the participants is also an indication of the interpolation of real life and fictional life.

In another conversation, the name of a character from the video game appears. In this conversation, there are four participants—the same three above with the addition of Dave.

Lana: [They all came from Jorji, Jorji's like "He:y!"
Sylvia: [Yeah.
Dave: ["He:y."
Fred: [So—
Lana: ["I make a passapo:rt[a:!"
Sylvia: [hahaha

The character of Jorji, a character who appears throughout the video game with false documents, stands in for participants' dealings with the bureaucracy of getting paid and being treated fairly in the work world. Immersion in the game world includes imitating the voice, accent, and situation of this character in the game, thereby developing an intertextual experience that only game players would fully comprehend. One of the participants, pseudonym Lana, even drew a mural of the housemates depicted as video game characters alongside their real cats, connecting the worlds of real and virtual communities. Through the participant observation methods, Sierra (2016) analyzes how the conversations, the imitative voicing, and the illustration of the participants as game characters create a speech community of video gamers with its insider and outsider status. This type of in-depth analysis and thick description of a community is only available through participant observation data collection methods, and in Sierra (2016), students find an example of a researcher using a community that they are already a member of, in this way moving from an emic to an etic perspective on the community. Exercise 5.4 invites you to discuss Sierra's topic in more depth, as well as how she was able to study in a group in which she was already a member.

EXERCISE 5.4: What would you like to know about Sierra's research?

Consider the following questions and topics about Sierra (2016).

1. In the Sierra study, the author is also a member—in fact, a housemate—of the group being researched. What strengths and weaknesses do you see in actually being "one" of the group? Contrast this with Reyes's participation in her study.
2. What kinds of internet groups are you a part of? Which types of groups do you think would be valuable to study? What problems do you foresee with doing Internet participant observation research?

3. Find the Sierra article on the *Language in Society* website. The article was published in 2016, vol. 45, pp. 217–45. What is Sierra's research question? What is the role of pictures in the study? How does she let her readers know the context of the study and why it is important and necessary? How and where does she define terms such as *keying, framing, intertextuality*, and *indexicality*?

RESEARCHER TO KNOW: Alexandra Jaffe

Alexandra Jaffe is Professor of Anthropology at the California State University at Long Beach (CSULB). She is a linguistic anthropologist who has done fieldwork studying language shift and revitalization for 30 years in the French island of Corsica. Her longitudinal and ethnographic study of Corsica has focused on language ideology and identity in the bilingual island and how it is taught in the schools, depicted in the media, and presented in language policy. She has also worked closely on orthography (spelling) and on nonstandard orthographies in sociolinguistic transcripts and has co-authored a book on the sociolinguistics of orthography with Mark Sebba, Sally Johnson, and Jannis Androutsopoulos, entitled *Orthography as Social Action* (2012). She also does research on how sociolinguistic variation is represented in the media—in movies, documentaries, online, and in broadcasts—and connects this to how we make meaning and to ideologies of language.

Use of participant observation data in student research

As we have seen from a few examples above, participant observation research is time-consuming, and we in no way feel that student researchers in a course have the time to provide the same type of thick description and triangulated data that were illustrated in the studies above. At the same time, many students value studying communities and social groups that they are already a part of, and can complete very powerful and interesting short pilot projects using participant observation methods. One example is our student Shirley Weng, who completed a research paper on code-switching between English and Chinese, what she termed *Chinglish*, in her own family. As she describes it, "My firsthand knowledge and experience with speaking a bilingual language offered me the chance to study Chinglish through participant observation." To conduct her study, she "took note of [her] own English-Chinese use" as well as that used by her mother, aunt, and uncle in naturally occurring conversations about topics such as food and clothing. Here is an excerpt of dialogue between the student researcher and her uncle, discussing a dish made with marshmallows and the cereal Rice Krispies:

Uncle: Yee dee deem yurng jaing gah?
(These, how are (they) made?)
Me: Mix ge marshmallow *tong ngow yauw.*
(Mix the marshmallows with butter.)
Uncle: Oh! Terrible!
Me: Haha, *mm hai gum daw ngau yauw,* but yeah, it's terrible.
(Haha, not that much butter, but yeah, it's terrible.)

As can be seen in the excerpt, Weng found that English is used for ideas that do not directly translate, like marshmallow. She also observed that English prepositions and conjunctions such as *but* in the above exchange may be used as fillers and connectors, but most noteworthy was her observation that "English is used to show a feeling of disagreement or discord." She acknowledges that this finding merits further research and Exercise 5.5 invites you to discuss Weng's topic and research methods.

> **EXERCISE 5.5: What would you like to know about Weng's research?**
>
> Consider the following questions about Weng's paper. A full copy of her text is available on the companion website.
>
> 1. What issues might arise if one is doing a participant research study with one's family? How would you deal with these issues?
> 2. What are the advantages of doing participant research with family? Or with close friends as Sierra (2016) did? What are the disadvantages?
> 3. What question would you like to ask Weng about her project?

Jack Kenigsberg conducted his student research project, "Speaking Geek: Intertextuality in an Online Community of Practice," by doing a participant observation analysis of a defunct online site, limerickdb.com, a group in which he had been a member until its demise. Kenigsberg explains the value of his participation in much the same way as Sierra (2016), noting, "Any communicative act is best understood by the community that produces it because only they can understand the full range of references that are needed to decipher the communiqué." Kenigsberg explains the reason why his participation in the group is critical because "not every reader is capable of recognizing the various references built into a text; recognition comes when one is part of the same community as the writer."

Kenigsberg chose some of the top 10 limericks that were shared by anonymous group members to illustrate how intertextual and self-referential the limericks were and how, although they could be read by anyone, they could only be understood by those who indexed themselves as "geeks." To rate them, limericks were tallied using plus [+] and minus [–] signs. The tallying was not a simple counting of positives and negatives; instead, Kenigsberg writes, "Two positive votes and one negative vote would give an entry a combined tally of 1; two negative votes and one positive vote would give an entry a combined tally of –1." In this way, the more positive votes are a reflection of the values of the community. As one example, Kenigsberg analyzes the number-one most popular limerick:

There once was a buggy AI
Who decided her subject should die.
When the plot was uncovered,
The subject discovered
That sadly the cake was a lie.

The limerick by itself makes little sense unless one has the "geek cred" to recognize the reference to the video game *Portal*, in which an artificial intelligence puts players through tests with the incentive of cake. In the video game, the players ultimately find graffiti on the wall that says, "The cake is a lie." The limerick summarizes the plot of the game and is only decipherable by those who know the game. The fact that non-gamers do not get the point is the point of the limerick. Its high value in the site attests to the idea that to index oneself as a "geek" and member of the community was to understand esoteric concepts not known by outsiders.

The third most popular limerick is more comprehensible by those who know about poetry types:

There was an old man
From Peru, whose lim'ricks all
Look'd like haiku. He

Said with a laugh, "I
Cut them in half, the pay is
Much better for two."

Using the conventional "There once was a [person] from [place]," this limerick assumes that readers know the form of a haiku as well as the form of a limerick.

Kenigsberg concludes that the Limerickdb site was a true community of practice with a special geeky language and fan group who, while remaining anonymous to each other, nonetheless became a speech community for those indexing themselves as the "smart masses." Kenigsberg's project is a good example of the use of online groups, social media, and gaming as data sources for participant research studies, and Exercise 5.6 invites you to think more about his research topic and data collection activities.

EXERCISE 5.6: What would you like to know about Kenigsberg's research?

Consider the following questions about Kenigsberg's paper. A full text is available on the companion website.

1. What are the challenges of doing online website research?
2. What are the advantages of doing online website research?
3. What types of social media that you are involved in might work well for participant observation research?
4. How can individuals be anonymous and members of a community?
5. What question would you like to ask Kenigsberg about his project?

Steps for doing participant observation research

Several steps are important in conducting a participant observation project, and students should consider these as they start a course-long project:

1. Select a community or group in which you are member and which will accept you as a researcher for your sociolinguistics class.
2. Keep the group small so you can hear and observe the conversation and the context or the events surrounding it.
3. Discuss with the participants the need for some kind of recording device—a smart phone and/or a video recorder.
4. Decide how many times and for how long you will record the activities of the group. (Keep in mind that you will need to transcribe and look closely at any video or photos you collect.)
5. Practice transcribing a short 2–5 minute conversation from your own recording of it or from a YouTube or podcast. Use transcription conventions as shown in Chapter 8.
6. Transcribe the material you collect.

7. Sort out and review your field notes and all data collected.

8. After looking closely at the data collected, choose the focus of your analysis if you have not already decided on this.

9. Decide on the best method for analyzing the data you have collected.

10. After the analysis, you may have a follow-up meeting with the participants to discuss your findings, both to validate your analysis and to continue the discussion with the participants. You may include parts of this final discussion in your final paper.

Finally, review the question in Exercise 5.7 to further develop your participant observation research project.

> **EXERCISE 5.7: Observation exercise**
>
> Conduct a practice observation of a particular social setting (e.g., a café, the student bookstore, a grocery store, or an exercise gym). Choose a place that you have easy access to and where you will be able to overhear conversations and language interactions. Complete the following tasks:
>
> 1. Observe the chosen site at least twice, for an hour each time.
> 2. Take notes about the people and how they interact. Write down information about how people are dressed, how long they stay, who sits with whom, how the store or restaurant is organized, and any other details that are important in describing the place to another person. Try to take notes on the four aspects of setting, systems, people, and behavior. Be sure to note any aspects of interactions or language use that appear to be outliers, as well as what appear to be some rules for interaction.
> 3. Interview at least two people at the site. Tell them that you are doing a class project and you are interested in learning about the place. Store clerks or wait staff would be good people to ask first as they may be the most friendly. Ask questions about why they work or come there, what they like about the site, and so on. (Provide the date and times of your observations/interviews in your reflection.)
> 4. Review your notes and perform an initial coding and/or memoing about them, offering initial analysis and asking questions about outlier data.
> 5. Prepare a 5–7 minute summary about your social setting, to share with partners. Include information on what sociolinguistic aspects of the social setting you would be interested in exploring in more detail and how you would go about conducting further research on your setting.

> **Further reading on participant observation data collection methods**
>
> In addition to our summary of participant observation research methods in this chapter, the following are excellent sources for further in-depth reading:
>
> DeWitt, K. M., & DeWitt, B. R. (2010). *Participant observation: A guide for fieldworkers*, 2nd ed. Lanham, MD: AltaMira Press.
> Guest, G., Namey, E., & Mitchell, M. (2013). *Collecting qualitative data: A field guild for applied research*. Thousand Oaks, CA: Sage.
> Jongensen, D. (1989). *Participant observation*. Newbury Park, CA: Sage.

6 Linguistic landscape and computer-mediated data sources

> **CHAPTER OVERVIEW**
>
> - Introduction: What Are Linguistic Landscape and Computer-Mediated Data Sources?
> - Preparing to Collect Linguistic Landscape and Computer-Mediated Data
>   - Research Questions and Data Sources
>   - Data Collection and Sampling Strategies
> - Use of Linguistic Landscape and Computer-Mediated Data in Published Research
> - Use of Linguistic Landscape and Computer-Mediated Data In Student Research
> - Steps for Collecting Linguistic Landscape and Computer-Mediated Data

Introduction: what are linguistic landscape and computer-mediated data sources?

Both linguistic landscape and computer-mediated data sources are relatively new areas of data in sociolinguistics research. Linguistic landscape (LL) research projects focus on how language constructs public spaces, or—as Landry and Bourhis (1997) define the term in their much cited article—linguistic landscapes are "the language of public road signs, advertising billboards, street names, place names, commercial shop signs, and public signs on government buildings . . . of a given territory, region, or urban agglomeration" (p. 25). Sayer (2010) in his study expands this description of the modern urban landscape to include signs "naming stores and streets, adorning T-shirts and backpacks, giving directions, peddling products and promoting politicians" (p. 144). Computer-mediated data sources, also referred to as computer-mediated communication (CMC), is an umbrella term which refers to human communication via computers or digital media such as email, social media sites, mobile messaging platforms, or educational and professional workspaces. Researchers often use distinctions between synchronous CMC, where communication takes place in real time such as during an online chat session, and asynchronous CMC, where interlocutors and community members are not necessarily online or communicating at the same time, such as communication through email or message boards (Simpson, 2002).

Research projects using these types of data are becoming more popular in sociolinguistics and other social science and humanities fields, and they offer student researchers the opportunity to collect data that comes directly from their daily lives and to apply different data collection methods depending on their research goals. Whereas linguistic landscape research is active and typically involves physical fieldwork, getting outside, taking photos, doing sketches, and making field notes, CMC research projects may involve more soliciting, organizing, and analyzing online data or data collected through digital communication. In fact, you may be communicating with your participants through the same medium that you are studying (i.e., texting with participants as a way to collect and analyze aspects of SMS communication). See Exercise 6.1 for another example of CMC and some practice analysis questions.

EXERCISE 6.1: Examining computer-mediated communication

In order to compare how features of CMC writing styles are different from traditional publishing sources, compare an article posted to one of *Scientific American*'s blog sites (https://blogs.scientificamerican.com) with one of the scientific papers that the blog is reporting on. Or find a similar magazine that offers presentation and discussion of academic research topics for a broader audience. Consider the following questions:

1. What are the linguistic differences between the blog post and the scientific papers in terms of word choice, sentence length/complexity, and organization of information?
2. Which writing would you characterize as more or less formal, and why? What information is left out or missing in the different forums and why?

As an additional activity, read some of the reader comments that appear at the end of blog posts on the *Scientific American* site. Compare linguistic or other content aspects of the reader comments with reader and user comments on other online media sites, for example comments on articles from a daily newspaper or comments on a YouTube video. How do comments differ in tone, language, and content across the various online forums?

Despite some differences in how the data is collected, we include both data sources together in this final chapter on data collection methods because we feel that both sources draw on multimodal resources and meaning-making affordances that can challenge and further many of our core understandings about language and communication in sociolinguistics. Both LL and CMC research projects draw on multiple data collection and analysis methods, from qualitative and ethnographic to quantitative and statistical analysis, and they can respond to research questions from all of the three major areas of sociolinguistics outlined in Chapter 1. Further, as Androutsopoulos (2014) writes, LL and CMC data "challenge traditional linguistic units of analysis such as clause or turn" and "extend what counts as sociolinguistic data as sociolinguistic scholarship moves on to examine language and discourse in new environments" (p. 75). Thus, for students, collecting and analyzing these data offer the chance to apply and analyze traditional sociolinguistic theories and beliefs and offer new insights to the field.

Preparing to collect linguistic landscape and computer-mediated data

As with most research projects, one of the first steps in planning a project is often to survey previous research and focus on a particular set of research questions. This is true in conducting LL and CMC research, perhaps even more than with other types of data collection. As mentioned above, LL and CMC studies often replicate or extend previous studies but then draw on new data and contexts that were not available or did not exist when previous studies took place. For example, Lawrence (2012) investigates William Labov's cascade model of language change through an analysis of public signs in different neighborhoods in Seoul, South Korea, and Kulkarni (2014) analyzes Roman Jakobsen's notion of phatic communication in instant messaging. In this way, a good place to start planning an LL or CMC study would be to identify a study or theory that you find particularly interesting and want to explore and analyze in more depth using online, digital, or multimodal data sources.

In addition, LL and CMC researchers at the start of their project planning need to decide from what perspectives they will approach their data collection activities, that is, do they view their data as "text," "place," or both? By this, we draw on Milner (2011) and Androutsopoulos (2014), who describe a "text" perspective as focusing on the written language itself, whereas a "place" perspective focuses on the social processes that take place within and in relation to the human-created spaces of linguistic landscapes and computer-assisted communication. Androutsopoulos (2014) offers the CMC example of a "Twitter as text" project, collecting a large amount of tweets and focusing on linguistic features in the tweets, perhaps comparing individual users with corporations or other categories of users (p. 77). She contrasts this with a "Twitter as place" project that would "examine how particular social actors use this medium in order to engage in social activities in the context of a particular event (say, a political rally), thereby shaping the course and social meaning of that event" (p. 77). Thus, as a starting point in beginning an LL or CMC project, researchers should first decide on whether they will focus on "text" or "place" perspectives during data collection. Of course, both perspectives are possible, especially in mixed-methods data collection designs, but this may involve more data and time than is possible to collect during a course-long project.

Once these framing questions have been addressed, researchers can outline their research questions, data sources, and sampling strategies in similar ways to other data collection methods. The rest of this chapter section focuses on examples and particular aspects of LL and CMC data collection that are slightly different from other data collection methods surveyed in previous chapters.

Research questions and data sources

After considering "text" or "place" orientations toward the study, LL and CMC researchers will want to think through a series of related questions in narrowing their research questions and determining where to collect data. Some examples are presented here:

- Will your study compare modes of communication (e.g., email vs. texting) or locations of signs (between neighborhoods)? Or will the focus be on intermode comparisons and detailing signs and language used within the linguistic landscape of one particular neighborhood or location?
- Will your study examine a larger theme or trend in how language is used in a particular speech community (e.g., the use of English as an international lingua franca)?
- Will your study focus on one aspect of communication (e.g., code-switching or translanguaging)?
- Will you collect only written language and examples, or are you also interested in participant feedback and perspectives? In other words, is your research question only about the language as "text" or are you also interested in user and resident experiences of the "place" you are studying?
- Are you interested in collecting and analyzing nonlanguage data and features such as the shape, placement, color, or any other multimodal aspects of the communication or linguistic landscape (e.g., emojis, physical shape of the sign, placement in relation to other texts or signs)?
- Will you analyze or consider grammatical features and translation aspects of the communication (both correct and incorrect)?

This list of questions is just a beginning point of places and topics to consider when defining your CMC and LL research questions, and they can help you consider the types of data and places where you will collect them.

As a further discussion of ways to focus your research questions and decide on your data sources, consider the following three examples of LL or CMC research that fall under our three general fields of sociolinguistic research.

Language variation: the Korean English linguistic landscape

In his study of the linguistic landscape of South Korea, C. Bruce Lawrence (2012) attempted to investigate a number of research questions about public signs. First, he writes that although English is widely studied in Korea, "the nation of Korea and the city of Seoul actually have a rather tenuous relationship" (2012, p. 71), and his study is an attempt to map and analyze how much English has been taken up in public signs in different neighborhoods across South Korea. In addition, he notes that sociolinguists from William Labov to Peter Trudgill have devised different theories—from gravity to cascade models—for how language changes spread and are taken up in a wider language community, and he planned to analyze these models through his data collection and analysis in regards to the spread of English on public signs. More specifically, he lists the following research questions:

- Regarding language, what is the percentage of English, Konglish, Korean, and Chinese in the signs?
- Regarding location, does the percentage change according to locale (main streets, alleys, inside stores, and on street vendor signs)?
- Does it change in relation to various districts in Seoul?
- Does it change in relation to other sites [in South Korea]?
- Regarding domains, are there certain domains where English can be expected to either exist or be absent?
- At the theoretical level, are the social stratification, gravity or cascade models supported by the data? (Lawrence, 2012, p. 75)

From these research questions, Lawrence (2012) then chose specific neighborhoods and devised particular qualitative and quantitative methods and sampling strategies for collecting and analyzing public signs in Korea. We can note that he started his project by first focusing on the bigger questions around the spread of English in Korea and the previous theoretical models used by sociolinguists to explain language change.

Languages in communities: responses to the linguistic landscape in Memphis, Tennessee

Garvin (2010) is an example of a linguistic landscape project that examines languages in communities and uses what the author termed "walking tour interviews" to analyze local residents' reaction to migrant and minority language signage in the Memphis linguistic landscape. In this way, her research questions and data sources focus on how residents of Memphis experience the linguistic landscape and not the "text" or variation focus of other LL studies such as Lawrence (2012). Garvin (2010) writes that she drew on and extended previous LL studies by situating her study and asking research questions about the lives and experiences of local residents or, as she explains, "the cognitive and emotional verbal responses elicited and triggered by close physical proximity and explicit reference to the LL" (p. 264). Specifically, she asks:

- In what ways do individual residents understand, interpret, and interact with the LL in their communities?
- What are their thoughts and feelings about multilingualism or changes in the LL?
- In what ways does the LL connect residents to their social and psychological identities? (p. 264)

From these research questions, Garvin (2010) located 10 informants and chose streets to take the participants on "tours" that had many multilingual signs, icons, and images. In order to find her participants, Garvin (2010) put up fliers in offices (both academic and nonacademic) and local stores and business. Five of her participants were considered native English speakers who had lived in Memphis all their lives, two from other areas in the United States, and the last three were non-native English speakers from Ethiopia, Mexico, and Cambodia. As a research plan, we understand that her research questions connect to her initial desire to study participants' lived experiences as well as connect these experiences and perspectives to their feelings about multilingualism and language change in their community.

Language in interaction: exploring instant messaging interactions

In Kulkarni (2014), we have an example of a CMC study that investigates a languages-in-interaction topic, specifically how conversation partners on an instant messaging (IM) platform establish, maintain, and terminate contact. Kulkarni (2014) is a good example of a study that draws on previous research and theories about how language works—in this case, how phatic, or interpersonal, communication is displayed and maintained—and draws on new CMC tools and spaces. For this reason, it is instructive to examine how the study is presented in the first paragraph of the article:

> The idea of phatic communication is traced to Malinowski (1923), who coined the phrase to refer to the language used to build ties of union with other members of the community. The linguistic function so conceived has some overlaps with the 'interpersonal' in Halliday's functional model (1973) and the "social" in Lyons's classification (1996). The concept is important because it counteracts the emphasis on the descriptive function of language and draws attention to the social, interpersonal use of language. Since Malinowski, researchers have observed the phenomenon in various interactional contexts. Most of this empirical research has been done in the face-to-face environment (Cheepen, 1988; Coupland et al., 1992; Holmes, 2000; Laver, 1975; Schneider, 1988; Tracy and Naughton, 2000; Yang, 2012) and some in mediated environments like telephone conversations (Cheepen, 2000; Drew and Chilton, 2000). In this research, I extend the enquiry to the online social world (see also Miller, 2008). The predominance of internet-based media such as instant messaging and social networking sites in facilitating our social interactions makes it pertinent to study phatic communion in this environment. (pp. 117–18)

As we see from the introduction to the study, Kulkarni (2014) clearly connects with previous studies of how language establishes contact between speakers, but effectively opens the space for a comparison with how CMC and IM communication change our understanding of this aspect of communication.

Later in the paper, Kulkarni (2014) lists more specific research objectives and data sources:

> The objectives of the analysis are twofold: first, to identify the various linguistic means used by participants to establish, maintain, and terminate contact (thus identify instances of phatic communion), and second to see what these suggest about the nature of contact in IM. A corpus of 60 IM interactions was collected from 20 respondents (three each). Since IM chats are private conversations, convenience sampling was used. Along with the chats, the participants were also asked to fill in a questionnaire which ascertained background information like demographic details, internet usage, and also details of the specific chats they had shared such as time and location from where they were chatting, their relationship with the other interlocutor, and frequency of contact between them. (pp. 119–20)

In this section, we can see again the movement between the specific data collection site and larger questions about how language is used in interaction. In addition, Kulkarni (2014) begins to outline the sampling strategy that was used in collecting the data, an important next step in preparing CMC and LL research projects.

Data collection and sampling strategies

As with most studies, your research questions will lead you to determining what data and what data sources can best answer your questions and become the center of your analysis. In the three studies summarized above, we can see that LL and CMC studies typically draw on two main types of data: (1) the text of the communication or signs themselves, and/or (2) talking with people about their computer-mediated communication or experiences with the linguistic landscape. Some decisions about data collection will depend on whether you are taking more of a "text" or "place" perspective in your research. For example, Garvin (2010) was interested in the different languages and code-switching on the public signs in the US city Memphis, but she was primarily interested in the ways residents interacted with the signs. Thus, she devised a data collection plan that focused on "walking tours" with Memphis residents, where she interviewed them and discussed their interpretations of the signs. In addition to the focus on collecting data from participants, Garvin (2010) is instructive as an example of purposive sampling because her participants were not randomly selected; rather, she purposely chose participants based on their characteristics and relevance to her "place"-based research questions.

Alternatively, Lawrence (2012) is more interested in mapping the placement, language, and physical characteristics of English signs in Korean cities, and his research methodology uses convenience sampling to focus on the English text on signs and to compare different neighborhoods and cities across Korea. It is important to note, however, that convenience sampling does not mean that Lawrence (2012) randomly collected images and examples of signs; rather, he created a systematic sampling strategy to record the different signs. As he writes:

> Upon exiting a subway station a direction was chosen and a count was made of how many out of 100 were in English, Korean and Chinese. This gave a rough estimate of the percentage of each. The nearest alley was analyzed using the same method. Then, the nearest store was analyzed according to the amount of the three languages on the menu and wall posters. Any small, mobile, street vendors in the area were also photographed and a rough estimate of the amount of the target languages on their signs or menus was made. These vendors may be permanent tents or mobile, electrically motorized carts with sheltering canopies, and they may sell anything from clothing and caps to freshly cooked seafood and drinks. (p. 75)

In this way, Lawrence (2012) followed the recommendations of Androutsopoulos (2014) when she writes that LL researchers need to determine the mode of analysis by answering questions such as "Is the unit of analysis the individual sign, the shop window, or a specific chunk of space on the street?" and "what aspect of the materiality (physical shape) of signs shall be taken into account in analysis?" (p. 85).

An additional sampling strategy that is useful when completing student LL and CMC research projects is theoretical sampling, in which researchers decide on particular themes or criteria for selecting data in order to respond to their research questions and often to generate a particular theory or explanation about a linguistic phenomenon or question. This type of theory building is associated with grounded theory and is an iterative process in which a researcher collects more and more data until a clear pattern emerges that can provide an explanation for the research question. This point is often referred to as data saturation. We refer to this type of analysis further in Chapter 7 on qualitative data analysis. This type of data collection and coding takes too long for a course-based research project, but students may start their data collection focused on particular themes related to their data sources and, based on those themes, collect further examples. Sayer (2010) is a good example of this type of theoretical sampling and thematic data collection. In his project, he began by collecting public signs with English words in Oaxaca, Mexico, based on whether they were cross-cultural (i.e., intended for an international or foreign audience) or intracultural (i.e., intended for a local, Mexican audience). He determined that the signs could be categorized into three main types, informational, iconic, and innovative, and began his data analysis from there. In their own projects, students may want to use preexisting categories such as the one Sayer (2010) has already outlined, or, time permitting, they may be able to collect data on multiple occasions after initial coding and analysis.

The previous examples of sampling strategies have all come from LL projects and are also examples of the beginning stages of data analysis that we discuss in more depth in the next section of the book. Similar strategies can be used in CMC research projects as well. For example, student researchers may use convenience sampling to collect as many examples of how communication occurs among a particular subgroup on a particular CMC platform, such as Reddit, in order to perform an initial analysis for a class project. Student researchers may also collect data from multiple CMC platforms about particular themes or topics, or researchers may look at how a particular feature, such as the acronym LOL (laughing out loud), is used on different sites. Further, CMC researchers may decide to focus on users themselves and draw on purposive sampling to interview participants about their use of a particular CMC technology. For example, our student Christy Ruschmeyer, whose paper we illustrate more in the next section, collected texts from her friends and surveyed them about how they interpreted silence and long waits between responses in particular conversations.

A final example of a sampling strategy that may be more common in CMC research is what Herring (2004) calls "sampling by time." In this strategy, researchers select particular times to collect data over a set period. In this way, research can examine changes in the language use over time and perhaps between different participants, and researchers can build more internal reliability into the data collection process by collecting multiple examples of the researched phenomenon from the same participants. Hutchby and Tanna (2008) offer an example study that uses sampling by time. As they write:

> The study is based on a corpus of some 1250 text messages sent and received by two selected SMS users over a six-month period in 2003. SMS exchanges occurring during six different one-week time periods spread out at various intervals over the course of the six months were recorded and transcribed. Approximately 30 individuals were the senders and receivers of the text messages comprising this data corpus. All individuals involved were informed (a) that the study was taking place; (b) of the dates within which data collection was being undertaken; and (c) of their right to decline to have messages transcribed. (p. 145)

In preparing for an LL or CMC research study, the key is that your data sources and data collection methods must be carefully chosen and based on your initial research questions, and often LL and CMC research methods and data sources overlap in mixed-methods and ethnographic research projects. In the next two sections of the chapter, we provide further analysis of two LL and CMC studies, one published study by Chun (2014) that examines protest signs featured in rallies, marches, encampments, and demonstrations, and a study by our student Christy Ruschmeyer on the interpretation of silence in text messages. For practice conducting LL research, see Exercise 6.2.

EXERCISE 6.2: Examining the linguistic landscape

Background: The three categories of public signs described in Sayer (2010)—informative, iconic, and innovative—are useful starting points to begin an examination of your local linguistic landscape. Informative signs serve to convey or translate important information about a local area or store. Iconic signs use language or images symbolically in order to index cultural significance and meaning, and innovative signs use language and symbols in new and interesting ways, often to catch the attention of shoppers or passersby. See Sayer (2010) for examples of each type of sign.

Activity: With a partner or small group, choose a neighborhood, urban area, or specific section of the region where you live. Walk, ride, or drive around the area, taking pictures of public signs, shop signs, or any other linguistic and symbolic information that catches your eye. Select the photos that you feel are most representative of the community, and as a group organize them according to the categories in Sayer (2010), informative, iconic, and innovative. Next, consider the following questions as a group:

- What types of signs appear the most? Where?
- How many languages are used in the signs? What is the relative status of the languages?
- Who appears to be the author(s) of the text? Who is the audience for each sign? How can you tell?
- Do any signs use a mixture of languages? Why? Are the different languages directly and correctly translated or are aspects left out? Explain.
- In non-English speaking countries, are there English signs? Why? In English-speaking countries, are there signs not in English or with limited amounts of English? Why?

When you have finished your analysis, prepare a short 5- to 7-minute presentation, including example photographs, for your classmates.

Use of linguistic landscape and computer-mediated data in published research

The previous sections have already drawn on multiple examples from published LL and CMC research studies, but in this section, we examine in more detail the research design and data collection methods of an example study. Chun (2014) is interesting because the author uses ethnographic and participant observation research methods and draws on data collected in person as a participant and spectator of the Occupy movement demonstrations in a public park in Los Angeles, California. In particular, Chun (2014) writes that he aims to expand the study of linguistic landscapes to include private signs displayed by individuals in public spaces that are "transgressive" and unauthorized (p. 654). He lists his research questions as the following:

> What is the role of this particular LL in transforming a public space? Second, what are the mediated interactions involved in the mobilities of this LL from its immediate "emplacement" (Scollon & Scollon, 2003) at the Park to broader platforms across time and space that enable its discourses to be taken up at these sites? Lastly, what are the discursive links between these protest signs and a cartoon published in mainstream media? (p. 654)

From his research questions, we can see how Chun (2014) will use a mixed-method approach to collecting and analyzing his data as the questions lead him to collect a variety of data sources.

Chun (2014) describes two methods that he used in his data collection. First, he draws on a visual and ethnographic method called a "photographic survey" that he describes as "attending, participating in, and visually documenting the rallies, marches, and encampment" (p. 657). Chun (2014) writes that he focused on both the use of the signs in marches as well as their subsequent placement in the park near demonstrators' encampments. Next, he adopts an approach that he calls "following the object" by picking out particular signs and slogans that held particular significance for the protesters or media and tracking their appearance and use in other media and online spaces. In the article, Chun (2014) specifically tracks and analyzes three protest signs that made reference to the game of Monopoly and the main character associated with the game, "Rich Uncle Pennybags," and signs that included the phrase "class warfare," which, according to Chun (2014), "was not a prominent topic in either the mainstream media or everyday discourse in U.S. society" (p. 658).

After selecting prominent phrases and images, Chun (2014) then tracks and analyzes their use in other spaces and finds an online video in which a commentator films and discusses one of the Occupy signs that referenced "class warfare." He also analyzes a discussion underneath an image of the "class warfare" sign on a community blog. Finally, Chun (2014) locates and analyzes three political cartoons published in the same period as his data collection and which all reference or include the images of "Rich Uncle Pennybags" or use the phrase "class warfare" in their text.

Drawing on different LL and CMC data sources, as illustrated in Chun (2014), can be useful for student researchers. For Chun (2014), the multiple sources allowed him to study questions about what is public, what is private, and what motivates people to display language. More practically, student researchers may not have time to do the extensive surveys, photographing, and analysis required in many large-scale surveys in LL and CMC work, but they can perhaps track one particular phrase, image, or linguistic feature across digital and physical spaces, offering revealing and interesting data and interactions not possible through in-person data collection methods alone.

RESEARCHER TO KNOW: Elana Shohamy

Elana Shohamy is Professor of Language Education in the School of Education at Tel Aviv University. Her research is about language policy and language justice in multilingual and multidialectal societies. She is interested in the role of language in immigration and has done linguistic landscape research, including examining the role of Arabic as a "minority language" in Israel. She has published some of her work on linguistic landscapes in two books, one she co-edited in 2009 with Durk Gorter, entitled *Linguistic Landscapes: Expanding the Scenery*; and another co-edited in 2010 with Eliezer Ben-Rafael and Monica Barni, entitled *Linguistic Landscape in the City*.

Use of linguistic landscape and computer-mediated data in student research

In her paper entitled "Speech, Silence, and Space: The Unspoken Dialogues of the Digital Realm," our student Christy Ruschmeyer illustrates a research study that examines both the "text" and "place" of CMC, in this case text messaging. In particular, Ruschmeyer is interested in how interlocutors use and interpret silence in their text conversations. As she summarizes in her introduction, sociolinguists have studied the role of silence in face-to-face communication in many contexts, but she points out that "it remains to be asked whether this peculiar melding of speech and silence in text message communication gives rise to conversational patterns that are distinct from those found during in-person exchanges" (p. 3). In this way, Ruschmeyer's study illustrates the common focus in CMC and LL studies mentioned earlier, which examined previously studied topics in sociolinguistics with new data, and these different aspects of the study are clearly articulated in her research questions:

> The present study aims to explore the murky boundaries between the norms of face-to-face and text-to-text interactions by pursuing two routes of inquiry: How can text-based conversations be compared to face-to-face conversations in terms of their structure, temporal pacing, and use of silence? Also, how do interlocutors conversationally employ and react to silence as an element of digital communication, and why might it occur? (p. 3)

In order to explore these questions, Ruschmeyer developed a mixed-method approach in which she asked her 10 participants to complete two separate tasks. First, she had her participants fill out a questionnaire designed to garner demographic information and details regarding their texting habits and opinions about text communication (see Figure 6.1). Next, she simply asked participants to collect and submit to her text-message exchanges that they had on their phones (see Figure 6.2). She writes, "No specific parameters were suggested for these chosen submissions. This ensured that the conversations suffered no bias in relation to the study, and could be judged as completely natural instances of text-based conversation" (p. 4). As we can see, the sample size is small and would very much be considered a pilot study, but Ruschmeyer is able to complete the study within the time period of a course and still offer a variety of data points to analyze and connect to larger topics in our field.

LINGUISTIC LANDSCAPE AND COMPUTER-MEDIATED DATA SOURCES   103

1. Age

2. Gender

3. Of the three, which is your preferred mode of communication?
   (a) voice call (b) email (c) texting

4. Which device do you usually use for texting? (a) phone (b) computer (c) other

5. How often do you communicate via text? (a) rarely (b) sometimes (c) often

6. Who do you text the most? (a) friends (b) romantic partners (c) family
   (d) coworkers (e) other

7. What are some reasons that you have not responded to texts in the past?

8. Are there communicative advantages/disadvantages to texting? If so, what are they?

9. When it comes to texting, what is your biggest pet peeve?

FIGURE 6.1   RUSCHMEYER'S SURVEY

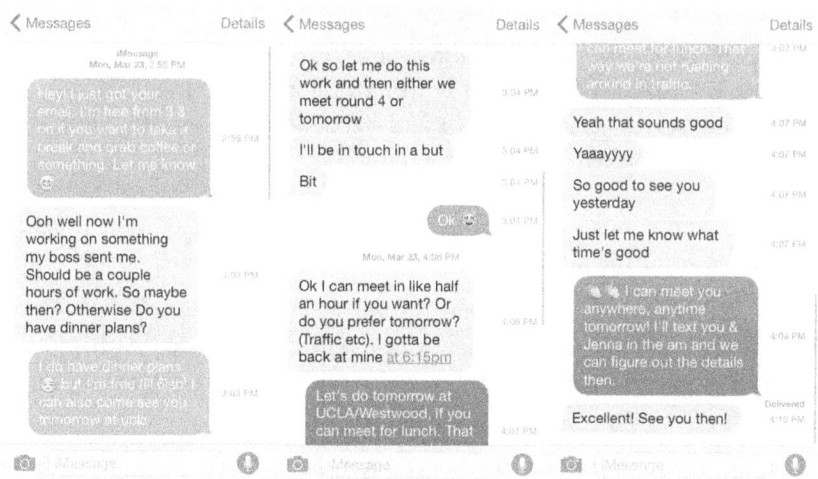

FIGURE 6.2   TEXT MESSAGE COLLECTED AS PART OF RUSCHMEYER'S CLASS PROJECT ON SILENCE AND TEXTING

> **EXERCISE 6.3: Collecting CMC data**
>
> Begin a small project collecting CMC data. First, decide if you want to collect intermode data (two or more CMC modes such as email and Twitter) or intramode (data from the same CMC mode such as male and female users of Snapchat). Some example topics are listed here:
>
> - Collecting and comparing text messages between you and a specific friend or group of friends versus text messages between you and a parent or relative (intramode).
> - Collecting and comparing Instagram hashtags and tags of two related groups for fans of rival sports teams (intramode).
> - Collecting and comparing your emails versus your text messages over a period of one week (intermode).
>
> Be sure to get the permission of your participants before beginning your data collection. As you collect the data, begin analyzing the linguistic aspects of the different modes and interlocutors, and prepare a brief summary of what you have found.

Steps for collecting linguistic landscape and computer-mediated data

As illustrated above, many linguistic landscape and CMC projects involve different types of data and use mixed methods for data collection. Many of the steps for collecting data in these types of projects will be similar to the participant observation, interviewing, or survey research outlined in earlier chapters. See Exercise 6.3 for help starting a pilot CMC project.

For LL research, Garvin (2010) and Sayer (2010) illustrate two specific examples for completing LL research. From Garvin (2010):

1. Select and contact participants for your study. You may want to talk to people from the area, to those who live outside the area, or to a small number from both.

2. Show the photos or take a walk with the participants, doing what Garvin refers to as a "walking tour" interview, asking the meaning and purpose of signs to the participant.

3. Record the responses or take careful notes.

4. Transcribe and analyze interviews and your field notes.

5. Have follow-up meetings with participants to validate your interpretation and findings.

The following is a slight revision of the stages described by Sayer (2010) in discussing data collection stages for LL research:

1. Selection of site to research

2. Walking the site, taking field notes and photos of signs, billboards, posters, and banners

3. Categorizing the photos into types or themes

4. Deciding whether the signs seem to be for cross-cultural purposes or intracultural purposes

5. Establishing whether the signs include translation from one language to another

6. Determining whether the signs are "informational," "iconic" (corporate logos and slogans), or "innovative" in some way

7. What seems to be the meaning of the signs? If they are in English in a non-English speaking area, why English? If they are not in English in an English-speaking area, what language are they in and why?

In addition to planning your data collection steps, you should also make plans to ensure the privacy of your participants. This is important in all data collection processes, but it is an issue to be particularly aware of in LL and CMC data collection because it may be easy to miss aspects of the data that reveal participants' identity. For example, posters and bloggers on public facing online blog or social media sites may use handles or pseudonyms that appear anonymous, but which may be able to be tracked back to the participants. If at all possible, it is important to obtain your participants' permission to use their quotes and text from their sites, especially if the information comes from private or restricted sites. In the same way, taking pictures of public signs for LL projects is typically considered appropriate because the signs are in the public domain, but you should be sensitive about not including pictures of people and their clothing without first obtaining their permission. Your instructor and university should be able to provide you with details and forms to use in order to follow local university and research board requirements for collecting data from both online and in-person participants.

> **Further reading on CMC and LL data collection methods**
>
> For students interested in reading in more depth about linguistic landscape and CMC data collection methods, we recommend the following materials:
>
> Backhaus, P. (2007). *Linguistic landscapes: A comparative study of urban multilingualism in Tokyo.* Clevedon, UK: Multilingual Matters.
> Kozinets, R. V. (2010). *Netography: Doing ethnographic research online.* Thousand Oaks, CA: Sage Publications.
> Shohamy, E., & Gorter, D. (eds.) (2009). *Linguistic landscapes: Expanding the scenery.* Clevedon, UK: Multilingual Matters.
> Shohamy, E., Ben-Rafael, E., & Barni, M. (eds.) (2010). *Linguistic landscape in the city.* Clevedon, UK: Multilingual Matters.

Part III
Data Analysis Methods in Sociolinguistics

7 Qualitative data analysis

> **CHAPTER OVERVIEW**
>
> - Introduction: What Are Qualitative Analysis Methods in Sociolinguistics Research?
> - Performing a Qualitative Analysis
>   - Organizing the Data
>   - Coding the Data
>   - Interpreting the Data
> - Qualitative Analysis Methods in Published Research
> - Qualitative Analysis Methods in Student Research
> - Steps for Completing a Qualitative Analysis of Your Collected Data

Introduction: what are qualitative analysis methods in sociolinguistics research?

As introduced in Chapter 1, qualitative research—along with its corollary quantitative research—is one of the two main research categories in sociolinguistics. Qualitative research encompasses many data collection methods, including participant observation, interviews, open-ended responses on questionnaires, discourse analysis, and other ethnographic and case study approaches to data collection. We deal with the specifics of performing a discourse analysis with your collected data in Chapter 8, but in this chapter we focus more broadly on ways to analyze all qualitative data.

As we also noted in Chapter 1, qualitative research is an inductive, emic approach to research, drawing primarily on textual data and examining it though an iterative, interpretive process in which data analysis may lead to further data collection in order to achieve thick description and data saturation or the point when new data only confirms a researcher's previous analysis. Croker (2009) notes that data analysis in qualitative research "will often steer data collection, as ongoing analysis indicates what avenues of research to pursue—who to observe or interview next, what questions to ask, and what documents to request" (p. 10).

Qualitative data analysis for students and for researchers may lead to new and expanded research questions while also providing insight on how their participants understand their world and use language to construct identities and group relationships, and student researchers should keep the two related concepts of social constructivism and indexicality in mind as they analyze their qualitative data. Social constructivism is based on the idea that there is no universal "truth" or meaning that can be accessed through the research process. Instead, social constructivists argue that the world is "constructed and maintained by social groups in their ongoing activities and interactions" (Riazi, 2016, p. 15), and research in sociolinguists uses natural settings and interactions in order to better understand the multiple ways people use language to make meaning, form social groups, and make sense of their specific contexts. In taking a constructivist approach to research, linguistic indexes or indexicality—that is, "the capacity of language to point to a meaning without directly referring to it" (Riazi, 2016, p. 139)—becomes an important theoretical tool and part of any textual analysis.

Of course, many qualitative research projects take a longer amount of time due to the need for data saturation and the cyclical research process of qualitative data collection and analysis, and students will most likely not have time to investigate every aspect of their research questions. And, as with all research, students performing qualitative research projects should avoid making their research questions and claims too broad and exaggerated to the point that no evidence for their interpretations exists. As Richards (2003) usefully points out, "Nearly all research is very modest indeed, playing an infinitesimally small but nevertheless valuable part in the advancement of our understanding. The aim, then, should be to share insights rather than change the world" (p. 264). For more guidance defining qualitative research methods and the differences with quantitative research, see Exercise 7.1.

EXERCISE 7.1: What is qualitative research and what is it not?

In Chapter 1, we asked readers to consider the differences between qualitative and quantitative research approaches and think about which orientation they preferred to read and which one they preferred to use for research. As an extension of that activity, you can now think more about what defines qualitative research. On your own or with a group, begin making a list in a two-sided column of aspects that define qualitative research and analysis (what is qualitative research?) on one side. On the other side, begin another list of what qualitative research is not.

What is qualitative research?	What is not qualitative research?

> Consider questions such as these:
> - What are the goals of qualitative research?
> - What counts as "proof" in qualitative research?
> - What is the role of quantification and statistics in qualitative research?
>
> As you read this chapter and continue to read more published sociolinguistic research studies, you can add to your table and compare your definitions and table with those of colleagues. Also, after you begin your table, you may want to compare it with a similar list found in Richards (2003, p. 10).

With these foundation points in mind, the next sections focus on the three aspects that all qualitative researchers perform as they analyze their data: (1) organizing, (2) coding, and (3) interpreting.

Performing a qualitative analysis

One of the most difficult aspects of any research project is deciding how to analyze the data and what you can conclude from that analysis. Numerous research guides and textbooks provide descriptions for qualitative analysis in much greater depth than we can provide here, and we list some of our favorite guides at the end of the chapter. For novice researchers, however, we expand on Creswell (2013) in presenting the three basic steps in qualitative analysis.

Organizing the data

The first step in data analysis—be it qualitative or quantitative—is organizing the data into a manageable format in order to begin a deeper investigation in response to the research questions. For qualitative research projects, analysis typically centers on coding bits of data and then organizing them into larger categories and themes, and it is important to develop a systematic way to organize, access, and review your data. Most researchers store interviews, observation notes, images, or any other pieces of data on computer hard drives with backup copies in different online storage programs. For audio or video recordings of interviews or observations, researchers typically transcribe verbatim the language and surrounding details of the interactions and dialogue and store these texts in word processing documents. We illustrate transcription systems and their different levels of specifics in detail in Chapter 8.

After determining where and how to store collected and transcribed data, the next step many researchers take is to sit down and reflect on the data collection process through a series of research memos or diary entries. These extended notes can be first impressions of what the researcher learned and should ideally be started during data collection. In this way, a research diary is the first attempt to make sense of the collected data and answer the questions "What is going on here?" and "What is the data saying in response to my research questions?" Research diaries should be different from any observation notes you made during data collection, where the aim was not interpretation, but more description and recording events and statements with as little analysis or subjective commentary as possible. Instead, research memos about data collection form the beginning of your analysis, and they will help you to decide on how to organize your data and what are some initial themes and codes to examine when first systematically coding the data. Students may not have time to write extensive notes about their data collection, but we recommend pausing for at least one or two moments in order to organize your own thoughts and feelings about your data before delving into the coding and interpretation steps of qualitative data analysis. Table 7.1 offers a few starting categories and example questions that we recommend using to begin a research diary for a course-long project after or toward the end of data collection.

Data sources	Do I need to collect data from any other sources? Have I collected enough information (albeit in a short, pilot project) to fairly represent all perspectives? Is anything missing from my data collection?
Research questions	Does my collected data respond to my research questions and goals? Do I need to change the goal or focus on my project or research questions? What new questions may be asked due to my findings?
Initial units of analysis and codes	What topics or ideas have you already noticed reoccurring throughout the data? How big or small is each unit of analysis (e.g., single words, sentences, or entire responses/interactions)? How do different pieces of data or topics relate to one another? Are there any outlier responses or data that do not fit well with other potential themes or categories?

TABLE 7.1 EXAMPLE RESEARCH DIARY TOPICS AND QUESTIONS

A final point to consider in organizing collected data is whether to use a qualitative analysis software program to help store and analyze the data. Although students can typically complete course-based projects using only word processing software or even just handwritten notes, they may take the opportunity to use a text analysis program that helps them search for terms and organize key examples in the text. Two software programs that our students have used and may be available for use through school or library licenses are NVivo and ATLAS.ti:

- QSR NVivo (http://www.qsrinternational.com).
  NVivo helps researchers organize qualitative data from interviews, open-ended survey responses, articles, social media, and web content. It enables researchers to search their entire set of transcripts and mixed-media data. It can display results graphically, work in multiple language at the same time, and merge data and findings from multiple researchers working together as a team.

- ATLAS.ti (http://atlasti.com)
  Similar to NVivo, ATLAS.ti allows researchers to quickly search and display results from a large corpus of collected and transcribed qualitative data. Data can be easily annotated and browsed with multiple researchers working on the same documents. Further, findings and analyses can be exported to statistical packages such as SPSS or HTML web files.

If these programs are not available through school licenses, both companies offer free 30-day trials, which should be ample time to complete a semester or course-based research project.

Coding the data

After organizing the collected data and then doing some initial reflecting and writing, researchers will typically begin analysis by writing short notes or memos about small meaningful segments of data. From these notes, researchers then develop codes on recurring topics that they see in the data. Researchers will then correlate the codes, either counting for frequency or identifying salient patterns, and from these codes larger themes will be developed that become the center of their analysis and responses to the research questions. As previewed in Table 7.1, coding will necessarily involve breaking the data into smaller units and assigning a name or tag to each unit. In their classic text, Glaser and Strauss (1967) recommend coding every line or section of data in order to create what they call axial codes or larger categories above the initial code that will then be compared and built into themes. Later, Glaser (1992) disavowed line by line coding as "helter-skelter" and over-conceptualizing an incident by generating too many categories. Much more detailed procedures and discussion of coding is available in the recommend books at the end of the chapter, and for smaller, course-long projects, we do not recommend coding every event or line of data or recorded dialogue. Instead, we recommend students selectively code key pieces of data based on the sections of data and interaction that they feel will best respond to their research questions.

Creswell (2013) writes that codes can be "in vivo," drawn from "the exact words used by participants" (p. 185) or come from "names the researcher composes that seem to best describe the information" (p. 185). He describes three types of data that are particularly salient to code in order to develop themes:

- Information the researchers expect[ed] to find before the study;
- Surprising information that researchers did not expect to find; and
- Information that is conceptually interesting or unusual to researchers (and potentially participants and audiences). (p. 186)

From these initial codes and impressions, researchers can then build themes through a process that Charmaz (2006) calls moving from focused codes to conceptual categories. A good example of this process comes from McPherron work on student English name choices (2009, 2016, 2017), in which he presented the many reasons for Chinese students to choose English names from his focused coding of his interviews, including: Chinese sounds, translations, cool sounds, the role of local and foreign teachers. He then connects these codes with the conceptual categories of "quest for uniqueness," "negotiation of English norms and standards," and "communicative competence as play." These codes were then further consolidated into a larger discussion of second language learner identity as determined by practices of resistance, play, and creativity.

Sayer (2010) is another excellent example of qualitative data coding that we often discuss with students and that was first introduced in Chapter 6. In his article, Sayer (2010) analyzes the linguistic landscape of Oaxaca, Mexico, by collecting 250 photos of signs, billboards, posters, and banners from public places that combined English with Spanish and other images associated with the United States and English-speaking groups. Unlike in McPherron's example, Sayer (2010) began with preexisting terms and drilled down into smaller analytical units instead of building up to larger conceptual categories. For example, he first coded the signs according to the sign's intended audience, either cross-cultural or intracultural. All of the cross-cultural signs were primarily intended to convey information to tourists or foreign visitors. He coded these types of signs as "informational." Sayer (2010) labeled most of the signs, however, as "intercultural" and aimed at a Spanish speaking and Mexican audience. He then categorized these signs into two types: (1) iconic signs that used well-known corporate logos or slogans such as "Domino's—The Pizza Delivery Experts," without translation; and (2) innovative signs that mixed English and Spanish in creative and novel ways, for example, a sign for the shoe brand Keds, which read *"Cool habla en todos los idiomas"* (p. 149). Sayer (2010) was most interested in the innovative signs, and he then further distinguished these signs according to six emergent themes that provide insight on the social meanings and use of English in the Oaxacan linguistic landscape:

Meaning 1: English is advanced and sophisticated.
Meaning 2: English is fashion.
Meaning 3: *English es ser cool* ('English is being cool').
Meaning 4: English is sex(y).
Meaning 5: English [is] for expressions of love.
Meaning 6: English [is] for expressing subversive identities. (pp. 147–50)

In addition to the emergent categories and themes found when coding textual data, language variation research projects often involve coding and analysis of specific phonological, syntactic, or lexical language features, and much of your time doing data analysis will be spent using statistical measurements to look for similarities and differences in the numerical data that are a result of your coding. For example, Becker (2009) knew she was interested in the use of syllable-coda /r/, so she transcribed over 3,000 examples of words from her corpus with syllable-coda /r/ and then coded whether the /r/ was pronounced [r-1] or was not [r-0]. She then had two other researchers code separately a random sample of 193 of the 3,000 examples to check for the reliability of her initial coding, and she found an overlap of 90 percent. This step of having more than one person code phonological data is important, as determining whether a particular variable was or was not uttered is difficult and may vary depending on the listener. In addition to coding for the phonological feature of syllable-coda /r/ and comparing grammatical features and characteristics of the speakers, such as age and sex, Becker (2009) also coded her interview transcripts for the topic of "neighborhood" and "non-neighborhood." Again, she asked a second reader to confirm her coding choices and found the second reader and Becker had a 96 percent agreement in their choices. After confirming her coding choice, she was then able to determine the statistically significant factors that influence the use of /r/. In this way, Becker (2009) was able to provide a broad analysis of various linguistic, age, and demographic factors that may influence /r/ use in the LES participants.

Interpreting the data

After developing codes into broader themes and categories, the next step in the qualitative research process is interpreting the data and responding back to research questions and broader ideas and theories in the field. In this sense, researchers are interpreting their data to answer the questions "What was learned during this project?" and "What is still unclear and in need of further study?" In some ways, this process can be creative or at least rely on the researcher's ability to pull together in some concrete form disparate pieces of data and themes. For novice researchers, one of the most straightforward paths to interpret your data is to examine how your study fits or does not fit into the results of a previous study or finding in the field. Many of the focal articles we summarize and mention throughout the textbook are good examples of studies that specifically draw on previous work when interpreting their collected data. We particularly recommend rereading Reyes (2005), Chand (2011), and Kiesling (2004) as examples of studies that draw on previous research and good articles to use as reference points for qualitative data analysis projects.

In addition to comparing themes and findings with previous students, another common and very useful way to interpret qualitative data is to represent your data in some visual format, for example, a table, graph, figure, or other image. For example, consider Figure 7.1, which presents the way McPherron conceptualized the changes in his students' English names once they left university and began their careers, along with the themes that each student's name choice reveals.

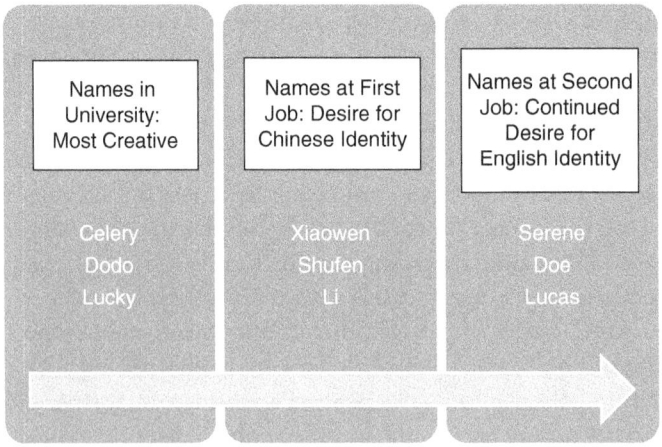

Figure 7.1 Trajectory of english name usage from university to professional life
Source: McPherron (2016)

Figure 7.1 helped McPherron when interpreting his data, and we encourage students to make similar figural or visual representations of their data. These figures may or may not be included in final written reports or presentations (McPherron did not publish the above image, but used it in conference presentations), but they help researchers, especially novice researchers, interpret their data and find connections between their themes.

Asking participants to review and comment on themes and findings that come out of the collected data is another activity that can help with data interpretation as well as add validity to the project. Creswell (2013) describes this as "member checking" and writes that it involves "taking data, analyses, interpretations, and conclusions back to the participants so that they can judge the accuracy and credibility of the account" (p. 252). Depending on the amount of time available, a student researcher may want to convene a small focus group of participants to discuss the data and conclusions or simply email some specific questions to a group or individuals and get their written feedback. Creswell (2013) makes the point that it is not necessary and perhaps not feasible to provide extensive transcripts or notes to participants. Instead, researchers may send participants parts of a written report or specific quotes along with interpretations and then ask for participant opinions. In doing this member checking or member validation (Richards, 2003), researchers do not need to feel compelled to change their themes or conclusions if participants disagree or offer disparate suggestions. Rather, in reporting your findings, it will be important to take into consideration the feedback you receive and build it into your analysis. In this way, member checking offers another source of data and an important aspect of validity and triangulation.

See Exercise 7.2 for practice performing a close reading of a transcript from McPherron's research.

EXERCISE 7.2: Practice analyzing qualitative data

As a way to begin analyzing qualitative data, read and begin taking notes, coding, and memoing for the following transcript from Paul McPherron's research. In the transcript, the Chinese students of English are at an evening English discussion club in 2007, and McPherron is asking them about their English names.

1 **Paul:** Do you have any other ways that you pick your English names (?) (1.0)
2 **Student 1:** By your major.
3 **Paul:** By your major (?)
4 **Student 1:** I know someone who chose their English name by their major.
5 **Paul:** So, like what (?)
6 **Student 1:** Like . . . business.

> 7   **Paul:** They—he named himself . . . Business.
> 8   **Students:** (laughing quietly)
> 9   **Paul:** Liberal Arts(?)
> 10 **Student 1:** No, I know one guy named . . . Lawman because a law student is a man who studies law and so he's a . . . law-man.
> 11 **Students:** (laughing loudly)
> 12 **Paul:** He's a *Lawman*.
> 13 **Student 1:** In that direction, I should call myself . . . Businessman. Okay (?)
> 14 **Students:** (laughing loudly)
> 15 **Paul:** Or, English *Man*.
> 16 **Paul:** [Looking at S2], your name used to be . . . CEO (?)
> 17 **Students:** (laughing loudly)
> 18 **Student 2:** Yes, I have two names before [his previous names were CEO and EFG].
> 19 **Paul:** Did you want to be a CEO (?)
> 20 **Student 2:** Yes, I want (.) ed (.) wanted to be a CEO. Someone will present you . . . your dream.
> 21 **Paul:** So you pick your name on what you want to be.
> 22 **Student 2:** Just a good pronunciation. EFG . . . I think it's a really good pronunciation.
>
> As you read over the transcript, circle key aspects of the transcript, either content or linguistic terms, that stand out and that you may want to investigate further. What are some questions you have after reading this transcript? What do you want to know more about? How—or by using what kinds of data—would you use to find out more about this context and these students?

Qualitative analysis methods in published research

In addition to the articles mentioned above as good examples of qualitative research analysis, we summarize here Julia Menard-Warwick's (2005) article, "Transgression Narrative, Dialogic Voicing, and Cultural Change" as a useful article for students to use as a template for doing qualitative analysis. The article represents a part of a larger interview study with immigrant Latina women in California, in which Menard-Warwick analyzed immigrant experiences and life histories. In this article, Menard-Warwick draws on six 1.5-hour-long interviews with one participant, Raquel, and in particular on one narrative Raquel told twice in different interviews about her uncle's enlistment in the Nicaraguan Sandinista military against the wishes of his family. Menard-Warwick classifies this story as a transgression narrative, defined as stories in which "the teller or a relative violate or contest norms held by other family members" (p. 539). Menard-Warwick developed that term and other themes that came out of Raquel's narrative through an analysis process that was inductive—based on coding particular statements and bits of narrative—as well as connected to previous research and topics in sociolinguistics, including dialogism and double-voicing (Bakhtin, 1981). In particular, the article helps students see the in-depth analysis that can be made from a relatively short narrative or text, as well as reveals the different terms and ideas already available to them to use for analysis from previous sociolinguistic studies.

In the article, Menard-Warwick (2005) begins by outlining her research question and data collection methods, including the following:

- *Research question:* "How does the teller orchestrate multiple voices and discourses to make sense of social and cultural changes in her community, both before and after immigration?" (p. 534)
- *Data collection:* "Thirty-three interviews with eight participants in the overall project and six with Raquel. All participants were students in an adult ESL program and were from Latin America." (p. 538)

In qualitative research analysis, it is important to list your research questions and data sources in as much detail as possible because the validity of your analysis stems, in part, from how well you represent your sources and context, and the face validity of your conclusions and claims.

Many researchers also feel that in qualitative research it is particularly important to offer some insight on the background of the researcher in order to understand better the dynamic between the researchers and participants and to reveal any of the biases that every researcher has in developing themes and conclusions. This idea of presenting aspects of research background is referred to as reflexivity, and Menard-Warwick adds these personal details at different points in the article, noting that she met all of the interviewees as an observer and participant in their ESL course, as well as pointing out the language of the interviews was mostly in Spanish but that she speaks English as a mother tongue and comes from an Anglo-American background.

Based on her initial readings and note taking for her interviews, Menard-Warwick separated parts of the interviews into discrete narratives that she would then assign to general themes. Of the hundreds of narratives in her entire data collection, she identified around 100 as related to what she calls social positioning, "the ways participants described ethnicity, immigration status, politics, and social status having affected their lives" (pp. 538–39). From those, she further classified 24 narratives as transgression narratives, one of which is Raquel's story analyzed here. Menard-Warwick writes that she chose to focus on Raquel's story because it was representative of the other transgression narratives in that it "attempts to make sense of cultural changes before and after immigration" (p. 539). In this way, the researcher has sifted through a large amount of data and narratives, selected particular units of meaning (here, entire narrative or story), coded and compared the narratives, and then selected one more or more for further analysis.

After Menard-Warwick chose Raquel's particular narrative to examine, she performed a more in-depth coding of each line or turn in Raquel's story, closer to the line-by-line type of coding recommended by Glaser and Strauss (1967). When performing this close coding, Menard-Warwick used codes from outside the story itself in order to label every instance she viewed as an evaluation by Raquel or someone in her story. For example, when Raquel says in Spanish, "My grandmother told him . . . 'you're crazy, you're going to die there'" (p. 540), Menard-Warwick codes this as both displaying affect and judgment. These terms come from a linguistic theory of meaning known as systemic-functional linguistics, and Menard-Warwick is specifically using the APPRAISAL framework of Martin (2000) for these categories. At the same time as she coded all evaluative statements for insights into how Raquel is positioning herself in relation to the events in her narrative, Menard-Warwick also coded parts of the story with similar "thematic, attitudinal, and often lexical content" (p. 540), eventually identifying three key themes that emerged from Raquel's story: Family Unity, Revolutionary Commitment, and Educational Advancement. From these two coding procedures, Menard-Warwick is able to offer insight on her research question in showing how immigrant women such as Raquel position themselves in relation to changing cultural norms and perspectives. More specific data examples can be found in the article itself, and we recommend reading this article as a good example of clear qualitative data analysis through the development of codes and themes both "in vivo" and in the existing literature.

RESEARCHER TO KNOW: Mary Bucholtz

Mary Bucholtz is Professor of Linguistics at University of California at Santa Barbara (UCSB), and describes herself as a sociocultural linguist. Her research focuses on social identities and how they are created through linguistic interaction, and much of her research is based in qualitative and discourse analysis methods. She is committed to interdisciplinarity, which is shown in her projects including the Center for California Languages and Cultures, which looks at the "diversity of linguistic and cultural practices within California, past and present" (http://www.ccalc.ucsb.edu). She also works with School Kids Investigating Language in Life and Society (SKILLS), a collaborative program that includes faculty and students at UCSB and Santa Barbara County high schools (http://www.skills.ucsb.edu). Her work with language in youth stems from her strong belief in promoting social-justice research on language and race.

Qualitative analysis methods in student research

Some student researchers will have time to interview participants in relation to their research questions in order to perform the type of thematic analysis we have described above. Others may find it necessary to examine existing data, often found online, in order to complete a short classroom project, and we summarize an excellent paper here by Alessandra Rosen in which she used two interviews with a famous yoga instructor, Dana Trixie Flynn, which she found on YouTube. As with all student papers referenced in Part II: "Data Collection Methods in Sociolinguistics," full transcripts of the papers are available on the textbook companion website.

For Rosen's project, she was interested in how yoga practices that have been taken from Indian religious roots have become modernized and secularized in order to reach a wider Western audience. In particular, she was interested in a recent call for authenticity in Western yoga communities and how celebrity yoga teachers such as Dana Flynn discuss the differences between traditional Hindu, Jain, and Buddhist yoga practices that are considered more authentic with the modern practices of most Western yoga studios. She asks: "How is this quest for authenticity reflected in the language of the modern yoga celebrity?" (p. 1)

In order to answer this question, Rosen chose Flynn because of her popularity as a "teacher's teacher" of yoga and the ultimate "yoga rock star" according to yoga publications. She found and transcribed the two online interviews with Flynn, began analyzing and coding lines and stories in the interview based on her initial assumption that Flynn would primarily be making arguments about her yoga teachings as authentic, and then developed different codes and understandings of Flynn's strategies for dealing with ethnic differences in yoga practice by drawing on previous writings about adequation or de-ethnicization from the sociolinguistic literature. Specifically, the three strategies that Rosen identifies in the Flynn interviews are as follows:

1. *Presupposition/reformulation:* For example, Flynn comments that "there's [sic] as many yogas as there are all of you." (p. 4)

2. *Embodied spirituality:* Rosen offers this example from Flynn's interviews: "So you can pull out the asanas—you're already made up of asanas. You're made up of mantras ... it's already who you are." (p. 5)

3. *Boundary cancellation:* For this strategy, Rosen offers this quote: "And even the cats that came before us didn't have a book to read. They explored. They wanted to know God ... And they started this way and that way ... to have an experience of oneness." (p. 6)

Rosen writes that through these three strategies Flynn reframes yoga as nonthreatening and nonreligious to Western audiences. Rosen argues that Flynn places yoga practices, history, and even Sanskrit words such as *asana* as part of the bodies of a Western audience, moving the practice of yoga away from a focus on authenticity and religious meanings and erasing any ethnic differences between past and present yoga practices.

Rosen ends her paper with comments about future directions to examine the process of authentication of Western yoga practices and the limits of her very initial look at the language of Western yoga teachers. We offer this paper as a good example of a very "doable" qualitative project that students could perform in many different contexts as long as they have access to prerecorded interviews online or through another local database. We encourage students to go through the steps of transcribing, journaling, coding, and building up themes as they respond to their research project topic and questions.

Steps for completing a qualitative analysis of your collected data

As we mention throughout the chapter, qualitative data analysis is a recursive process in which analysis may lead back to refining of the research question and more data collection. In addition, different types of data may involve different steps and analysis procedures, as we examine in more depth in terms of discourse analysis in Chapter 8. Summarizing the various aspects we discussed in this chapter, however, we can offer the following broad steps involved in completing a qualitative analysis of data:

1. Organizing the data
2. Writing data collection journal entries
3. Coding the data
4. Building themes
5. Connecting themes to research questions and previous literature
6. Checking interpretations with participants
7. Refining the research questions and deciding what further data is needed (if any).

Finally, in working through these data analysis steps, it is important to continually keep in mind aspects of reliability and validity in qualitative data analysis that we have mentioned at different points in this chapter. Providing explicit insight into the background of the researcher and detailed descriptions of the participants and context of the study are good starting points to ensure the reliability of your study. In addition, in writing up your research, you should define all terms and constructs as specifically as possible if they are used to code data and make generalizations. In terms of validity, checking interpretations with participants is a good place to start, and you may also ask colleagues or other researchers to examine their interpretations of the data and suggest connections to other research sites; this will indicate aspects of both the reliability of the conclusions as well as ways in which the findings could be generalizable.

Writing about qualitative research analysis, Richards (2003) points out that the terms *reliability* and *validity* are primarily used in statistical and experimental research designs and may not apply well to qualitative research. This is the reason that many qualitative researchers may use alternative terms, such as Richards's coinage of *member validation*, noted previously, when justifying the soundness of their research analysis and conclusions. Richards (2003) summarizes three aspects of validity in qualitative research that we find particularly useful for students doing shorter qualitative analysis projects (p. 285), and we summarize here the three aspects in our own words, with questions that students should ask about their project as the complete their data analysis:

- *Description validity:* Has the researcher provided full and accurate descriptions of the data, participants, and context?

- *Interpretive validity:* Has the researcher explored all aspects of the data, including any negative evidence, in drawing his or her conclusions?

- *Theoretical validity:* Has the researcher clearly identified the concepts and ideas used to explain relationships and examples in the data, and do those relationships make sense?

Further reading on qualitative data analysis methods

For more in-depth guides to conducting qualitative research analysis, we recommend the following materials:

Creswell, J. W. (2013). *Qualitative inquiry and research design: Choosing among the five approaches,* 3rd ed. Thousand Oaks, CA: Sage.
Glesne, C. (2015). *Becoming qualitative researchers: An introduction,* 5th ed. New York, NY: Pearson.
Maxwell, J. A. (2013). *Qualitative research design: An interactive approach,* 3rd ed. Thousand Oaks, CA: Sage.
VanderStoep, S. W., & Johnson, D. D. (2009). *Research methods for everyday life: Blending qualitative and quantitative approaches.* San Francisco, CA: John Wiley & Sons.

8 Discourse analysis

> **CHAPTER OVERVIEW**
>
> - Introduction: What Are Discourse Analysis Methods in Sociolinguistics Research?
>   - Subfields of Discourse Analysis Methods
> - Performing a Discourse Analysis
>   - Creating a Transcript
>   - Coding and Interpreting the Data
> - Discourse Analysis Methods In Published Research
> - Discourse Analysis Methods In Student Research
> - Steps for Completing a Discourse Analysis of Your Collected Data

Introduction: what are discourse analysis methods in sociolinguistics research?

Discourse analysis (DA) is a popular tool for students to use in their research, perhaps because at first it seems like a natural process to listen carefully or read carefully what someone has said or written and then to analyze it. What is different from the ordinary act of listening and/or reading language is that in discourse analysis research, we focus on linguistic features or variables and analyze their use and meaning in a particular context—time, place, and interlocutor.

Discourse analysis fits in with our discussion of qualitative analysis methods that are used to better understand the role of language in social interactions and practices. Commonly used as a tool by students, it is also used by professional sociolinguists, often in part of a larger study. Although definitions vary widely as to the focus of DA and the various subfields, most sociolinguists agree that DA involves analysis beyond the sentence and focuses on linguistic features of people in action. Some sociolinguists such as Sean Sutherland focus on simple definitions that describe DA as "the study of language in use" (Sutherland, 2016, p. x), whereas others, like Anne Curzan and Michael Adams, describe DA in more broadly linguistic terms as "the systemic study of connected text, or units of language above the level of the sentence, and the utterances of which they are composed" (Curzan & Adams, 2012, p. 237). For us, one of the most useful definitions is James Paul Gee's (2011) description of discourse analysis as a method by which we "make things new and strange that we usually see as completely 'normal' and 'natural'"(p. 8). Gee (2011) goes on to say, "To do discourse analysis, we have to see what is old and taken for granted as if it were brand new. We need to see all the assumptions and information speakers leave unsaid and assume listeners know and will add in to make the communications clear" (p. 8).

> **RESEARCHER TO KNOW: James Paul Gee**
>
> James Paul Gee is the Mary Lou Fulton (MLF) Professor of Literacy Studies and Regents Professor at the MLF Teachers College Center for Games & Impact at Arizona State University. His research interests are multifaceted. Gee's *Social Linguistics and Literacies*, 5th ed. (2015) was foundational in the formation of New Literacy Studies. Gee's *An Introduction to Discourse Analysis: Theory and Method*, 4th ed. (2014) and *How to Do Discourse Analysis: A Toolkit* (2011) are used by many universities to introduce and explain discourse analysis. Most recently, he has become interested in the intersections of learning, literacy, and identity development using digital technologies, specifically video games, and his book *Teaching, Learning, Literacy in Our High-Risk High-Tech World: A Framework for Becoming Human* (2017) broadens his perspective beyond video games to include all the ways we learn, make meaning, and form our varying identities, as well as an examination of new kinds of teaching and learning emerging from digital technologies.

In this chapter, we explore the process of conducting research using discourse analysis as the study of "language in use," with particular attention to Gee's discussion of DA as a way to look at and analyze something that at first may seem ordinary and "natural." As an example, if you hear someone say, "I'm done" and you want to analyze what it means, you need to think about who said it, where, when, and why it was said. A child who does not want to eat something on the plate may say, "I'm done," meaning that the child is refusing to eat anything more. A person who has eaten a large meal may touch his or her stomach and declare, "I'm done," to indicate fullness and enjoyment of a meal. A student taking a test, and especially someone who has finished before the other students, may raise a hand and announce loudly, "I'm done," to show that the student is smarter and faster than the other students. Someone arriving home after a day of school and work announces to everyone, "I'm done," meaning the person does not have any more energy to do anything and is indirectly telling everyone not to ask the person to do one more thing. After an argument, one member of a couple turns to the other and says, "I'm done," meaning the relationship is over and the person is leaving. Notice that to better understand the communicative value of the phrase, it is helpful to describe the speaker, the situation, and the possible motivation for the statement. Additionally, Gee (2011) tells us, when we do discourse analysis, we have to think about "the knowledge, assumptions, and inferences we bring to any conversation" (p. 8). Gaining access and analyzing these multiple perspectives on a discourse or speech event are central to doing DA research projects and an important goal of DA research to keep in mind as you develop your own project and read the example studies, research steps, and tips in the next sections. See Exercises 8.1, 8.2, and 8.3 for additional practice and examples of doing discourse analysis and considering the types of analysis performed in DA studies.

> **EXERCISE 8.1: Introducing discourse analysis**
>
> Let's take a simple example of how this might work in our everyday life: Your friend says "Do you want to go to the movies tonight?" Here are several responses:
>
> "I have a lot of homework, but—well, I don't think so."
>
> "I'd love to, but I'm broke."
>
> "I have to wash my hair."
>
> "Tonight? I have an 8 a.m. class tomorrow."
>
> Each response suggests that the friend cannot go to the movies but for different reasons. What is the difference in these responses? How do you interpret them? How might you respond to each of them?

Subfields of discourse analysis methods

Just as we have said that discourse analysis can be described in a variety of ways, it is also true that research using DA can occur with different goals and rely on different theoretical frameworks, and it is useful to compare different frameworks before beginning analysis with any collected data. Here, we look briefly at four of them:

Variationist discourse analysis

Variationist discourse analysis involves an analysis of transcripts focusing on specific discourse features that can be counted, such as the frequency of the use of specific linguistic features and phrases such as *like, you know, well,* curse words, interruptions, the use of *go* or *be like* as a quotative, and so on. Although many researchers in variationist discourse analysis focus on words and phrases, researchers may also find connections between those features and factors such as age, class, region, race, and ethnic differences. Look at the factors that seem the most salient aids to your analysis of social identities. This can be part of the triangulation process, where more than one variable is used to come to a conclusion in the research. For example, much of the research on the use of *like* has focused on the word as well as on the age and gender of the informants. Later in this chapter, we look at student Zayneb Almiggabber's paper focusing on the use of Arabic code-switching in a bilingual community. As in those pieces of research, variationist discourse analysis is often qualitative and quantitative, involving both an analysis of specific interactions as well as frequency counts and visual materials such as charts to support findings.

Conversation analysis

Conversation analysis (CA) examines the structure of conversations and concentrates on real-life, authentic, naturally occurring interactions and detailed interpretation of those interactions. CA depends on recordings and detailed and carefully constructed transcripts of these recordings. Researchers often choose to analyze episodes from longer transcripts to interpret the interchanges from a few different perspectives. One perspective that CA often focuses on is turn taking, for example, to see how conversations open—who speaks the most in a conversation, who speaks the least, who opens a topic, who interrupts and how that individual does so, and who changes the subject or ends the conversation. The study may look at overlaps, hedges, evidences of listening, and of taking someone else's turn or giving up one's own turn. Some questions that might be addressed include the following: Is there a shared sense of a conversation where there is a back and forth? Or does someone monopolize the conversation? Who speaks first? What is the response? What evidence do you have that interlocutors are or are not listening to each other? How does the conversation close? How does one hold or lose the floor? How is silence handled? What happens when turn taking is violated and someone interrupts or overlaps another speaker? The key in CA is that the interactions are real life and focus on turn taking and often politeness. Part of CA involves extremely detailed transcriptions, with the goal of discovering patterns in the micro-level linguistic interactions. Despite the detail and close analysis involved, many sociolinguists rely on the insights that CA can provide, and it is therefore used to some degree in almost all varieties of discourse analysis.

Critical discourse analysis

Critical discourse analysis (CDA) is related to CA in that it may examine the structure of conversation in real-life transcripts and interaction, but in CDA the focus is squarely on power relationships and how power privileges those with it and discriminates against those without it. In this way, CDA researchers connect face-to-face interactions with larger sociopolitical issues around power and ideology. For example, a CDA researcher examining a conversation will not be as interested in general features for how turn taking is handled, but will ask questions about how gender, class, ethnicity, and/or race influence aspects of who speaks first, who holds the floor, and who has the right to interrupt and change the topic of conversation. In short, the focus in CDA studies is on privilege and power. Students have conducted CDA studies in their dorms, at family dinners, and in club meetings, focusing on who speaks loudest, who speaks first, who interrupts, who settles arguments, and so on. These often involve some recording of conversations and transcripts. These studies may also use video and TV sources to study the use of power in political debates, panel discussions, and news reporting. As an example, we suggest that you look at the analysis in Reyes (2005) to see how she used CDA techniques in her participant research project.

EXERCISE 8.2: Conversation analysis exercise

Two people meet on the street. They know each other from school but are not close friends. The following interchange occurs:

A: Hi, you're in my bio class, right?
B: Yes. With Dr. Majors, right?
A: How's it going for you?
B: Okay. And you?
A: Don't ask. I'm so behind. I just can't catch up. Majors talks so fast and doesn't make any sense. I don't think she cares about any of us. Maybe you get some privilege because you sit in the front. I've been sick as a dog.
B: Oh, [I]—
A: [Look], I have a headache and a sore throat. I think I'm getting a cold. My sinuses hurt too. It's been tough for me all around.
B: That's too bad. [I'm]—
A: [It] just isn't my semester. I've been feeling miserable all week. I can't do my work. Plus I have to go to work. Do you have notes from our last class?
B: [I]—
A: [Never] mind. I can get them from someone else. See you around.

Thinking about CA, how would you analyze this conversation? How does turn taking function in the conversation? Who begins and ends the conversation? Who changes the topic? What do you learn about each participant?

Interactional sociolinguistics

Interactional sociolinguistics emphasizes the role of social context in the discourse that occurs with people in interactions. Researchers use multiple tools such as ethnographic observations, field notes, interviews, and transcripts to explore how social identity is constructed through social practice and triangulate findings. Interactional sociolinguistic studies use a combination of the discourse analysis tools described above including deeper description of the context and field notes.

Discourse analysis studies may examine group interactions, as Reyes (2005) did, or even focus on two-person interchanges, as occurred in the research conducted by Negrón (2014) that we discuss later in this chapter. Students in our classes have done discourse analyses of college clubs, family dinners, and blog or forum threads, just for some examples. One student studied the interactions of customers and greeters at a series of low- to high-priced restaurants, focusing on the differences in ways customers were treated, as well as the number of words spoken and the type of language used in each instance. Studies vary, but the overall goal of DA is to look closely at the social context and to examine how social meanings are created, how identity is formed, and the overall effect of the context of the interaction.

EXERCISE 8.3: Discourse analysis exercise with address terms

As part of gaining a better understanding of what we can learn from DA, let's think about how differently we address people we meet and how and why these differences occur. Think about the following situations and what you might say in greeting to the individuals listed below. Choose from among the people in the list, and write the phrase you are likely to use when you encounter the person for the first time in a day:

Your parent(s)_____

Your best friend_____

Your best friend's parent(s)_____

Your partner/significant other_____

Your professor_____

Your next-door neighbor_____

Your roommate _____

Your doctor_____

A law enforcement officer_____

Review the differences in the phrases you used with a partner in class, discussing why you use different phrases and what those phrases suggest about the relationships you have with those people. What terms of address or titles do you use? Why? What is the role of politeness in your choice of greeting phrases? Notice the differences in levels of formality, friendliness, academic language, and the use of slang. The types of changes in your vocabulary, intonation, and politeness level are referred to as style shifting—something that we all do as a means of creating our identity and positioning ourselves in societal interchanges.

Performing a discourse analysis

As summarized above in the text and in Exercise 8.4, the focus and analysis methods for a discourse analysis project may vary depending on the goals of the subfield and what you find most interesting to emphasize and explore in your collected data. In the following sections, we focus on two aspects common to all discourse analysis projects: transcribing and coding your data. Then we offer a summary of key research terms used when performing and writing up a discourse analysis.

> **EXERCISE 8.4: Planning a discourse analysis project**
>
> Think about your potential research project. What feature or variable interests you? What group of people do you have access to? What aspects of their relationships would work well with a discourse analysis project? Which of the above types of discourse analysis would seem to work best with your project? List the first three steps that you might take to begin your research.

Creating a transcript

Transcripts are extremely useful for discourse analysis, but they are time-consuming to create. The first step in creating transcripts is for you to listen to everything that you have recorded, including pauses, backchanneling, laughing, and so on, and to take notes as you listen, including marking the times of what seem to be relevant interactions if they are available in the recording software or smartphone that you use. Next is to choose a list of conventional transcription markers so that when you type up your transcript, you can indicate pauses, laughter, raising or lowering of the voice, lengthening of words or phrases, interruptions, latching, and/or talking over one another in the transcript. Table 8.1 is a slightly adapted transcription convention list similar to what Reyes (2005) used in her research, which you will notice in her bibliography was adapted from Goodwin (1990). When using transcripts in your research paper, you need to include a list of the conventions that you used. You also should number each line to make it easier to refer to as well as to make it easier for your readers to follow your analysis.

Transcription feature	Meaning
<u>word</u>	(underline) utterance stress
word?	(question mark) rising intonation
word,	(comma) falling-rising intonation
wo::rd	(colon) elongated vowel or consonant
°word°	(circles around word) utterance is quieter than surrounding talk
wo(hh)rd	(hh) laughter breaking into utterance
(.)	(period in parentheses) a pause of less than 0.5 second
(0.5)	(number in parentheses) a silence measured in 0.5 second or more
[word [word	(brackets) simultaneous talk or overlap by two or more speakers
word= =word	(equal sign) continuous talk, latching no interval between turns
(word)	(parentheses) doubtful transcription or conjecture
(?)	(question mark in parentheses) inaudible utterance(s)
…	(ellipsis) break in transcript; omitted lines
<word> OR ((word))	(arrows or double parentheses around word) transcriber's comment
.hh	inbreath
Hhh	outbreath

TABLE 8.1 TRANSCRIPTION CONVENTIONS
Source: Adapted from Reyes (2005) and Goodwin (1990)

The next step after listening carefully several times to the data you have recorded is to decide on the data that is most relevant in answering your research question and then to transcribe it. In most projects, it will be important and necessary to provide a close transcript of every line of recorded data. This will allow you to analyze all pauses, interruptions, hesitations, backchanneling, laughter, and so on, in order to make as accurate a rendering of what was said as possible. These close transcriptions take time and practice, and you may want to start by transcribing one or two minutes so you can get used to listening to the voices, the intonation, and the accents or pronunciation patterns of the participant(s). On average, you will need about an hour or more for transcribing 10 minutes of dialogue. Even though it can be a slow process, it is a vital part of discourse analysis, and in addition to having a detailed account to use for analysis and in a final presentation of your report, you will learn about the participants and begin analyzing your research questions as you transcribe.

Close transcription of all data is the expectation for most students, but in studies where discourse analysis may be part of multiple data sources and the researcher cannot take the time or spend the money to transcribe every recorded interaction, it may be possible to simply listen to all of the data, take notes, and then make an informed decision about which parts of an interview, recorded conversation, and so forth to transcribe. This is particularly true with some interview studies that are focused more on the content of participant responses, and we certainly recommend that students working on a shorter pilot project not feel that they have to spend the time to transcribe all of their data. In addition, the research may decide that not all of the features listed in Table 8.1 will necessarily need to be noted. For example, although Reyes (2005) recorded data over several years, she carefully chose the excerpts that she transcribed closely and ultimately analyzed. The excerpts showed participants using the slang terms she was studying so she could analyze the context, the roles of the participants, the use of the slang, and ways that in and out groups were established. Similarly, Negrón (2014) collected months of material in a range of settings, yet she chose to transcribe and analyze the interactions between William and Roberto that illustrate how the participants revealed and performed their Latino identity, the subject of her study. In this sense, creating transcripts can be strategic, particularly in short-term student projects, in that you are trying to examine a research problem and are looking for transcript data that will help you do that. You will want to listen and take notes on all of your transcripts, but you may not have time to transcribe every line of recorded data.

Coding and interpreting the data

The question of how you interpret your data takes you back to your research problem, the subfield of discourse analysis you are interested in, and more specifically to your research question(s). In addition to the qualitative, inductive coding procedures we discussed in Chapter 7, in which you build up themes to interpret relationships and language use in your data, you may have preset categories and linguistic features that you are interested in examining in your transcripts. There are multiple topics, theories, and methods for coding and interpreting discourse data, and we offer a list of recommended books for further reading at the end of the chapter. As an introduction to interpreting discourse data, we summarize here the five categories of analysis proposed by Sutherland (2016) in his guidebook to discourse analysis. Student researchers may find it useful to focus their reading, coding, and interpreting of their data on one or two of the following categories.

Text

At perhaps its most basic level, discourse analysis is concerned with how words or linguistic units join together in a clause or sentence in order to create meaning in a text. Discourse analysts look for patterns in the way parts of a clause, sentence, or passage in a text connect together, a feature often referred to as cohesion. At this clause or textual level, key features that analysts look at in a text include reference, substitution, ellipsis, conjunction, and lexical cohesion. Reference involves the way a word can point to another word, idea, or section of the same text. Examples include something relatively simple, such as personal pronouns (he, she, they, we, etc.) referring back to earlier references of actual people or the more complex analysis of comparative reference in which something such as a comparative adjective like *bigger* implicitly refers to a previous and perhaps cultural definition of "bigness."

Substitution and ellipsis are related features in that substitution is a device that adds cohesion to a text by replacing one word with another (e.g., the use of *one* for cookie in "I don't want the chocolate chip cookie. I want the peanut butter one"), whereas ellipsis is a cohesive device that eliminates redundant or unneeded information (e.g., the dropping of "likes parsnips" in the second clause of "Johnnie likes parsnips; I don't, but I will cook them for her anyway").

Conjunctions are terms that show a relationship between parts of a clause or sections of a text (e.g., the *so* in "Clinton was predicted to win the election, so most Americans were surprised to see Trump elected president of the United States" shows a cause-and-effect relationship). And lexical cohesion is the way certain words have meanings and associations with other words or simply are often used in conjunction with other terms, a feature called collocation that is studied by corpus linguists and discussed further in Chapter 10.

The linguist M.A.K. Halliday and others using a systemic functional linguistic (SFL) approach to discourse introduced and defined these discourse features, and they offer a relatively simple way to gain some initial understanding of how language is used in a particular text. Once researchers determine how features such as reference, substitution, ellipsis, conjunction, and lexical cohesion work in one text, they can compare the way these features work in similar and different texts and context.

Meaning

Sutherland (2016) writes that when discourse analysts examine the meaning in texts, they are considering "how people make sense of the multiple possible meanings of language in use" (p. 37). There are multiple theories of meaning and terms and features that an analyst can use when exploring how meaning works in a text, including examining how and what verbs are used (e.g., the differences between modal verb uses in sentences such as "You should speak in English" vs. "You need to speak in English") and what information is assumed to be shared and known by the speaker or writer of a text. This information is related to the notion of *schema*, or the mental picture of words, processes, and actions that speakers share. For example, a discussion about parenting and childrearing between speakers from different cultures may involve different schema and understandings of parent–child relationships. These schemas will affect the information that is presented about the topic and how different terms and phrases are interpreted. In addition, a focus on meaning may lead a discourse analyst to examine what are considered the unmarked and marked usages and meanings in their data and what this might reveal about the speakers and the interaction. For example, it is conventional in US English to say, "How tall are you?" instead of "How short are you?" The use of *tall* is the unmarked version of the question, and the use of marked alternatives may indicate an implicit meaning by the speaker and may lead to misunderstandings or conflict.

Producer and context

In addition to aspects of linguistic variation associated with studies on dialect, linguistic variables, and standard/nonstandard language usage, features of discourse analysis focused on the producer and context—namely, register, genre, and stance—can be useful entry points for analysis of discourse data. In discourse analysis, *register* may refer to how language is different in different contexts. For example, Trudy may adopt a more professional and formal style when leading a class in comparison with when she and Paul are discussing how their class session went the previous day. In both contexts, the topic and information may be similar, but word choices and other linguistic features will differ; in other words, she is using two different registers. In this way, *register* refers to the lexical choices and style that speakers use in different situations. However, the term *register* is also used in sociolinguistics to refer to the jargon or special language used by a particular group or organization. For example, lawyers learn a technical, legal language with particular terms and meanings associated with courts and legal proceedings. This can be referred to as a legal register. In analyzing discourse data, researchers may code for examples of particular registers as well as note the uses and contexts in which participants change their use of different registers.

Whereas registers refer to overall variation in language use based on context, discourse analysts examine *genres* in the use of language in their data as the language used for specific purposes, functions, and communicative events. For example, the statement-of-purpose genre that is often used when applying to higher education institutions may vary depending on context, but the purpose and function of the statement connects these texts together as a genre. Comparing the language of a particular genre that is used by participants in your collected data can reveal information about the genre itself, and how it is changing, as well as the way a particular genre, for example, spoken word poetry, is taken up by different speech communities.

A final aspect of discourse that we point out for student researchers to consider as they begin their interpretation and analysis of their data is the more complex notion of *stance*, which Johnstone (2009b) defines as "the methods, linguistic and other, by which interactants create relationships with the propositions they utter and with the people they interact with" (pp. 30–31). In other words, stance or stance taking includes all of the ways we use language to communicate our evaluation of a situation, belief, or argument. Is our opinion strong, weak, or tentative? Do we have sympathy for another's position or experience? There are multiple ways to communicate our evaluations with both linguistic and nonlinguistic ways, such as gestures. To illustrate just one example of stance taking, Sutherland (2016) offers a typical argument between children about who was responsible for breaking an item, in which one child argues, "You broke it," and the other child responds, "Did not" (p. 97). The use of the past tense *did* signals certainty about who broke it (not the speaker) and sets the frame for the argument as an either/or situation in which no doubt can be introduced. Either one speaker or the other did it; there is no modality or entertaining alternative scenarios.

These types of fine-grained analysis based on textual features and the way meaning is constructed by the speakers in particular contexts reveal the complexity involved in even everyday interactions, and it can be very easy for students to become lost in trying to determine what exactly to focus on. We recommend starting small, and once you see a pattern or feature of language being used, listen to recordings and read over your notes to see similar examples, keeping in mind the categories and terms listed above and in the next sections of this chapter.

As a further summary of some key aspects of discourse that you may want to look for and use as part of your analysis and in response to your research questions, we summarize in Table 8.2 a few more key terms used in DA research.

Interlocutor	Each person who takes part in the conversation or exchange
Participant	Each person who takes part in the research you are conducting
Style shifting	The shift in vocabulary; use of "in" words or foreign words, phrases, or pronunciation; changes in tone; and the level of politeness used in our interchanges. These shift or change depending on the situation and the ways we use language to index or position ourselves as friends, family, parents, students, teachers, bosses, workers, enemies, etc.
Code-switching	Switching between languages, usually among bilingual or multilingual individuals. Linguists suggest multiple reasons for this, including group solidarity; establishing identity; establishing intimacy and terms of endearment; and "crutching," which occurs when someone doesn't know a word or phrase or when there is a better word or phrase in another language.
Discourse markers	Seemingly meaningless words and phrases that perform multiple functions in keeping a conversation going: 1. Adverbs such as *so, however, then*, and *like* 2. Interjections such as *wow, gee, huh,* and *well?* 3. Quotatives, words that introduce a direct quote, such as *say, go,* and *be like* 4. Conjunctions such as *and* and *but* 5. Phrases such as *you know, I mean,* and *I think*
Hedges	Words and phrases like *kind of, sort of,* and *I think* that seem to indicate tentativeness.
Tag questions	Short question phrases tacked onto a statement. such as "It's cold today, isn't it?" "That was a great book, wasn't it?" "That's what you mean, sí?" Early research done by Robin Lakoff associated the use of tag questions with women. More recent research questions that conclusion. This makes researching the use of tag questions a relevant research project.

High-rising terminal (HRT) or uptalk	These interchangeable terms refer to when someone ends a statement with a rise in the voice that makes it sound like a question. Use of uptalk has been associated with young women. Some interesting longitudinal research suggests that the use of HRT is not only gender related but also age related and that when women mature, they do not employ this speech pattern.
Falsetto	The raising of the vocal register to the top of the range; usually associated with men.
Creaky voice/ vocal fry or glottal fry	Interchangeable terms that refer to a deepening of the voice to the lowest vocal register. It is produced through a loose glottal closure. This vocal characteristic has been associated with young women and is discussed in the research conducted by Patricia Yuasa on page 68.
Turn taking	This point of analysis looks at the structure of the interchange—how it opens or begins, how the conversation is maintained and how topics are chosen, and how the conversation closes and who makes that decision.
Interruptions and overlap	Interruptions occur when someone cuts off someone else's turn before that person is ready to stop talking, and are related to overlaps that occur when someone starts speaking at the same time as someone else.
Backchanneling	This involves someone showing that he or she is engaged in the conversation by nodding one's head, giving a thumbs-up, or making sounds such as *hmm, uh-huh, yeah, no way,* or *well*?, or tsking (tsk, tsk) to show disapproval.
Latching	This discourse feature occurs when someone starts speaking as soon as the other person stops or takes a breath without any pause in the conversation.
Silence	Silence and the amount of time that people can abide silence before speaking may indicate something about the comfort level of the group

TABLE 8.2 KEY SOCIOLINGUISTIC TERMS AND PROCESSES ANALYZED IN DA RESEARCH

Discourse analysis methods in published research

Rosalyn Negrón, in her article "New York City's Latino ethnolinguistic repertoire and the negotiation of latinidad in conversation" (2014), uses discourse analysis to understand and present her findings about how speakers, specifically Latinos in NYC, actively construct their identities through situated social practices such as switching between Spanish and English. As an example study, students can use Negrón (2014) as exemplary for both her data collection and discourse analysis methods as well as how she connects the relevance of her study to previous work on Spanish communities, code-switching, and shared notions of "latinidad."

> **RESEARCHER TO KNOW: Rosalyn Negrón**
>
> Rosalyn Negrón is Associate Professor of Anthropology in the College of Liberal Arts at the University of Massachusetts, Boston. Her areas of research include sociocultural urban and linguistic anthropology, international migration, and ethnic flexibility and multiethnicity. Her research on the linguistic and ethnic flexibility of Latino immigrants is discussed in this chapter and in greater detail in her 2011 book *Ethnic Identification among Urban Latinos: Language and Flexibility*. She is interested in how the daily negotiations of ethnicity and language take place and shape people's relationships. She has conducted this research in Jamaica, Florida, New York City, and Boston

The article starts by setting the context and giving an historical perspective on the rise and diversity of the Latino population in the United States. Negrón (2014) states that demographic changes offer "both challenges and opportunities for the formation of panethnicity," or what she labels "latinidad" (p. 88), and she is interested in the ways in which bilingual New York City Latinos index themselves through strategic appropriation of linguistic patterns and variables in everyday social practices. Negrón explores panethnicity and latinidad through participant observations and recordings of the conversations and interactions of two men in Queens, NYC, Roberto and William, as they go about their daily lives. William, a self-described Nuyorican (New-York-born Puerto Rican), is a developer of a community-based website promoting Latino culture and the manager of a cell phone store. Roberto, who has lived in the United States most of his life, is a Venezuelan-born entrepreneur trying to promote his street fair business. Negrón chose these two participants for analysis because of the complexity in the way they used multiple linguistic features to highlight their ethnic identities.
Some of the features that Negrón found to be salient in her choice of participants in her study include the following:

1. Knowledge of multiple language varieties

2. Highlighting of ethnolinguistic identities in work-related domains

3. A preference for the use of the term *Latino* (inclusive/familiar) rather than *Hispanic* (bureaucratic) in referencing the panethnicity

4. Ethnic ambiguity (a physical appearance that does not readily mark a specific ethnoracial identification) as presenting opportunities for or complicating ethnolinguistic identification (p. 95).

The recordings of William and Roberto are just part of a larger study of over 11 participants and over 500 hours of recordings, and from this enormous body of data, Negrón only analyzes seven "extracts" from five conversations between William and Roberto in William's store for her article. She also includes two interviews between herself and Roberto in which she attempts to understand how Roberto chooses what variety of Spanish he will use and even if he will speak Spanish in his encounters.

To illustrate Negron's data analysis, take, for example, the first extract that she included in which Roberto first entered William's cell phone store, looking for a business deal where he could rent his canopies to William for a future street fair. This is a conversation between strangers, and takes place after they had talked entirely in English for several minutes, during which time Roberto tells William that he rents canopies, tables, and chairs, and William reveals that he has another store and might be interested in doing business with Roberto. At exchange number 39 in the extract below, Roberto gives William his business flyer and William says he will give him information about how they will set up for future business:

```
39   William:    Let me give you some information.
40               (5.0)
41   William:    Roberto? ((Finding Roberto's name on Roberto's flyer))
42   Roberto:    Yeah.
43   William:    I had a couple of other customers that that (.) do
44               fairs and stuff.
45   William:    O?k.
46               (2.0)
47   William:    °Try to give you some info.°
48               (2.0)
49               ((William searches for business card))
50   William:    °(Okay)° ((William hands Roberto a business card)) (p. 98)
```

Negrón (2016) noted that Roberto had been speaking in a New York–accented English, signaling his "initial assessment that William should be approached in English. ... As William turned away from Roberto to retrieve his business card (line 40), he looked at Roberto's flyer to confirm Roberto's name and [Negrón maintained] to gather clues about Roberto's ethnoracial background" (p. 99). William pronounces Roberto's name with a Spanish pronunciation, changing the "footing" of the relationship,

> **EXERCISE 8.5: Analyzing transcripts in Negrón (2014)**
>
> After finding a copy of Negrón (2014), discuss the following two passages with a partner.
> - Read the interchange [39–50] between Roberto and William. What do you notice about their conversation that Negrón does not focus on in her analysis? What do you make of the brief pauses between answers?
> - Read the interchange [53–67] between Roberto and William. What do you notice about their conversation that Negrón does not focus on in her analysis? When do they seem to index each other as Latinos or latinidad and people with a shared identity, as almost "friends"?

thereby indexing himself as Latino and revealing their shared Latino ethnicity. In her analysis, Negrón (2016) referenced a theory of footing or how alignments emerge and change between participants linked to spoken utterances and receptions to those utterances or other sign-mediated interactions (Goffman, 1981).

In a follow-up interview between Roberto and the researcher, Negrón asks him about his use of Spanish and particularly his use of Puerto Rican and Caribbean Spanishes; he tells her that it depends on his surroundings and that there are places where he uses a more mellow Colombian Spanish or a Cuban or Venezuelan Spanish. Negrón asks him to describe the Venezuelan Spanish, and he tells her it is "just a flow" and that he pronounces "the *s*'s and the *r*'s. He pronounces everything." Overall, Negrón (2014) concludes that "the distinct ways that Roberto and William negotiate latinidad demonstrate how the junctions and disjunctions of latinidad play out at the microlevel of everyday social practice. Latinidad emphasizes the shared aspects of the Latino experience in the United States, even as it encompasses significant heterogeneity across multiple domains of social organization: demographic, linguistic, racial, socioeconomic, and so on. … One takeaway from my analysis is that when little else is known among strangers, latinidad provides an entryway through which mutually beneficial opportunities can be explored" (114). This corresponds to Reyes's (2005) finding about the "benefit" of using slang to index group membership as well as its use as an identity marker.

For students, Negrón's study is a good example of the way that language is used in interactional studies and is a resource for participations to index local contexts and create a multiplicity of identities. Moreover, the multidimensionality of her discourse analysis—including descriptions of the community, the participants, and the conversations—enables Negrón to interpret both the social and the linguistic aspects of the situation to better examine her research problems and questions. Students should respond to the questions in Exercise 8.5 for further insight into Negrón's analysis methods.

Discourse analysis methods in student research

In her paper "Call Me *Habibi:* Generational Code-Switching in Arab-American Communities," student Zayneb Almiggabber asks the following research questions:

- What is the distinction between code-switching among older generations of Arabic speakers and younger generations of Arabic speakers?
- In what context does code-switching typically occur?
- How is linguistic identity shifting, and how does it tie into cultural and ethnic identity?

To gather her data about her eight bilingual subjects, she recorded and observed them in various settings, including a home, a college campus, and a local Arab restaurant. She transcribed her findings and made several observations. In class, we had discussed the multiple uses of *like* by young people, and Almiggabber discovered how a similar word was used by her bilingual participants. She writes:

> The word *ya'ny* means "like" and is used as often as American millennials use *like* between words within a sentence. One participant, named Maha, was telling a story in English, and before she clarified a certain detail, she said *ya'ny*. At the end of a conversation, most of the subjects would say *khalas*, meaning "enough" or "that's it." The Arabic term itself usually indicates the end of something, and it was interesting to see the word used as often as it was.

Almiggabber also noted that code-switching frequently occurred during moments of affection, and the most common terms of endearment spoken in Arabic were *habibi*, meaning "my love," and *hayaty*, meaning "my life." This finding helped her find the title for her paper "Call me *Habibi*," keeping in mind its literary reference as well.

Context played a role in Almiggabber's findings. The above findings were in public places, but in the home she found that code-switching was less frequent and served a different function. One participant she profiled,

Ahmed, was speaking to his mother in an Arabic-dominant conversation but code-switched in order to explain things that his mother understood better in English. Almiggabber points out that some terms were easier for Ahmed and his mother to understand in English. For example, on his way out, he told his mother, *"Ahna hanrooh el park,"* meaning "We're going to the park" with *park* being the only English term used in that interaction.

As we have discussed earlier, discourse analysis is a useful tool in combination with other data collection and analysis methods, and Almiggabber not only analyzed transcripts, but she also interviewed her participants and included a chart of the Arabic terms used, the context of the conversations, the number of incidents of switches, and the length of the conversations that she observed. See Table 8.3 for a summary of her data and findings; the full paper can be found on the course website.

From this student example, we can view Almiggabber's paper as a good example of a student project that collected varied recordings, transcribed selected passages, and then performed a close analysis of her participants' use of Arabic and English in a variety of settings. This allowed Almiggabber to offer a deep analysis of her own culture and the role of English and code-switching.

Steps for completing a discourse analysis of your collected data

Here are some of the steps in conducting a discourse analysis study:

1. Decide what you are interested in researching. Look at the list of possible approaches in discourse analysis, and choose whether several seem appropriate to your study.

2. Clarify your research problem or question, and write it out in question form.

3. Do a literature review to find relevant research on your topic.

4. Identify a community of practice, group of people, or situation where you can gather data to do your research.

5. Obtain permission from the individuals and group participants to record and/or video them.

6. Take field notes and audio- or video-record when it is appropriate.

7. Listen to all audio recordings and watch videos. Look for patterns or elements that stand out and would be interesting in answering your research question. Take notes as you listen and/or watch.

DISCOURSE ANALYSIS 143

Subject name	Arabic term(s) used	Context of conversation	Age	Number of switches	Length of conversation documented
Ahmed	• *Habibti* (my love) • *Min fadlik* (please) • *El mohem* (anyway) • *Ya'ny* (like)	He was telling a story to Maha, seated next to him, who he is also dating.	27	4	3 minutes
Maha	• *La* (no) • *Ya'ny* (like) • *Wallah* (I swear to God)	She was responding to Ahmed in conversation at the restaurant.	28	3	2 minutes
Noha	• *Hamdellah 3al salama* (welcome back) • *Mish adra* (I can't) • *Ya'ny* (like)	She is greeting another bilingual speaker.	24	3	2 minutes
Reem	• *Ya'ny* (like) • *Sah* (right?) • *Min* (from) • *Museeba* (issue) • *Mashrou* (project)	She is in conversation with another bilingual speaker.	24	5	3 minutes
Mahmoud	• *Ya'ny* (like) • *Kessir* (break) • *Wil'it* (It's lit)	This subject used the largest number of recontextualized terms.	22	3	2 minutes
Tanya	• *Ma biddi* (I don't want to) • *Yallah* (used as "let's go")	She did not code-switch as much as the others.	28	2	2 minutes
Nadia	• *Ya'ny* (like) • *Sah* (right?) • *Lazem takly* (You need to eat)	She was speaking to her aunt, who understood some English.	26	3	2 minutes

TABLE 8.3 SUMMARY OF ALMIGGABBER'S DATA AND ANALYSIS

8. Create transcripts of the material that you will analyze. Choose the parts of the transcripts that you will focus on. Notice that both Negrón and Almiggabber did not include every word from their transcripts, but focused on the parts that fit with their research problem and interests.

9. Analyze your findings, focusing on the data you found, and connect it to prior research or readings you have done on the subject.

You may not do all of the steps listed above, but you will want to choose the group with which you will do your discourse analysis carefully and early in the semester because in a one-semester course, you will be conducting a relatively short and very focused research project with a limited number of participants. This means that you need to identify your participants and the context early on, so you can record or video the interactions and have time to transcribe and analyze your data.

Further reading on discourse analysis research methods

We list here the following books as good places for further investigation of discourse analysis research methods:

Cameron, D. (2001). *Working with spoken discourse.* London, UK: SAGE

Gee, J. P. (2011). *How to do discourse analysis: A toolkit.* Abingdon, UK: Routledge.

Gee, J. P. (2014). *An introduction to discourse analysis: Theory and method,* 4th ed. Abingdon, UK: Routledge.

Johnstone, B. (2018). *Discourse analysis,* 3rd ed. Oxford, UK: Wiley-Blackwell.

Jones, R. H. (2012). *Discourse analysis: A resource book for students.* Oxford, UK: Wiley-Blackwell.

Schiffrin, D. (1994). *Approaches to discourse: Language as social interaction.* Hoboken, NJ: John Wiley & Sons

Sutherland, S. (2015). *A beginner's guide to discourse analysis.* London, UK: Palgrave Macmillan.

Tagliamonte, S. (2011). *Variationist sociolinguistics: Change, observation, interpretation.* Oxford, UK: Wiley-Blackwell

Waring, H. Z. (2017). *Discourse analysis: The questions discourse analysts ask and how they answer them.* New York, NY: Routledge.

Wortham, S., & Reyes, A. (2015). *Discourse analysis: Beyond the speech event.* Abingdon, UK: Routledge.

9 Statistical analysis

CHAPTER OVERVIEW

- Introduction: What Are Statistical Analysis Methods in Sociolinguistics Research?
- How Do We Perform a Statistical Analysis of Our Collected Data?
  - Variables and Hypothesis Testing
  - Descriptive versus Inferential Statistics
- Statistical Analysis Methods in Published Research
- Statistical Analysis Methods in Student Research
- Steps for Completing a Statistical Analysis of Your Collected Data

Introduction: What are statistical analysis methods in sociolinguistics research?

Often, our students choose projects that use the discourse and qualitative analysis methods presented in Chapters 7 and 8. This is because many of our students come from a humanities background and prefer to discuss and collect data on language topics using interview and observation techniques. In addition, for semester or course projects, even students who have a background in statistics may not have the time to organize and collect the appropriate data necessary to perform in-depth statistical analyses. Guy (2014) writes that the field of sociolinguistics originally came out of the field of linguistics and was influenced by its humanistic traditions in which language was studied categorically, that is, something was grammatical or it was not. Many topics in sociolinguistics, particularly studies of language variation and attitudes, however, are studies of relationships that are "relative, not absolute; that is, relations of *more* and *less* rather than of *either/or*" (p. 195). In other words, as we have seen and will illustrate further in this chapter, sociolinguist studies of language variation, attitude, and use are rarely if ever absolute and rarely offer universal tendencies; for these types of studies, statistical analysis methods can give us an important tool when analyzing these types of data. In this way, statistical analysis can investigate the central tendencies—some strong, others weaker—that can lead us, as researchers, to interpretations and conclusions about group behaviors, language change, and the indexical nature of language.

For most students enrolled in a sociolinguistics course with a term-length research project, a basic summary of statistics in sociolinguistic research as provided in this chapter will suffice as an introduction, and we understand that most students will need an entire course or two and many guidebooks to become proficient in using the statistical analyses used in sociolinguist research in order to complete a statistical analysis on their own. Some sociolinguistics instructors may choose to focus their entire class around a quantitative data collection project and lead their students through the statistical analysis, as illustrated in Tagliamonte and Hudson (1999) and Tagliamonte and D'Arcy (2004), and this chapter can provide a background for that type of in-depth group project as well. Our goal in this chapter is that after reading and examining key aspects of statistical research design and the research examples profiled here, readers will have a better sense of what statistics are used for and how they may incorporate some aspect of statistical analysis into their research projects. As with previous chapters, we can then point readers to more in-depth texts and introductions of statistical analysis if they do want to add more than a descriptive statistical analysis to their course projects.

How do we perform a statistical analysis of our collected data?

Variables and hypothesis testing

In Chapter 1, we discussed the sociolinguistic variable as a linguistic feature that may have two or more alternative forms with the same meanings (but different social significations and indexes). The sociolinguistic variable is typically the central point of analysis in language variation studies and is often analyzed using the broader categorizations of types of variables used in statistical analysis. Following is a list of the key types of variables used to study sociolinguistic features such as the sociolinguistic variable.

- **Independent variable:** This is the variable that the researcher expects to influence the other variables under examination. For example, age in Becker (2009)—a study introduced in Chapter 4 and further analyzed later in this chapter—appeared to influence the use of syllable-final /r/ among her participants; thus, age was an independent variable.

- **Dependent variable:** This is the variable that is changed by the presence of the independent variable. For example, /r/ usage changed among the participants of Becker (2009) based on the independent variable of the topic of "neighborhood talk" or "non-neighborhood talk." Sociolinguists typically examine sociolinguistic variables as dependent variables that rely on an independent variable such as class, gender, or age.

- **Nominal variable:** These are variables that are considered mutually exclusive, such as sex or social class; or a linguistic variable such as word order, number, tense, or case.
- **Continuous variable:** These are variables such as age or income that exist on a continuous scale with greater and lesser values.
- **Ordinal variable:** These continuous variables are defined by the order in which they are ranked, that is, first, second, third, and so on, but the distance between each ranking is not necessarily the same or clear. For example, Morris (2014)—whose study was introduced in Chapter 4 and further analyzed in this chapter—described his participants' ranking of their Welsh abilities as on a continuous, ordinal scale from 1–7 because there was not a consistent distinction between each number, on the scale. For example, participants may understand the difference between scores of 6 and 7 as smaller than the difference between scores of 4 and 5.
- **Interval variable:** This continuous variable provides a fixed definition between two points on a scale. For example, participants' scores on a language proficiency test are arranged on an interval scale because a 5-point difference between, for example, 70 and 75 would mean the same thing as the 5-point difference between 60 and 65. This measurable difference between points was not clear in the Likert scale used in Morris (2014).

In performing a statistical analysis, it is important to clearly designate and define the type of variable or variables that your study is examining and what relationships exist between the variables you are examining. To do this, you need to first define the construct or idea that you are studying and then make a case for how that construct can be validly measured as a variable in your collected data. You will also need to decide how you view the variables in your study in terms of independent, dependent, continuous, or interval. For example, if you were interested in studying the use of a nonstandard form in English, such as *ain't*, you would first need to decide what social categories you are going to examine. If you consider *ain't* as a dependent variable that will be influenced by a person's gender, class, or other identity characteristics, you will need to decide how you will determine your independent variables. You will have to answer questions such as "What will be considered markers of different social class (e.g., household income or neighborhood of residence)? How will you determine a person's biological gender? And will it be self-reported?" In short, you will need to provide specific definitions for how you are defining independent and dependent variables.

Guy (2014) writes that the traditional assignment of a sociolinguistic variable as a dependent variable is challenged if we view social identity as a set of performances and practices. Further, he writes:

> Gender identities—masculinity and femininity—as well as ethnic identities and social relationships like boss, teacher, friend, and so on are all at least partially constructed through linguistic practice, such that making certain linguistic choices contributes to the establishment and maintenance of the identity. From this perspective, one might reasonably construe the linguistic variables as independent and the social identities as dependent. (p. 198)

However you decide to assign your independent and dependent variables—to social or linguistic categories—the key point is that you need to be clear how you are defining or operationalizing the constructs that underlie your variables. By doing this at the beginning of your research project, your study will gain what Nunan (1992) calls construct validity, or the ability to confidently answer the question "Is the study actually investigating what it is supposed to be investigating?" (p. 16). If your constructs and variables are clearly stated, you improve your ability to confidently draw conclusions and generalizations from your collected data and measurements. Further, as you complete your analysis and write up your results, you can refer back to your variables and how you have defined the constructs. Exercise 9.1 provides practice operationalizing underlying constructs as variables in sociolinguistic research.

Hypothesis testing and generalizability

In Chapter 1, we noted that quantitative research design generally starts with a hypothesis that the study wishes to test through various means of numerical analysis. A hypothesis is the researcher's initial statement, based on previous research and theory, that states what the researcher predicts or expects when analyzing the collected quantitative data. A hypothesis is stated as something to test, such as, "In this study, we test whether…" or "An examination of the collected data will reveal whether…" Just like research questions, hypotheses need to be as narrow as possible in order for the data to support or disprove the claim. For quantitative researchers, the use of statistical analysis to test a hypothesis allows for generalization to a larger population than the number of participants in a study. In addition, many of the statistical tests used in sociolinguistics are based on the notion of a null, or zero, hypothesis. The null hypothesis is the idea that there is no correlation between the variables and the groups studied. In other words, the null hypothesis is the opposite of what is expected in the stated hypothesis. By rejecting the null hypothesis through statistical analysis, researchers are able to draw conclusions and generalizations about their data, participants, and predictions.

> **EXERCISE 9.1: Connecting variables with constructs**
>
> Before analyzing any data, a quantitative researcher must transfer an abstract idea or construct into a measureable variable. As Lowie and Seton (2013) write, "The transfer of a construct into a variable is always the researcher's own choice; and the validity of the outcomes of the investigation may strongly depend on it" (p. 20). For the following constructs, provide at least two ways to operationalize the construct as a measurable variable.
>
> - A person's spoken proficiency in a language
> - A person's membership in a political party (at one point in time)
> - A person's membership in a social group (i.e., a member of the burned-out burnouts in Eckert, 1989, or our student April Polubiec's study of power lifters versus body builders)
> - Use of a nonstandard grammatical form such as *ain't* or marked pronunciation features such as vocal fry
> - A group or individual's attitudes toward language education policies
> - Different neighborhoods or zones in an urban area
> - Add your own construct and propose two different ways of operationalizing it as a measurable variable

Descriptive versus inferential statistics

Researchers use two main types of statistical data analysis when testing hypotheses. First, descriptive statistics include measures that broadly summarize the characteristics and distribution of the data. Key measures of descriptive statistics include the following:

- **Mean:** Mean is the arithmetic average. Researchers compute this number to see the basic tendencies of data sets. For example, Kiesling (2004) reports the results of his survey questions as the basic averages (means) of participant responses.
- **Mode:** The mode is the most common response. It is particularly useful for reporting nominal data.
- **Median:** The median is the middle number in a list of values in which the same number of values appears above and below the median number. For example, Morris (2014) reports the median response to his survey items. The median is often reported as a central tendency in order to eliminate extreme values that may skew the average to look greater or smaller than that of the majority of respondents.

- **Ratio:** This involves comparing the percentage of instances of a variable to the number of times other variables of the same type were used. For example, in Moore and Podesva (2009), many of their graphs compare the percentage of different forms of tag questions (e.g., nonstandard vs. standard) to the total number of tag questions in the data set.

- **Standard deviation:** This statistic is used to show how close the data in a set are to each other, or, in statistical terms, "how cases differ from each other around the mean" (Riazi, 2016, p. 303). This is important because the standard deviation reveals whether the data values are widely spread over a range. For example, two sets of data may have the same mean, but their standard deviation may differ, revealing differences in the data sets.

Because of the students' lack of previous training, their projects typically draw only on descriptive statistics in their course projects, but inferential statistics are the primary tests researchers use to make inferences and generalizations to a larger population outside of the data sample. It is important for novice students to have a general knowledge of inferential statistical tests in order to read sociolinguistic research as well as consider ways to expand their course research experiences into larger projects. Using inferential statistics, researchers use a wide range of tests in order to show whether a pattern or correlation between data sets, variables, or other values is significant. In other words, researchers can use inferential statistical equations and measures in order to make reasoned generalizations about a study's variables based on the limited amount of data collected. Some common inferential statistical measures in sociolinguistics are listed here:

- **T-test:** The t-test is used to compare the means of two sets of data for continuous dependent variables. It is based on the null hypothesis and assumes that your data will assume a normal, bell-shaped curve. You cannot use a t-test to examine an independent variable that has more than two groups.

- **Chi-square test:** The chi-square test is used to test the data collected about nominal variables in comparison with what would be expected if all of the variables were independent and showed no relationship.

- **Multivariate analysis:** Sociolinguists use multivariate analysis to examine the correlation that exists between multiple independent variables in order to see how likely it is that any one of the multiple independent variables affected the appearance of the dependent variable. As illustrated in Morris (2014) and Becker (2009), multivariate analysis is very common in sociolinguistic research. Many researchers use software programs such as Goldvarb, Varbrul, and Rbrul to perform these analyses.

- **Factor weights:** When performing multivariate analyses, software programs report each variable according to its factor weight, which is basically the degree to which each independent variable affected the linguistic variation or variant that is being examined. For example, Becker (2009) reports on the factor weights of the multiple variables that influenced the production of syllable coda /r/ among her participants.

- **Correlation:** Tests of correlations examine the relationship between two variables. For continuous, ordinal scale data, Pearson's r statistic is used. The statistic is reported on a scale of -1 to $+1$, where $+1$ describes a perfect correlation (both variables increase together at exactly the same time) and -1 describes an inverse relationship (where you have one variable, you never have the other). An r of 0 reveals no relationship between the two variables. Another common statistic of correlation used in sociolinguistics is the Mann-Whitney U test. This test of correlation is used to test the relationship between ordinal variables and nominal variables. Morris (2014) used the Mann-Whitney U test to test the relationship between participants' responses on a language attitude survey with the home language and area.

The key component in all of these tests is determining the significance, or p-value, of the relationship that the test is analyzing. All inferential statistics include significance tests that measure how likely it is that the data collected would continue to be the same if researchers collected more data from the same population. Significance tests draw on the null hypothesis in order to show that there is little chance that there is no relationship between the variables studied in the data. Depending on the test used, most sociolinguists consider p-values under 0.05 to be statistically significant. This means that the null hypothesis has only a 5 percent chance of being true.

These are just a few of the main descriptive and inferential statistical measures and terms used in sociolinguistic research. The descriptions are provided for you to better read quantitative sociolinguistic research and understand some basic ideas about how you could examine language variation and other sociolinguistic topics quantitatively in order to better read published papers of language variation research studies. At the same time, many students do compute the basic descriptive statistics such as the mean, mode, median, and ratios when doing their class projects, and in some cases they use one of the inferential statistics tests, such as the t-test in the student example later in this chapter. Even drawing on some basic descriptive statistics can allow students to make general comments about their variables and research topics, and analyze the central tendencies that they have found in their data collection. We offer a list of additional readings on statistics and quantitative analysis in sociolinguistic research at the end of the chapter, as well as a list of commonly used statistics software programs.

Statistical analysis methods in published research

Of course, there is much more to conducting a statistical analysis than selecting variables, collecting data, and then plugging your data into a statistics software program. As we further illustrate in taking a close look at two example studies in the next section, Becker (2009) and Morris (2014), statistical analysis involves decisions at every stage of the research process, including questions about sampling methods, data coding, and interpretations of the data. As we discuss Becker (2009) and Morris (2014), we continue to provide tips and note aspects of completing your own statistical analysis, or key points to focus on when reading studies using statistics.

Becker (2009) revisits the location of William Labov's foundational work in variationist sociolinguistics on the Lower East Side (LES) of Manhattan in New York City. Instead of focusing on language variation as a means of analyzing social stratification, as in Labov (1966), she connects place and meaning in examining one feature of New York City English (NYCE), non-rhoticity, or r-less speech. In particular, Becker (2009) draws on quantitative analysis of interviews with seven long-term LES residents of European ancestry to reveal the continued presence of non-rhoticity as a feature of NYCE and, more importantly, the way /r/ is used as an index of place and identity for long-term LES residents. Becker (2009) is a useful example for sociolinguistics students because her research design draws on classic studies of language variation that have used statistical analysis, but she broadens her analysis to examine place, identity, and social meaning as well as variation.

The data that Becker collected with her seven participants included (1) a general interview and discussion about the neighborhood, (2) the reading of a short passage, and (3) the reading of a list of words. She used all three sources of data to perform her quantitative analysis in which she found 3,000 words with a syllable-code /r/. She then coded each instance in which the speaker pronounced the /r/ as [r-1] and each instance in which the /r/ was not pronounced as [r-0]. In total, Becker (2009) reports that the coders agreed on 90 percent of the instances where either [r-0] or [r-1] were heard. Table 9.1 summarizes some of the statistically significant factor groups for [r-1] found in her data.

In reading Table 9.1, we can see that for each factor group, Becker (2009) reports the number of times (N) that [r-1] was pronounced (or realized) in the interview and what percentage [r-1] accounted for all instances when [r-1] or [r-0] were possible. As we can see, the highest percentages of [r-1] occur in more careful speech styles and when preceding a vowel. In addition, younger speakers use more [r-1]. In these quantitative studies of linguistic variation, the factor weight decimal reveals the degree to which each factor influenced the use of the linguistic variable under examination. For example,

Factor group	Factor	Percent [r-1]	N	Factor weight
Preceding vowel	[i]	42	278	0.44
	[e]	40	260	0.41
	[ɑ]	47	480	0.61
	[o]	42	592	0.49
Following context	consonant	33	2,269	0.44
	pause	30	405	0.41
	vowel	78	326	0.91
Topic	neighborhood	33	1,385	0.47
	other	39	916	0.55
Speech style	interview	35	2,304	0.46
	reading	41	572	0.58
	word list	67	124	0.78
Age	older (70+)	29	2,054	0.39
	younger (45–55)	57	946	0.72

TABLE 9.1 SUMMARY OF SELECTED QUANTITATIVE ANALYSIS OF [R-1]
Source: Becker (2009)

high factor weights such as 0.72 for younger speakers and 0.78 for word list confirm the strong influence of age and close attention to speaking in the use of [r-1] among the interviewees.

In addition to revealing that non-rhoticity, or [r-0], remains a feature of NYCE, Becker (2009) noted the different factor weights according to neighborhood talk. She analyzed this factor by coding her interview transcripts according to topics that concerned the LES neighborhood—such as local food, changes in the neighborhood, narratives located on the block, and memories of the block—and general "non-neighborhood topics"—such as food, spirituality, career, and schooling. In doing this, she was able to perform a microanalysis of each interview and reveal the way [r-0] was used more often in neighborhood talk. Further, when discussing the differences between neighborhood and non-neighborhood talk, Becker (2009) provided an example from one of the interviews:

Lindsey: It really has changed, and, I just never[r-0] thought it would get that high. But it has. And I'm forty[r-0]-five, so I didn't really anticipate things getting so expensive.
Kara: Do you find, being in the neighborhood hard—I don't know groceries, and things like that?

Lindsey: Well, we only have, really have like one super[r-1]market[r-0].
Kara: Where do you guys go now when you go out—I don't know, restaurants or, [other places to go.
Lindsey: We or[r-1]der[r-0] in. (laughs) Well we or[r-0]der[r-0] from Odessa's and that's a landmark[r-0], that's been here for years. (p. 650)

Through her quantitative examples interspersed with these excerpts from the interviews, Becker (2009) reinforced her key finding that use of non-rhotic speech has moved beyond a marker of social class in NYCE and now provides long-term LES residents with resources to indicate their authenticity as a "true resident of the Lower East Side" (p. 653).

Statistical analysis of language variation research often involves coding and analysis of specific phonological, syntactic, or lexical language features, and researchers need to ensure that their coding choices are systematic and not based on their own biases. For this reason, Becker (2009) first transcribed the 3,000 examples of words from her corpus with syllable-coda /r/ and then coded whether the /r/ was pronounced [r-1] or was not [r-0]. She then had two other researchers code separately a random sample of 193 of the 3,000 examples to check for the reliability of her initial coding, and she found an overlap of 90 percent. This step of having more than one person code phonological data is important, as determining whether a particular variable was or was not uttered is difficult and may vary depending on the listener. In addition to coding for the phonological feature of syllable-coda /r/ and comparing grammatical features and characteristics of the speakers such as age and sex, Becker (2009) also coded her interview transcripts for the topic of "neighborhood" and "non-neighborhood." Again, she asked a second reader to confirm her coding choices and found the second reader and Becker had a 96 percent agreement in their choices. After confirming her coding choice, she was then able to determine the statistically significant factors that influence the use of /r/. In this way, Becker (2009) was able to provide a broad analysis of various linguistic, age, and demographic factors that may influence /r/ use in the LES participants.

Morris (2014) offered a good example of a mixed-method data collection approach that used statistical analysis to compare the similarities and differences between Welsh speakers' backgrounds, language attitudes, and languages skills. Specifically, he compared two cohorts of 27 students, one from North West Wales in a Welsh-dominant area and one from North East Wales in an English-dominant area. To ensure validity, Morris (2014) had similar numbers of participants from each cohort group, and the study found that although attitudes toward Welsh and the value of Welsh-English bilingualism were positive among all participants, only participants from

Welsh-speaking homes in North West Wales showed high degrees of Welsh use and self-confidence in their Welsh proficiency.

The data collection process can be described as a "qual → QUAN" study (see Dörnyei, 2007) in which a questionnaire study is facilitated and informed by a preceding interview. In Morris (2014), the interviews both informed the subsequent questions on the questionnaire as well as provided data for analysis in the manuscript, particularly related to participants' attitudes toward learning and using Welsh in school and in their personal lives. As illustrated in Chapter 3, for the questionnaire, Morris (2014) used a 7-point Likert scale, with the first point correlating with "Strongly Disagree" and the last point indicating "Strongly Agree."

After collecting the survey and interview data, Morris (2014) grouped the questions on the questionnaire according to similar themes such as Welsh in the Area, Opinion of Welsh, Use of Welsh, Opinion of English, and Self-Reported Ability in Welsh. He then tested the reliability of the question responses in each theme, using Cronback's Alpha; the correlation between different themes, using Pearson's r correlation coefficient; and the relationship between attitudes and participant areas and home languages, using the Mann-Whitney U test.

Overall, Morris (2014) found that there was extensive support and positive attitudes for learning and using Welsh, but participants from homes lacked confidence in Welsh even though they had over 10 years of immersion school experience in Welsh.

Despite these positive views of Welsh use, there was a statistically significant correlation between Welsh home language and both ability and use. Further, Morris (2014) reported on data from the interviews in which participants narrated examples of segregation according to the language groups and negative experiences with learning Welsh among some English home language participants. For example, one North West Wales English home language participant explained:

> I think I can't [speak Welsh] though 'cause I remember the school was quite bitchy 'cause I was in primary school; they used to start on me for it a lot for not being able to say it properly. 'Cause I was like one of the better performing kids in my year for everything apart from reading Welsh ... and that was really embarrassing, and I think that's why I don't like it ... I got good [grades] in the GCSEs [General Certificates of Secondary Education], like I got Bs and stuff, but I just don't like it. Jen (p. 77)

Further, a North West Wales home language Welsh speaker described the following student cliques in his Welsh interview:

> Mae gynnych chi'r criw Cymraeg a'r criw Saesneg … a'r half and half 'de, hanner Cymraeg, hanner Saesneg. … Iaith oedd y clics mwy 'na dim byd.
> [You've got the Welsh crew and the English crew … and the half and half like, half Welsh half English. … Language is the cliques more than anything.] (p. 81–82)

Morris (2014) concludes that the issue of speaker confidence and the role of group affiliation has been missing in previous work on Welsh, which focused more on "the dominance or prestige of English in the wider community and in youth culture or to negative opinions of the language amongst certain groups of young people" (p. 87), and he argues for more research and exploration of speaker confidence as a barrier to Welsh language use both inside and outside the classroom.

When working with survey data or doing quantitative analysis, researchers define and label independent and dependent variables that they are interested in examining before collecting data, rather than looking for themes and patterns to emerge from the data after they have finished collecting all of their data, as is done in qualitative data analysis. In Morris (2014), the researcher was interested in comparing participants' use of Welsh at home, their self-reported abilities in Welsh, and whether they lived in a Welsh-speaking area (all independent variables), with their opinions and attitudes about Welsh (dependent variables). Based on his statistical analyses, Morris (2014) found a significant correlation between participants' self-reported ability in Welsh and their opinion of Welsh and promotion of Welsh. In other words, if a participant was highly proficient in Welsh, her or she was also likely to have a high opinion of Welsh and want to see the language promoted. Although she did not perform the same statistical tests as Morris (2014) in order to show correlations between variables, if we look back at Jessica Balgobin's paper (introduced in Chapter 3 and available on the book's website), in her survey participants she examined variables such as whether they identify with the South Asian community, whether their family comes from the Caribbean or South Asia, and whether language is an important marker of identity. Balgobin reported the overall averages or means of her survey items and drew some conclusions from these results. In this way, Balgobin was using descriptive statistics to analyze her research questions, and Morris was drawing on inferential statistics to show the statistical significance of the correlations between themes or variables. The next section of the chapter offers another example of a student paper in which descriptive statistics were computed in its analysis, and some conclusions were drawn based on inferential statistical measurements.

As a final point in this section about what we can learn from published research, we find it instructive to point out how Morris (2014) used two cohorts of participants in his data collection, one from North West Wales and one from North East Wales. Comparing two similar groups that differ in one key characteristic, in this case English- versus Welsh-dominant areas, is a classic research and analysis method in linguistics and sociolinguistics. In this way, data analysis and initial conclusions are set up by the comparison of the two groups: if similarities are found, they should be reported and an analysis of why these similarities exist should be undertaken; if specific differences between the two groups are found, the same reporting and analyzing process should occur. For students, this ensures that no matter how participants respond, they will have some results to discuss. As we often tell our classes, even finding the opposite of what you expected to find is a finding in itself!

See Exercise 9.2 for further practice analyzing the statistical methods in Morris (2014) and Becker (2009).

> **EXERCISE 9.2: Analyzing Morris (2014) and Becker (2009)**
>
> Locate copies of Morris (2014) and Becker (2009), or see the links to the articles on the companion website. For each article, perform the following tasks, and then be prepared to share your responses with a group.
>
> 1. *Data/findings:* List or describe data, findings, or analysis that you think are particularly significant and interesting. Or list and describe data, findings, or analysis that you find are misleading or lack validity. State briefly why you think so.
> 2. *Connections:* Write a short statement (one to three sentences) describing how what you've read connects to your previous knowledge on the topic (both from academic studies and personal experiences) and/or course readings and discussions.
> 3. *Question or comment:* Briefly note any thoughts, including questions, that the article has raised for you, and/or propose further research studies and topics based on the findings or data in the article.

Statistical analysis methods in student research

For her class project, April Polubiec drew on the same initial data collection and analysis methods as Morris (2014) in that she chose to examine the similarities of two related but distinct speech communities, in her case bodybuilders and powerlifters. She writes that the sports and athletes may seem similar, but "the foundational difference between bodybuilding and powerlifting is that the former's goal is to build an aesthetically pleasing figure (which is defined by symmetry and low body fat) while the later aims to be as strong as possible (which is defined by the amount of weight one can lift)" (p. 2). From this difference, Polubiec built her research questions, data collection, and data analysis methods. Her questions included the following:

1. Can bodybuilding and powerlifting be considered two distinct speech communities? If so, are they nested within the larger speech community of athletes, or are they different altogether?

2. How do males and females index their gender identity through language within the sports of powerlifting and bodybuilding?

In order to address these questions, Polubiec collected caption and hashtag data from the public Instagram profiles of 40 bodybuilders (20 male and 20 female) and 40 powerlifters (similarly, 20 male and 20 female). The caption data consisted of all text included alongside the images except the language following a hashtag. The hashtag data included just the text used following a hashtag. Polubiec writes that the only hashtag data included in the caption data were hashtags that were necessary for the sentence structure (e.g., "Today I trained #legs). In order to choose her participants, Polubiec searched for public profiles on Instagram that used hashtags such as #bodybuilding, #powerlifting, and various hashtags used by professional bodybuilding and powerlifting associations such as #npc (National Physique Committee), #ifbb (International Federation of Body Building and Fitness), #uspa (US Powerlifting Association), and #usapl (USA Powerlifting). Polubiec only chose to include profiles from participants with 1,000-10,000 followers to ensure that the participants were not stars in their fields and would represent more genuine comments for comparison, as researchers have found that the larger a person's social network, the more likely he or she is to disclose positive rather than negative emotions.

In this way, Polubiec collected her data and was able to create distinct collections of text also referred to as corpora, and she used statistical and corpus analysis tools to analyze her data. We address corpus analysis research methods in more detail in Chapter 10, but in this chapter we can look more specifically at the statistical measurements Polubiec used to compare similarities and differences between her corpora. In performing her analysis, Polubiec first coded her data and created different corpora according to the specific groups she was interested in comparing, including the following: all powerlifter data, all bodybuilder data, male bodybuilder captions, male bodybuilder hashtags, female bodybuilder captions, female bodybuilder hashtags, male powerlifter captions, male powerlifter hashtags, female powerlifter captions, and female powerlifter hashtags.

Next, she computed and presented some of the descriptive statistical data, including percentage of different topics in bodybuilder versus powerlifter pictures and the 25 most frequent hashtags by female and male bodybuilders and powerlifters (see Figures 9.1 and 9.2, and Tables 9.2, 9.3, and 9.4).

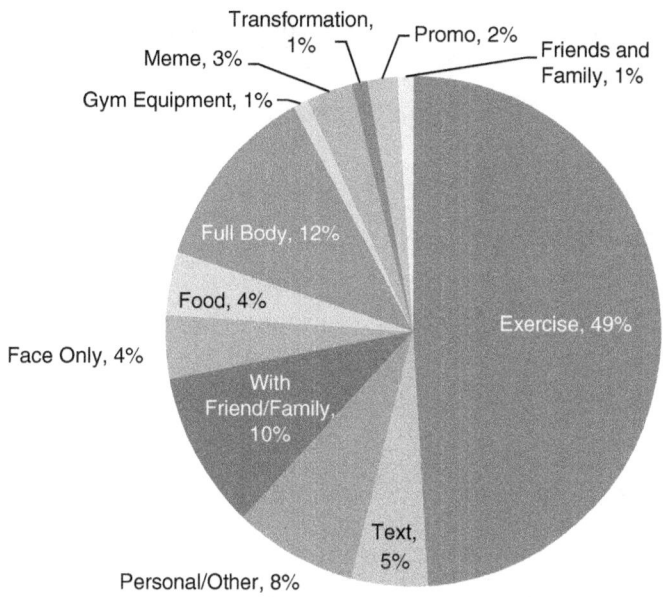

FIGURE 9.1 CONTENT OF POWERLIFTERS' PICTURES AND VIDEOS

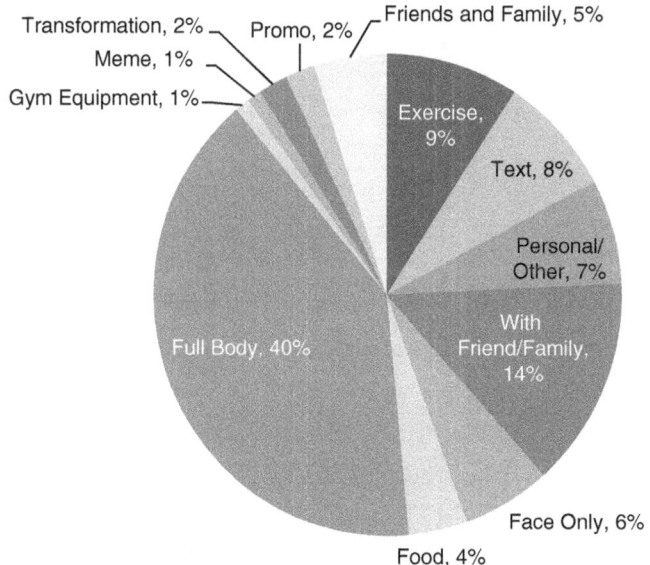

FIGURE 9.2 CONTENT OF BODYBUILDERS' CAPTIONS

Next, in order to address her research questions, Polubiec used a corpus analysis software program called Linguistic Inquire and Word Count (LIWC) to perform independent t-tests on her caption corpora in order to

Females (*n* = 6,023)	Males (*n* = 6,581)
npc	npc
fitness	bodybuilding
fitfam	fitness
girlswholift	fitfam
npcbikini	fit
fitspo	physique
fit	gym
girlswithmuscle	fitspo
bodybuilding	mensphysique
fitchick	aesthetics

TABLE 9.2 TEN MOST FREQUENT BODYBUILDER HASHTAGS

Females (*n* = 4,798)	Males (*n* = 1,811)
powerlifting	powerlifting
girlswhopowerlift	uspa
fitness	uspal
girlswholift	fitness
bodybuiling	fitnessmotivation
fitfam	power
powerlifter	powerbuilding
squat	bodybuilding
fitspo	powerliftingmotivation
usapl	roadto

TABLE 9.3 TEN MOST FREQUENT POWERLIFTER HASHTAGS

compare similarities and differences between the two sports and between genders within the sports. LIWC codes and calculates the text in a corpus according to 96 different dimensions ranging from linguistic categories, such as "words per sentence," to affective categories, such as analytical thinking, clout, authenticity, and emotional tone. There is not enough space to detail all of the comparisons, LIWC category definitions, and statistics that Polubiec reports, but her full paper is available on the companion website. Table 9.4, however, summarizes the results of one of Polubiec's key comparisons between bodybuilders and powerlifters. To take one example, the table reveals that bodybuilders are shown to have a score of 59.58 on the "clout" dimension in LIWC, which was significantly higher than the powerlifters score of 46.91; t(75) = 3.33, p < 0.01. High clout numbers suggest that the speaker is confident and speaking with assumed expertise. In comparison, powerlifters' score of 79.01 on the "analytic" dimension was significantly higher than the bodybuilders' score of 57.18; t(78) = 3.21, p < 0.01. A high analytic score reflects more logical and less personal narrative explanations. Along with her other analyses, Polubiec writes that she can confirm her hypothesis that powerlifting and bodybuilders are separate speech communities, but her results reveal differences between the genders in each sport, with male bodybuilders, in particular, using significantly more speech associated with masculinity.

LIWC summary dimensions	Powerlifting M(SD)	Bodybuilding M(SD)	Test statistic
Word count	782.88 (430.83)	623.95 (314.44)	t(78) = 1.89
Analytic	70.07 (14.39)	57.18 (20.89)	t(78) = 3.21**
Clout	46.91 (15.19)	59.58 (18.640)	t(75) = 3.33**
Authentic	66.01 (19.87)	64.97 (21.40)	t(78) = 0.23
Tone	74.83 (19.80)	75.76 (24.46)	t(78) = −0.19
Words per sentence	11.72 (3.66)	11.08 (2.96)	t(78) = 0.87

TABLE 9.4 COMPARISON OF BODYBUILDERS AND POWERLIFTERS ON LIWC DIMENSIONS**
** = Significant at p < 0.01.

In summary, Polubiec's project illustrates the utility of analyzing data by creating independent and dependent variables in relation to two or more distinct groups and comparing the variables and groups through a statistical analysis of data points, for example, the use of a sociophonetic variable (Becker, 2009), their attitudes toward different languages (Morris, 2014), or the language of captions and hashtags of the group on social media. Further, Polubiec's paper illustrates the way descriptive statistics can reveal important trends that can be analyzed in shorter-term projects if students do not have the time or background to complete inferential statistical measurements. For example, a simple summary of the most commonly used words in hashtags or the types of comments made in captions revealed differences in the two groups that Polubiec was analyzing.

> **RESEARCHER TO KNOW: Kara Becker**
>
> Kara Becker is Associate Professor of Linguistics at Reed College in Portland, Oregon. She is a sociolinguist who does research in language variation and change, ethnicity, sex, and gender. She maintains an interactive website (www.newyorkcityaccents.com), which includes a series of quizzes testing one's ability to identify a NYC borough accent, as well as a place to add your own voice. She is working with her students on vowel production in Oregon and co-authored a 2016 paper with her students, "Variation in West Coast English: The Case of Oregon." Becker also developed The Sociolinguistic Artifacts website (http://www.reed.edu/slx-artifacts/), an educational site with videos, images, websites, audios, and articles that is open to the public for research as well as for submissions.

Steps for completing a statistical analysis of your collected data

In Chapter 5 of their handbook, Lowie and Seton (2013), authors of one of the books we recommend for further exploration, offer the following steps in completing a research project using statistics:

1. *Operationalization:* This involves operationalizing the constructs into variables, as discussed above.

2. *Forming hypotheses:* Also discussed above, the second step involves making clear what hypothesis is being tested and what alternative hypotheses need to be considered.

3. *Selecting a sample:* We have discussed different ways to select a sample in the data collection chapters. For statistical analysis, Lowie and Seton (2013) argue that the sample must be random either from the entire population or from a specific subpopulation. Of course, as we previously discussed, this is difficult for students in a semester course (as it is for most researchers), and students may use other nonprobability sampling techniques such as snowball sampling or convenience sampling, as described in Chapter 3. Adopting these sampling strategies, however, will limit the validity of the results and the ability of the research to generalize to a larger population.

4. *Data collection:* In addition to our previous points and examples about data collection, Lowie and Seton (2013) point out the need to ensure as much as possible that participants in a quantitative research study do not know the hypothesis that is being tested and that their responses are not affected by the presence of the researcher or the data collection tool.

5. *Setting the level of significance:* As discussed above, for sociolinguistic students of variation or language attitudes, the level of significance is

typically under 0.05. This means that the null hypothesis has only a 5 percent chance of being true.

6. *Statistics:* After calculating the descriptive statistics and inspecting tendencies and anomalies in the data, the best inferential statistical choice is chosen depending on the number of variables, the type of variable, and the relationships between the variables. Table 9.5 summarizes some of the main inferential statistics tests and the types of variables and questions they answer.

Statistical test	**Variables used**	**Purpose of analysis**
T-test	1 nominal independent and 1 continuous dependent	Compares whether the differences between two sets of scores are "real" and generalizable or simply based on random variation; for example, are there significant differences between men and women on language attitudes surveys?
Chi-square tests	1 nominal independent and 1 nominal dependent	Determines whether a significant relationship exists between nominal variables; for example, was there a significant relationship between voting choice and gender orientation in an election?
Factor analysis	1 or more nominal and continuous variables (both independent and dependent)	Compares which independent variable was more likely to have influenced the dependent variable(s); for example, if data were collected on various factors influencing a child's proficiency in learning English as an additional language (age when began learning, mother tongue,

		teaching methods, etc.), factor analysis tests would determine the most influential factors.
Correlation tests	1 nominal or continuous independent variable and 1 continuous dependent variable	Tests the extent one variable predicts or correlates with another; for example, is there a positive or negative correlation between age and ability to learn a foreign language?

TABLE 9.5 Choosing the right inferential statistical test for your hypothesis and data
Source: Based on Dörnyei (2007), Guy (2014), and Smakman (2018)

7. *Interpretation of the data:* If your results show significant correlations or relationships between your variables, you can go back to your hypothesis and constructs, and form conclusions and make generalizations about the speech community or group of participants in your study. When interpreting your results, you should always refer to previous studies and how your results do or do not fit with those of previous studies. In addition, as we discuss in more depth in Chapters 11 and 12 on writing up your study, the end of your paper will typically state any concessions or limitations to your research and look forward to future studies based on your results.

Further reading on statistical data analysis methods

For those seeking further in-depth guides to quantitative and statistical analysis in sociolinguistic research, we recommend the following titles:

Drager, K. (2014). Experimental methods in sociolinguistics. In J. Holmes & K. Hazen (eds.), *Research methods in sociolinguistics: A practical guide* (pp. 58–73). Malden, MA: Wiley-Blackwell.
Guy, G. (2014). Words and numbers: Statistical analysis in sociolinguistics. In J. Holmes, & K. Hazen (eds.), *Research methods in sociolinguistics: A practical guide* (pp. 194–210). Malden, MA: Wiley.
Lowie, W., & Seton, B. (2013). *Essential statistics for applied linguistics.* London,: UK: Palgrave Macmillan.
Macaulay, R.K.S. (2009). *Quantitative methods in sociolingustics.* London, UK: Palgrave Macmillan.

10 Corpus data analysis

CHAPTER OVERVIEW

- Introduction: What Is a Corpus and What Are Corpus Analysis Methods in Sociolinguistics Research?
- Performing a Corpus Analysis
  - Research Questions: Corpus-Based or Corpus-Driven
  - Choosing and Building a Corpus and Choosing a Software Program
  - Key Processes in Corpus Analysis
- Corpus Analysis Methods in Published Research
  - Mautner (2007): Using Existing Corpora
  - Tagliamonte and Roberts (2005): Using Television Show Dialogue in Corpus Studies
  - Grundmann and Krishnamurthy (2010): A Corpus-Based Approach to Analyze Climate Change Discourse
  - Deumert and Lexander (2013): Texting Practices in Africa
- Corpus Analysis Methods in Student Research
- Steps for Completing a Corpus Analysis

Introduction: What Is a Corpus and What Are Corpus Analysis Methods in Sociolinguistics Research?

In recent years, corpus linguistics—known as "the study of language based on examples of real life language use" (McEnery & Wilson, 2001, p. 1)—has grown as a method of analysis in sociolinguistics, and students may choose to use corpus analysis methods for all or part of their research project. The *corpus* (from the Latin term for "body") of corpus linguistics refers to a collection of digital language data that either are (1) compiled by other researchers or research institutions and available for independent researchers to use as data sources; or (2) compiled by the researcher as part of the data collection process. Corpora can be large and contain millions or even billions of words, are built by collecting language-related data from a variety of sources, and include both oral and written examples as well as different genres and registers. For example, large, general corpora such as the British National Corpus (BNC), over 100 million words, or the Corpus of Contemporary American English (COCA), over 560 million words, are described as "equally divided among spoken, fiction, popular magazines, newspapers, and academic texts" (Davies, 2008). By using these large collections of language data, students can compare the results of their own analysis (both qualitative and quantitative) to common usage patterns from a wider range of speakers and speech communities, or students may choose research questions that can be answered through analysis of data from these or other large databases.

In addition to large, general corpora, there are a number of specialized corpora, focused on a particular genre, dialect, register, or context that may be useful for student research projects. For example, linguists have built a number of corpora, such as the Michigan Corpus of Academic Spoken English (MICASE) and the British Academic Written English (BAWE), that consist of academic writing or speaking. These corpora have been created for pedagogical purposes but can provide insightful sources for comparing the use of particular grammatical or discourse features of academic writing with more informal registers or dialects from interviews from participant observation data. Alternatively, some researchers create their own corpora from their collected data or from existing transcripts or media sources and then analyze the data using corpus analysis methods and software programs. Baker (2010) points out that some corpus linguists would not classify as corpus linguistics studies that do not use established corpora such as the BNC and MICASE, but instead focus on one author's novels or the transcripts from one television show. Baker (2010) calls these smaller collections of data "textual databases," but he writes that researchers can still use corpus techniques and analysis with these smaller samples (p. 7). Because students may decide to use a smaller corpus of data, as with all research analysis, Baker (2010) notes that a smaller corpus or textual database will simply limit or affect in some way the ability of the researcher to make generalizations to a larger population.

One of the strengths of corpus analysis is that corpus techniques can be used in conjunction with many other data analysis methods in sociolinguistics, both qualitative and quantitative, and they can add more evidence to what may seem anecdotal. In particular, corpus analysis can be an important aspect of language variation studies that attempt to answer questions about how differences in language use are related to social factors such as gender, age, class, and geography, and other social demographic features. In this way, corpus linguistics can provide a wide lens into how language is used currently and how it is changing over time in a particular community or dialect, but the ability to examine large amounts of actual language use makes corpus analysis tools useful for many projects outside of language variation, from language in interaction studies of media and political persuasion to language in communities studies of language shift and multilingual practices.

In the following chapter sections, we highlight and summarize examples of general, personalized, and researcher-created corpora from a variety of sociolinguistic fields as a way to provide examples of how corpus analysis research methods can be useful for student research projects. One of the central aspects of corpus analysis methods is the use of computer software programs that can provide quick and complex analysis of large amounts of data. The next section focuses on these software programs and the key analysis processes that they can provide to students analyzing their collected data. In this way, as with previous chapters, the chapter focuses on practical, specific information for performing corpus analysis, and we again provide a list of more in-depth guidebooks and readings on corpus analysis research methods at the end of the chapter.

Performing a corpus analysis

As with most research analysis procedures, the first step is typically to organize your collected data in a way that will make it possible to analyze, compare, and cross-check your results. In corpus analysis, this involves either transcribing your data into digital records that can be used by a software program or choosing the correct corpus that will allow you to make comparisons with your collected data and respond to your research questions. Finally, you need to understand the different analysis procedures available in each software program and how their results connect to your research questions. The next sections first focus on the different types of research questions and available corpora as well as how you may want to build your own corpus. Then, a section summarizes key corpus analysis processes.

Research questions: corpus-based or corpus-driven

A student's research questions guide what existing corpus or source of texts will be most useful or whether the researcher needs to collect data and build his or her own corpus before analysis can begin. For example, our student April Polubiec, whose paper we summarized in Chapter 9, was interested in the language use and differences between bodybuilders and powerlifters, as well as the differences between male and female athletes in both groups. April was not aware of any existing and accessible corpus of language use of either group, so she decided to create her own corpus based on Instagram hashtags. In this way, April's research question and design could be described as corpus-based because the researcher already had questions that she was exploring, and the corpus was used as a way to confirm or tweak preexisting ideas about differences between speech communities (Flowerdew, 2012; Tognini-Bonelli, 2001). The four articles summarized in the following section are also primarily corpus-based studies, and so is the student paper we profile by Ryan Sukhnandan.

A corpus-based approach is often contrasted with corpus-driven research questions in that, in a way, researchers use the corpus to determine their research questions and focus. Baker (2014) writes that a corpus-driven approach asks, "What is distinctive about this corpus?" or a bit more specifically, "In what ways do male and female language differ?" (p. 111). Thus, the results from analysis of corpus may lead the researcher to focus on certain linguistic features that are prominent or revealing, and build an analysis of language from the corpus results themselves. Many dictionary-building projects such as Collins COBUILD Advanced Learners English Dictionary and some corpus-based discourse analysis projects that consider multiple aspects of a corpora, such as the language of university teaching (Biber, 2006) or professional discourses (Connor & Upton, 2004). Most student projects, however, are typically more corpus-based because they need to be focused on finding data and analysis on a specific linguistic feature or group; in the end, most projects are both corpus-driven and corpus-based, as we may start with a specific phrase or topic in mind when examining a corpus, but the results of initial data analysis will lead to new questions that, in a sense, are "driven" by the corpus. Mautner (2007), on use of the word *elderly*, and Tagliamonte and Roberts (2005), both detailed in more depth in the next section, are good examples of corpus-based studies that become more corpus-driven after initial analysis.

Choosing and building a corpus and a software program

In deciding whether to build a new corpus of texts or use an existing one, time may play a role, as you will need to transcribe any spoken data and save the transcripts on digital files for computer analysis. It may be much easier and simpler to collect and organize written, electronic data, such as April's example of Instagram hashtags or Tagliamonte and Robert's (2005) use of the transcripts to all of the episodes of the television comedy *Friends* that were available online for free download. Or in organizing your corpus based on your research questions, it may be as simple as choosing the correct settings in an existing corpus that will search and provide examples from a particular subset of the corpus. For example, the COCA corpus allows researchers to examine the use of different terms in the entire corpus or in smaller sections such as all spoken, fiction, magazine, newspaper, or academic texts. It also can organize the data according to year. Each corpus has its own built-in search and analysis program that can be used for performing analyses of the corpus, and each stand-alone software program that can be used to analyze constructed corpora will allow a variety of different tools for organizing and comparing data. Before deciding on a corpus or software tool, we recommend comparing the features of different programs. Tables 10.1 and 10.2 summarize some existing corpora and programs, and Exercise 10.1 offers some activities and questions that introduce the basic features of these corpora and software programs.

Corpora name	Brief description	Website
The Corpus of Contemporary American English (COCA)	COCA is the largest, free corpus of American English and includes more than 560 million words (from 1990 to the present).	https://corpus.byu.edu/coca
Michigan Corpus of Academic Spoken English (MICASE)	Over 1.8 million word corpus of transcribed speech (200 hours of recordings) from the University of Michigan, USA. MICASE includes class lectures, labs, discussion sections, and advising sessions.	https://quod.lib.umich.edu/m/micase
British National Corpus (BNC)	BNC includes British texts from the 1980s and 1990s including spoken, media, academic, and fiction genres. It was originally created by Oxford University but now can be accessed through a number of corpus linguistics research project websites.	http://www.natcorp.ox.ac.uk
British Academic Written English Corpus (BAWE)	BAWE contains around 3,000 student assignments (6,506,995 words) from British universities. All assignments received high marks and represent over 30 discipline areas.	www.coventry.ac.uk/bawe
The *Time* Magazine corpus	The *Time* corpus contains 100 million words from 275,000 *Time* magazine articles from 1923 to 2006.	https://corpus.byu.edu/time

TABLE 10.1 SOME EXISTING ENGLISH LANGUAGE CORPORA AVAILABLE FOR SOCIOLINGUISTIC RESEARCH

Tool name	Brief description	Website
AntConc	Free, multifunctional analysis toolkit with ability to run standard corpus concordance, keyword, and frequency test.	http://www.laurenceanthony.net/software/antconc
WordSmith	Well-known corpus tool that provides concordance, keyword, and frequency tests as well as a number of advanced statistical tools; requires a license fee.	http://www.lexically.net/wordsmith
Linguistic Inquiry and Word Count (LIWC)	LIWC reports on percentages of words within each text along multiple dimensions, including negative and positive emotions, cognitive processing, grammatical categories, and content categories.	http://liwc.wpengine.com

TABLE 10.2 THREE CORPUS ANALYSIS SOFTWARE PROGRAMS

EXERCISE 10.1: Practice using existing corpora and corpus analysis software programs

On your own, complete one or both of the following activities, and be prepared to discuss with your classmates.

1. Choose a term or linguistic feature in English that you would like to know more about (i.e., how the term has been used over time, where it has been used, or by whom). You can consider spoken or written language and another language if you have access to corpora using that language data. Choose a corpus or multiple corpora to view examples and data about how the term has changed over time or in different contexts. Write out some brief thoughts about how and why the term is used and how it may have changed over time.

2. Choose a corpus analysis tool such as AntConc or LIWC and create a small corpus of texts from your own writing (e.g., a group of texts sent to your friends, or a sample paper you have written over the past academic year). Use the analysis tool to run some basics tests of frequencies,

> keywords, collocations, and so on. Next, create or find a second corpus to compare with your first. For example, use the COCA or create a second corpus that is related to your first (e.g., texts sent to friends vs. texts sent to family members). Write out some brief thoughts about how and why the results in the two different corpora differ.

Key processes in corpus analysis

Included in our list of recommended sources for additional reading, Baker's (2010) book *Sociolinguistics and Corpus Linguistics* is one of the best introductions to the specific ways corpus tools can be used in sociolinguistic research, and we draw on his introductory chapter's identification of the following key processes of corpus analysis: frequency, concordance, collocation, keyword, and dispersion.

Frequency

On one level, the measure of frequency in a corpus is simply the raw number of occurrences of a particular word or multiword units in a corpus. Different software programs may be able to calculate other categories of interest (e.g., grammatical features such as the total number of intensifiers, past tense verbs, or other grammatical category in a corpus). Often, frequency counts are the initial data researchers will examine, but they may not be useful or relevant until compared with the frequency of other frequency counts. In order to make these comparisons more salient, frequency counts can be calculated in terms of occurrences per million words and then compared to the percentages or proportions of the term(s) in other corpora with related terms.

As an example of frequency lists, Figure 10.1 shows a basic frequency analysis of the term *fake news* from COCA. From the figure, we can quickly see the increase in use of the term after 2015 as well as the tendency for it to be used more in spoken contexts than written and, at least in early 2018, the small number of uses in academic contexts. From this data, we could compare the term *fake news* to the use of other related terms such as *false news* (only 27 occurrences in COCA) or *faux news* (only five occurrences). We can then connect reasons for its increase in usage to the 2016 presidential election in the United States, as well as begin to examine the specific examples and sources by examining the concordance lists.

Concordance

A concordance, or in some software programs what is referred to as a keyword in context (KWIC), is a list of the occurrences of the linguistic search term or terms within its spoken or written context (i.e., a few words before and

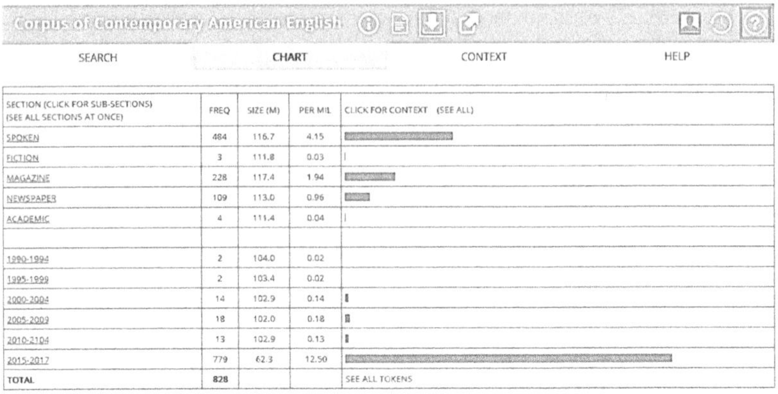

172   THINKING SOCIOLINGUISTICALLY

FIGURE 10.1   FAKE NEWS FREQUENCIES IN COCA

after where the term(s) occur). For example, Figure 10.2 shows 20 lines from the concordance data for *fake news* in COCA. Depending on the software program, researchers can manipulate concordance lists to code or display a certain number of places to the right or left of the search term(s), which allows the researcher to inspect the list for patterns in the language context of the search term(s). In addition, as illustrated in the COCA example, programs or corpora can code the grammatical category of the words before and after the term(s), and many can order the concordance list in alphabetical order based on adjacent items.

Figure 10.2 displays only 20 examples of *fake news* from COCA, but this short list already reveals some patterns and collocated terms and ideas. As already revealed by the frequency lists, most of the items come from 2017 or 2016, but we can now begin to confirm that *fake news* is most often used in relation to the 2016 US presidential campaign and in reference to

FIGURE 10.2   EXAMPLE CONCORDANCE OF FAKE NEWS IN COCA

President Donald Trump or as a direct quote from him. In addition, we can see how *fake news* is primarily used as a noun (e.g., "fake news about Clinton"), but it is also used as an adjective in constructions such as "fake news accounts" . We can also begin to examine the verbs that might occur next to fake news, such as *calls, accuse,* or *highlight*, as well as other key ideas such as *propaganda*.

Just examining 20 lines of concordance data reveals initial insights about the distribution of an item, and researchers can then develop new searches and terms to search in the same corpus or others. It may seem daunting, however, to inspect and form questions for analysis if the list of concordance lines is in the hundreds or thousands (remember, there were 828 examples of *fake news* in total in COCA), and for students there may not be time to examine each occurrence and context. Corpus linguists have advocated various methods around analyzing 30 concordance lines at a time, noting key patterns and terms, and then comparing these initial insights to another 30 items until the researcher is confident about the patterns. In this way, the researcher performs a similar process of coding and developing themes as was described in Chapter 7 on qualitative data analysis. For students, this may mean that not all lines are coded and inspected, but the student researcher can argue for the validity of the insights based on this inductive process.

Collocation

Collocation is the analysis tool that reveals the relationships between words. In this way, two words are collocates if they tend to occur near each other. Corpus programs can inspect the strong collocates of an entire corpus or search for collocates for specific search term(s). Often, the most frequent collocates of search terms are functional words such as determiners, pronouns, or other items from closed-class grammatical categories. These collocates can reveal the typical grammatical context the term(s) occur in, but it may be more useful to understand the common lexical items that co-occur with the search terms, and corpus linguists have developed tools such as the measure of mutual information (MI) that reveal how often terms occur together in relation to how often they occur apart. For example, the MI score is higher if the terms more often occur together than apart. Figure 10.3 reveals common collocates with high MI scores for *fake news* in COCA.

Collocations provide a quick view into a word's context that is less detailed than a concordance list but can offer terms and ideas that may be worth examining in more depth in the list of concordances. In addition, lists of collocates of terms in different corpora that represent different social groups or different times periods can be compared and provide insight into how a term is changing over time or varying in usage and meaning among different groups. In addition, once collocation patterns are determined, researchers

Corpus of Contemporary American English

SEARCH | FREQUENCY | CONTEXT | HELP

1	NEWS	863	181642	0.48	8.68
2	MEDIA	37	82620	0.04	5.27
3	FAKE	36	10212	0.35	8.25
4	STORIES	31	67225	0.05	5.31
5	STORY	27	176743	0.02	3.72
6	TRUMP	20	58202	0.03	4.89
7	FACEBOOK	17	13659	0.12	6.74
8	RUSSIA	16	37927	0.04	5.18
9	SPREAD	15	39144	0.04	5.04
10	SITE	13	70898	0.02	3.98
11	CNN	12	33680	0.04	4.94
12	TERM	11	48934	0.02	4.27
13	ELECTION	11	55432	0.02	4.09
14	PROPAGANDA	9	5638	0.16	7.10
15	FOUNDER	9	13378	0.07	5.86
16	SITES	9	34687	0.03	4.48
17	TYDN	8	9	88.89	16.22
18	TECHNOLOGIST	8	336	2.38	11.00
19	RUSSIAN	8	35130	0.02	4.29
20	RISE	8	41604	0.02	4.05
21	COVERING	7	15935	0.04	5.24
22		7	36397	0.02	4.05
23	COMEDY	6	14689	0.04	5.14
24	COMEY	5	2086	0.24	7.69
25	FLYNN	5	4040	0.12	6.74
26	SPREADING	5	8194	0.06	5.72
27	SO CALLED	5	19086	0.03	4.50
28	FALSE	5	19169	0.03	4.49
29	THROW	5	28017	0.02	3.94
30	CALLING	5	43932	0.01	3.29

FIGURE 10.3 COLLOCATES OF FAKE NEWS IN COCA

also can gain insights into the connotative meanings and associations of terms that may reveal unconscious biases. For example, Baker et al. (2006) note that *innocent* is the most often used collocate of *bystander* in the BNC, "suggesting that even in cases where bystander occurs without this collocate, the concept of innocence could still be implied" (p. 38).

Keywords

Keywords are terms that appear more frequently than others and more frequently than would be expected if compared to another corpus of equal or larger size. Each software program will use a statistical measure to determine keywords that can be used to reveal how particular corpora differ or have changed over time. Baker et al. (2006) refer to keywords as giving "an indication of the 'aboutness' of a text" (p. 98), and they offer the example of an examination of student essays from learners of English that can reveal distinctive features such as spelling errors (e.g., *tenis, beatiful,* or *voleyball*), use of a limited number of adjectives (e.g., *nice, good, lovely,* or *big*), and the insight that most essays are first-person narratives through their use of personal pronouns (e.g., *I* or *my*). Student researchers may use keywords to then go back to their concordance lists or other collected data and look more closely at how participants use or do not use the distinctive keywords from their collected corpus.

Corpus analysis methods in published research

Instead of focusing in-depth on one or two example studies, as we did in previous chapters, we provide here shorter summaries and examples of work using corpus analysis methods to research sociolinguistic questions. This allows us to survey the wide range of uses of corpus analysis in sociolinguistics, and we hope to inspire student researchers to use some corpus tools as part of their research project.

Mautner (2007): using existing corpora

In Mautner (2007), the researcher investigated the use of the term *elderly* in the corpus known as Wordbanks Online, which is a smaller, widely accessible subset of the larger and not easily accessible Bank of English corpus. Mautner began her investigation and article by detailing her initial assumptions about the use of *elderly* as a pejorative term that has been labeled as ageist, connoting limited mental and physical abilities. Her researcher questions are thus:

- What is it about *elderly* that makes some users, individual as well as institutional, reject it as "ageist"?
- What attributes and activities are older people commonly associated with, and what dominant roles and identities emerge as a result? (p. 52)

To address these questions, Mautner (2007) used the software already built into the Wordbanks Online corpus to generate concordance lists, collocations (including high MI scores), and overall frequencies of use. She then used the statistical data results, such as combining lists of collocates that were both frequent and had a high MI score, in order to guide a qualitative examination of the concordance lists. Overall, she observed how *elderly* is often collocated with terms related to disability, passivity, victimhood, and vulnerability, in particular when *elderly* is used as a nominalized form, such as in "the elderly," and she was able to argue that the term cannot be glossed as a synonym of *old* or *aging*, as it often is in dictionaries and usage manuals. For students, Mautner's work (2007) is a good example of a project that uses an existing corpus to investigate preexisting research questions and usage questions through both quantitative and qualitative analysis.

Tagliamonte and Roberts (2005): Using television show dialogue in corpus studies

Tagliamonte and Roberts (2005) offered an example of the creation of a corpus from online, existing transcripts as a "surrogate to 'real world' data in sociolinguistic research" (p. 280). In this case, they used transcripts from eight seasons of the popular comedy *Friends* in order to examine variation and change in the use of intensifiers in English, such as *really*, *very*, and *so*. In addition to creating and examining the *Friends* corpus, the authors compared the intensifier use in *Friends* with an existing corpus of spoken language, The Bergen Corpus of London Teenage Language (COLT), as well as historical surveys of intensifier use from Old English through Modern English and recent work on Canadian English. In this way, the article revealed how media language, at least the language of popular programs, reflects ongoing language change and to an extent drives some of the change.

In particular, the researchers were interested in the increasing preference for *so* instead of *really* in contemporary English. In order to examine this usage, they first made careful distinctions about how the study would define intensifiers and what contexts were included as possible places to use an intensifier. This lends validity to the study's findings and allows for cross-corpus comparisons because the researchers used similar definitions as in the existing literature. Next, the authors offered frequency results from their corpus in terms of (1) total number and percentage of occurrences for each intensifier (*so* is the most common at 44.1%); (2) comparisons between male and female usage of each intensifier (women in general use more intensifiers and they use *so* and *really* significantly more than men); and (3) data that point out contexts when different intensifiers are used more often (e.g., with emotional adjectives). They also offered comparisons of intensifier use in the other corpora and sociolinguistic studies in order to conclude that *so* is rapidly replacing *really* and *very* in overall, spoken English usage, particularly when an intensifier is used for an emotional appeal (e.g., "I'm so jealous you're all going!" (p. 289). Students may be able to use similar techniques to compare the use of intensifiers or other linguistic features in transcripts of other television shows or movies. Alternatively, as illustrated in our student example below, the *Friends* transcripts can be a rich source of data about North-American English language use at the turn of the twenty-first century because, as the authors pointed out, the show was widely popular and has now made its way to many countries around the world.

Grundmann and Krishnamurthy (2010): A corpus-based approach to analyze climate change discourse

Grundmann and Krishnamurthy (2010) provided an example of a research project that used an existing database of media articles, Nexis, and a corpus analysis software program, WordSmith Tools, to examine media reporting on climate change in four different countries, France, the United States, Germany, and the United Kingdom. The researchers first created their own corpus of articles by downloading all of the articles from the Nexis database between 1980 and 2007 and organizing them according to country and year. They then chose search terms related to climate change that had been used in previous research as well as through Google searches and their own knowledge and intuition about terms related to climate change in the four countries and three languages. The search terms allowed them to examine the number of articles over time about climate change in each country's media, the frequency and collocation lists of each term related to climate change, and the specific contexts of each term in concordance lists. The specific search terms for each country were the following:

United States and United Kingdom: global warming, climate change, and greenhouse effect

France: *changement climatique, effet de serre, réchauffement de la planète,* and *réchauffement climatique*

Germany: *klimawandel, globale erwärmung, treibhauseffekt,* and *klimakatastrophe*

From their analysis of the use of the above search terms in media articles in the various countries, the authors noted that the topic is much more important in France and Germany in terms of overall number of articles in their corpus and number of words related to climate change in those two countries. Further, the researchers coded and analyzed the collocation lists provided for each of the search terms according to whether the term fit with a political frame, science frame, action frame, or moral frame. These frames were taken from previous writing about climate change reporting and provided insights into each country, such as the dominance in the United States of a scientific frame (e.g., collocation words such as *carbon, emissions, energy, ozone, scientists,* and *researcher*). In comparison, the European countries use more terms associated with political frames (e.g., *international, intergovernmental, conference*) and moral frames (e.g. *lutte* and *kampf,* meaning "fight" in French and German, respectively; or *responsables* and *verantwortlich,* meaning "responsible," respectively). The authors wrote how the use of a scientific frame in the United States and the few articles in the 1990s in the US press may have contributed to a belief in the United States that climate change can be controlled through scientific progress alone, and there is still debate about the causes and overall effects of climate change. These insights on a current policy issue such as climate change reveal to student researchers how they can use corpus techniques in order to provide new perspectives on questions from fields related to sociolinguistics, such as media studies and public policy.

> **RESEARCHER TO KNOW: Ruth Wodak**
>
> Ruth Wodak is Emeritus Distinguished Professor at Lancaster University in the United Kingdom. She is currently the lead investigator at the University of Vienna's multiyear project "Discursive Construction of National Identity." Wodak does critical discourse research, examining the connections between discourse and politics, including most recently the rise of right-wing populism in Europe, and she continues to write surveys and guides for student researchers, including her paper "Language and Politics" in the 2018 edited book *English Language: Description, Variation, and Context*.

Deumert and Lexander (2013): Texting practices in Africa

Our final example is a corpus-based study that compiled over 3,000 text messages from five African countries—Ivory Coast, Ghana, Nigeria, Senegal, and South Africa; conducted 150 ethnographic interviews with participants from South Africa; and collected 500 questionnaire responses from participants in all five countries. From all of this data, Deumert and Lexander (2013) attempted to examine texting practices from an area of the world that is often neglected in research about texting and digital language use. The authors were particularly interested in how texters "play with words" and "articulate meaning through the skillful use of both global and local forms" (p. 522). For example, the researchers examined their corpus for examples of when English, French, and other non-African languages are used in comparison to when Wolof, isiXhosa, and other African languages are used. In addition, similar to many studies of texting in North America and Europe, they were interested in the use of nonstandard forms and "what linguistic forms are being literalized in the messages and for what purposes" (p. 523).

For this article, Deumert and Lexander (2013) primarily used the corpora of text messages to examine frequency counts of the use of nonstandard orthographic forms and to compare the prevalence of these forms in African and UK texters. They found that South African, Nigerian, and Ghanaian texters use forms such as /u/ for *you*, /2/ for *to*, and /r/ for *are* at much higher percentages than UK texters, as seen in this sample text from a Nigerian participant:

> Wassup! Just wan'd 2 tel u dat we have kinda settled tins. Gues tins uld b beta. Thanks!
> ("What's up! Just wanted to tell you that we have kind of settled things. Guess things should be better. Thanks!") (p. 533)

Deumert and Lexander (2013) argue that the widespread use of nonstandard forms reveals not only the value African texters place on displaying knowledge of global languages and creative forms but also the ability of a texter to innovate and reappropriate global forms for local audiences as well as display features of local dialects such as Nigerian Pidgin. As one interview participant noted, the use of nonstandard writing in text messages reveals the texter as not a "newcomer" (p. 535). The authors provide numerous other examples of innovative, multilingual texts and written forms along with interview data that contextualizes the examples from their corpora. In this way, the article provides a useful example for students of how a corpus can be compiled and used as a part of a research study in combination with other qualitative and quantitative data such as interviews and surveys.

Corpus analysis methods in student research

In addition to the corpus analysis project by our student April Polubiec that we summarized in Chapter 9, we include in the companion website a paper completed by our student Ryan Sukhnandan, in which he also compiled and analyzed a corpus of language use data, using corpus analysis research methods. Specifically, Sukhnandan used the Tagliamonte and Roberts (2005) article as a basis to perform further investigations into the language used during the many seasons of the popular comedy show *Friends*. For his project, Sukhnandan was initially interested in examining the differences in uptalk between male and female characters in the show and how the use of uptalk may have changed over the course of the show. Uptalk, also referred to as high terminal rising (HRT) or upspeak by linguists, is the use of rising intonation at the end of a phrase that is not a question. For example, Sukhnandan uses the following example from the *Friends* character Rachel when she was discussing why she joined a group of smokers outside her office, even though she was not a smoker. He uses the symbol "?" to denote a rising, then falling pitch movement.

> You know it got kinda lonely up/there? So I just thought I would come out/here? And get some fresh air. (S5, E18:35)

Linguists continue to debate the phonetics and pragmatics of uptalk, including when and how it is realized in a sentence and what additional meaning it conveys, but in popular culture and thought, the consensus belief has associated uptalk with female speaking patterns, often assuming that uptalk reveals a speaker's insecurity and positions women as less authoritative in comparison to men. In his analysis, Sukhnandan did find that the female characters used uptalk more overall than the male characters, but as Figure 10.4 reveals, male characters used uptalk often over the course of the show's 10 seasons. As illustrated in Figure 10.5, Sukhnandan found the increase in the use of

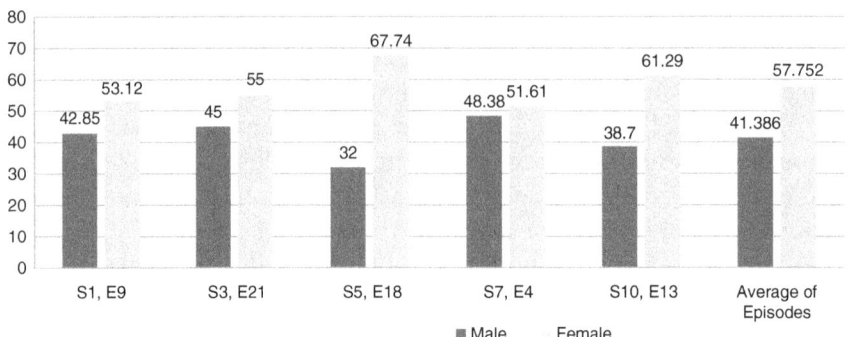

Figure 10.4 Percentage of male and female uses of uptalk in Sukhnandan corpus

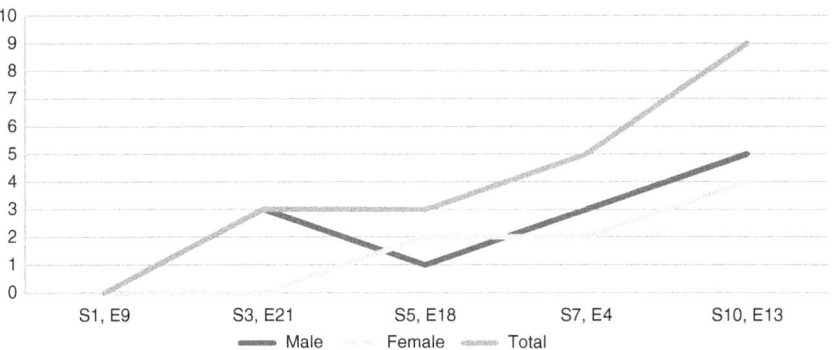

Figure 10.5 Frequency of uptalk use in the middle of a phrase

uptalk in the middle of a phrase in the later seasons by both male and female characters more revealing of language changes.

As illustrated in Figures 10.4 and 10.5, for his corpus Sukhnandan did not use transcripts from all episodes from all seasons of *Friends*, as Tagliamonte and Roberts (2005) did. Instead, in order to be able to complete his research project during a semester-long course, Sukhnandan randomly chose five episodes to catalog, code, and analyze. Reducing the size of the corpus was important because Sukhnandan had to inspect every line of dialogue, while listening to audio of the show, in order to mark where uptalk occurred. After inspecting and coding all five episodes, he could then look for frequencies and other contextual factors for using uptalk. In this way, Sukhnandan did not use a corpus software program, but he was able to find very interesting patterns in the data about the use of uptalk that connect to current discussion in sociolinguistics about the function of uptalk in different positions of a phrase. And if he or other students are interested, it would not be difficult to now put his coded data into a corpus program and perform further analysis about collocations, keywords, or other patterns that emerge in relation to occurrences of uptalk.

Steps for completing a corpus analysis

Completing a corpus analysis project follows similar steps as other qualitative and quantitative research designs, but we list some of the key questions, actions, and decisions that are specific to corpus studies in the following list of steps.

1. *Focus of the study:* What linguistic term or terms are you interested in studying? In what language, dialect, and context? Is a corpus study the best research design for examining your chosen topic?

2. *Review previous work:* What previously published studies have examined your topic, either using corpus analysis or other sociolinguistic analysis methods? What are the results, and how might your study connect to previous findings? Do you intend to replicate the data collection and analysis methods of previous studies? Will you use previously collected data or corpora in your research design or analysis? What terms, codes, or other data analysis methods from previous studies will you replicate when analyzing your data?

3. *Research questions:* What are your specific research questions? Will your study primarily be corpus-based or corpus-driven?

4. *Research design and data collection:* Will you use a preexisting corpus or data that you collect yourself? How will you collect the data? Will you need to collect other types of data such as survey, interviews, and so on? How will you ensure that you have collected data from multiple sources and that it is representative of the entire speech community or group you are interested in studying? If creating your own corpus, what software programs will you use to analyze the data? What codes will you choose to use, and how and when will you code the data?

5. *Data analysis:* Are the differences between the language uses of groups in your data generalizable to a larger population? What variety exists in language use among speakers from the same social group or speech community? Can you explain this variety? What are the outlier data points or examples in your data, and how can you explain them?

6. *Report results:* What graphs and charts are most useful for presenting your results? What new questions do you have about the term or terms based on your findings? What other data could be collected to further explain the use of your chosen topic?

> **Further reading on corpus data analysis methods**
>
> We list here the following titles for those seeking more in-depth guidance on corpus analysis methods in sociolinguistics:
>
> Baker, P. (2010). *Sociolinguistics and corpus linguistics.* Edinburgh, UK: Edinburgh University Press.
>
> Baker, P., Hardie, A., & McEnery, A. (2006). *A glossary of corpus linguistics.* Edinburgh, UK: Edinburgh University Press.
>
> McEnery, T., & Hardie, A. (2012). *Corpus linguistics.* Cambridge, UK: Cambridge.
>
> McEnery, T., & Wilson, A. (2001). *Corpus linguistics: An introduction*, 2nd ed. Edinburgh, UK: Edinburgh University Press.
>
> McEnery, T., Xiao, R., & Tono, Y. (2006). *Corpus-based language studies: An advanced resource book.* New York, NY: Routledge.

Part IV
Putting It All Together and Finding Your Voice

11 Organizing your research paper

CHAPTER OVERVIEW

- Introduction
- Organizing Your Research Paper
  - Title and Title Page
  - Abstract
  - Introduction
  - Defining Terms and Concepts
  - Literature Review
  - Methodology
  - Results, Discussion, and Conclusion
  - Appendix
  - References

Introduction

Now that we have summarized some of the major data collection and analysis methods in sociolinguistics, we hope that you are ready to start collecting data and completing a sociolinguistic research project. As you finish your collection and analysis, you will inevitably start to think about how to present your data in both written and oral presentations, and the purpose of this final section of the book is to help you organize and present the research that you have conducted through the writing of a research paper that uses appropriate academic language typical of a sociolinguist; as well, we offer some tips and ideas for classroom and conference presentations. In short, if the previous chapters emphasized "thinking like a sociolinguist," the next two chapters focus on "sounding like a sociolinguist."

Here in Chapter 11, we focus on the parts of a typical undergraduate sociolinguistics research paper. We draw on examples from the articles that we have discussed throughout earlier chapters as well as excerpts from student papers, both of which can serve as models or even inspiration for your work. Throughout the chapter, we offer "model" phrases and sentences that are lists of sentences or sentence stems that we have pulled from example papers (both published and student papers). Our students have found it useful to have some example sentences to examine and perhaps use in their writing as a way to organize their ideas at different points of their manuscript. The idea to provide model sentences comes from using the book *They Say/I Say: The Moves That Matter in Academic Writing*, 3rd ed., when teaching first-year university composition courses (Graff, Birkenstein, & Durst, 2014). We agree with the authors of *They Say/I Say*, who write that providing example sentences, or what they refer to as templates, does not mean that students have to use every model sentence verbatim, perhaps stifling creativity. Instead, they write that by using models, instructors can "focus writers' attention not just on what is being said, but on the forms that structure what is being said. In other words, they [templates] make students more conscious of the rhetorical patterns that are key to academic success but often pass under the classroom radar" (p. xxi). Thus, in the following sections, we offer lists of example sentences and sentence stems from sociolinguistic articles and our student writing as examples for students to use in constructing their own manuscripts. We encourage students and instructors to add to our lists when reading other sociolinguistic manuscripts, in this way creating your own dictionaries of sociolinguistics writing examples.

The assumption of these chapters is that you have found, read, and annotated your resources, and that you have collected your data. However, not all researchers write their research manuscript after data collection, and you may find it useful to write parts of your paper as you conduct the research. In this way, your paper works as a scaffold for the research project, and you may find that by writing up the methods or beginning to analyze the data in writing, you find holes in your research plan and new sources of data or analysis that you would like to explore. Whenever you decide to begin writing your manuscript, it is important to always remember that writing takes time and effort. If you plan out your writing and do not wait until the last minute, you will have most of the parts of your paper already in good shape soon after finishing your data collection, and you will be ready to assemble and revise your notes into a clear and informative research paper.

Organizing your research paper

Although not all professors require every part of a research paper discussed here, it is important that you know what they are and how each section of a research paper is constructed.

Title and title page

Student research papers should have a title just as the professional articles you read do. Although you may not write your title until the very end of your research project, the title is important. It states what your topic is, suggests the scope of your research, and tells a little bit about you as a researcher. Sometimes it is quite original and funny, and sometimes it is more formal. Some titles have two parts connected by a colon. Look at the following examples and consider why a researcher might want a two-part title or prefer a shorter title, and see Exercise 11.1 for more examples:

- "The Influence of Social Factors on Minority Language Engagement amongst Young People: An Investigation of Welsh-English Bilinguals in North Wales"
- "Elite Positionings Toward Hindi: Language Policies, Political Stances, and Language Competence in India"
- "Appropriation of African American Slang by Asian American Youth"
- "Texting Africa: Writing as Performance"
- "Dude"
- "Tag Questions and Cross Examinations" (student paper)
- "Made For Yoga, Made for Manduka™: Recontextualizing Yoga in Terms of Brand Identity" (student paper)
- "I Can Speak Konglish" (student paper)

> **EXERCISE 11.1: Looking at titles**
>
> Looking at both the professional and student titles listed above and in other chapters of our book, what would you think the papers are about just by reading their titles? What differences do you notice? What seems to be the function of the colons in the titles that include colons?

According to APA (American Psychological Association) format, the first page of your paper should be a title page that includes your title centered on the upper half of the title page. APA recommends titles should be 12 words or less, but as illustrated in the example papers, not all published papers in sociolinguistics follow this recommendation. APA also recommends that the title should not include abbreviations or unneeded words. In addition to the title, your title paper should include the author's name (first name, middle initial, and last name), institutional affiliation, and a running head. The running head is a shortened version of the title that is less than 50 characters and is placed in the header (flush left in all caps) of each manuscript page (except the first page). On the title page, the running head also includes the term, "Running head," but on subsequent pages, just the shortened title appears. Thus, Figure 11.1 illustrates the title page of one of our student's papers.

Running head: SPEECH, SILENCE, AND SPACE

Speech, Silence, and Space: The Unspoken Dialogues of the Digital Realm

Christy Ruschmeyer

Hunter College

FIGURE 11.1 Example title page

Of course, professors may ask that you add further information such as your name, the course name and number, the date, and your professor's name, and they may prefer another formatting style such as MLA or Chicago. Always, check with your professor, and if possible, request an example paper or guide for formatting your paper.

Abstract

Many sociolinguistics professors require students to write an abstract as the first section of the research paper. As you have seen in other research articles, the abstract is a short summary of the work that has been done, and includes a preview of the study's key findings. The abstract is intended to introduce readers to the main ideas of the research and to encourage readers to read the rest of the paper. The abstract is usually made up of four general parts: (1) a statement of the research problem or motivation for the research, (2) a description of the methods for conducting the research, (3) the findings or results of the research, and (4) the conclusion, including how the research contributes to the field and perhaps a suggestion for future research. Although we are describing the abstract first because it belongs at the very beginning of the paper underneath the title and your name, most researchers do not write the abstract until they have written the rest of the paper, because it is a summary of the entire paper. On the other hand, some researchers find writing an abstract first may help them organize and focus their paper before they write the entire manuscript. See Exercises 11.2 and 11.3 for more guidance and examples about writing an abstract.

EXERCISE 11.2: Examining abstracts from the sample papers

In this exercise, we look closely at several abstracts from some of the articles discussed in this book.

1. First, review the abstract from Kara Becker's (2009) article, "/r/ and the Construction of Place Entity on New York City's Lower East Side" that we summarized in Chapter 9. It is available on the *Journal of Sociolinguistics* website (vol. 13, no. 5, pp. 634–58) and on this book's website. She begins by telling her readers the argument of her paper. Look at the verbs and tenses that Becker uses throughout the abstract. Notice that she uses present tense and active voice in each of the five sentences. She focuses on the results of her research. She begins, "This paper argues that a group of white residents on the Lower East Side of Manhattan use a New York City English (NYCE) feature—non-rhoticity in the syllable coda—in the construction of place identity, one aspect of identity tied to localness and authenticity" (p. 634). What does this tell you about the content of Becker's article? What does she assume that her readers already know? At the end of the abstract, Becker lists seven key words or phrases. Researchers do this both to assist readers' understanding of the research and to enable the article to be listed in databases so that other researchers can find it.

    Next, see the abstract from Jonathan Morris's (2014) article, "The Influence of Social Factors on Minority Language Engagement Amongst Young People: An Investigation of Welsh-English Bilinguals in North Wales" that we also summarized in Chapter 9. It is available on the *International Journal of the Sociology of Language* website (vol. 230, pp. 65–89) and as an attachment on this book's website. In Morris's eight sentences, we see more variety in the verbs and tenses. Underline the verbs and identify the tenses used. Morris also uses both active and passive voice. When does he use each? After setting up the situation he is researching, Morris explains in sentence 3, "This article examines the correlation between speakers' backgrounds and their language attitudes, self confidence in their language use, and use of Welsh." What does this tell you about the content of his article?

    Finally, read the abstract from Ana Deumert and Kristin Lexander's (2013) article "Texting Africa: Writing as Performance" that we summarized in Chapter 10. It is available on the *Journal of Sociolinguistics* website (vol. 17, no. 4, pp. 522–46) and on this book's website. In the eight sentences in their abstract, they use a variety of tenses and both active and passive voice. Identify the verbs and tenses. When do they use each? Their paper begins with the following sentence: "This paper discusses African multilingual digital writing focusing on one digital genre: texting." What does this tell you about the content of the article?

2. Compare the three abstracts and decide which you prefer and why. Compare the three sentences listed above that explain the purpose of the studies. Which is clearer? What makes it so?
3. Review the three abstracts, analyzing the order of the content and whether they each contain in some form the four elements that generally comprise an abstract for a research paper:
   - Statement of problem or motivation
   - Method of research
   - Findings
   - Conclusion and contribution of research

EXERCISE 11.3: Writing your own abstract

Now that we have reviewed three example abstracts, either (1) draft an abstract for your paper; or (2) find a published article on a sociolinguistic topic and write an abstract for the paper without reading the article's abstract.

In a peer group or with a partner, review the abstract, making sure that you include the four elements described above. Identify four or more keywords that are important to understanding your paper or the example paper, and list those. Why did you choose these words?

Introduction

The introduction is the section of the paper in which you establish what you are looking at and why it is interesting and important to you and to your readers. The introduction is a vital part of your paper and for many it takes the most time to write. The introduction is where you accomplish the following:

1. State your research problem or question. You may also present your thesis or position—what you have learned from your research. This can be as simple as a sentence like, "Doing research on the use of 'you know' has shown me the importance of looking at language change and finding out how people respond to the changes."

2. Establish the importance or relevance of the topic and why it is interesting to you. You may do this formally by briefly describing and then listing some of the research that has been done on your topic and that you have read, informally by explaining why the topic mattered to you and using the first-person *I*, or a combination of formal and informal by explaining a brief personal reason that you have researched the topic and a sentence or two telling about the research done on the subject and that inspired your work, including the name of the researcher and the date of the research.

3. Show that there is a gap or limitation in what has already been found and how your research can fill that need.

4. Define terms or concepts that are important to understanding your topic, approach, and findings. This is especially important if you are using an approach or term that has not been discussed in class.

5. Include questions that you asked to inform your research. This may be a list of two or three questions that were the focus of your study and that will help your reader understand your paper.

6. Briefly describe your approach to the research, and explain your principal findings and why your study matters.

The list above includes both required and optional elements. The following list includes the elements that are required of a good introduction:

1. State your research problem or question.

2. Establish its importance.

3. Briefly summarize previous research or history of your topic and mention the gap or need for more research.

4. Briefly describe your approach to the research and your participants.

5. Explain your principal findings and the value of your study.

Let us now consider the introduction in Negrón (2014). She begins in the following way:

> The rise of a collective Latino panethnicity in the U.S. has largely been described in political terms, emphasizing the ways Latinos of different national backgrounds strategically mobilize around their collective interests (Padilla 1985; Stokes 2003; Martinez 2008; Barreto et al. 2009). The Latino population grew by 43 percent between 2000 and 2010, accounting for more than half of the increase in the

overall U.S. population (Ennis, Ríos-Vargas and Albert, 2011). As the Latino population has grown, so has its diversity, offering both challenges and opportunities for the formation of panethnicity. (p. 88)

Negrón has established the importance of the topic and has included previous relevant research. She continues giving more information about the topic and ends her introduction in the following way:

> In this article, I argue that latinidad is best understood by taking into account everyday, situated social practices and the negotiations of collective identities that take place in daily interactions. Specifically, I show how latinidad is affirmed through ethnic alignment in routine conversation. I ask: how do Latinos invoke latinidad in their everyday interactions, and to what end? To answer this question, I examine a conversation between Roberto and William, two New York City (NYC) Latinos who employ various linguistic and discursive strategies to ethnically align with each other. (p. 89)

Notice Negrón's use of first person as well as her statement of her thesis. Like Morris (2014), Negrón ends with a question, but she follows this with her approach to the research and the way she will answer her question.

Let us now look at the introduction to Reyes (2005):

> African Americans have contributed enormously to American English slang over the past several decades (Eble, 1996). Many scholars argue that slang terms rooted in African American culture, such as *cool, hip*, and *gig*, are taken up by mainstream Americans because non-mainstream lifestyle and speech are seen as inventive, exciting and even alluringly dangerous (Chapman, 1986; Eble, 1996). Yet that non-African Americans benefit from appropriating the verbal dress of a group that has been the target of much discrimination and racism in the United States is a complex subject that deserves more attention from scholars of language and ethnicity. Eble (2004) notes, "Adopting the vocabulary of a non-mainstream culture is a way of sharing vicariously in the plusses of that culture without having to experience the minuses associated with it." (p. 383)

Notice how Reyes uses both paraphrases and quotes from Connie Eble's research to set up her own research interest, and in sentence 3, Reyes uses the phrase "complex subject that deserves more attention." This suggests the gap in the research that her study will attempt to fill. Why do you think Reyes uses the Eble quote instead of paraphrasing it?

> "In the present study, I examine _____. I first present data _____. I then provide findings _____." (Yuasa, 2010).
>
> "This article compares ... The article contributes to previous studies of _____." (Morris, 2014)
>
> "This article aims to ..." (Moore & Podesva, 2009)
>
> "This article outlines the patterns of use for _____ and its functions and meanings in interaction and provides some explanations for its rise in use ..." (Kiesling, 2004)
>
> "This paper presents sociolinguistic data from speakers who _____." (Becker, 2009)
>
> "The present study identifies a _____ feature ... and describes the ways that this feature _____." (Becker, 2009)
>
> "To answer this question, I examine _____." (Negrón, 2014)
>
> "In this article, I present the concept of _____." (Sayer, 2010)

FIGURE 11.2 WRITING EXAMPLE 1: VALUABLE PHRASES FOR YOUR INTRODUCTION

Turning now to some example introductions from student papers, our student Rachael Holborn's paper about language endangerment and revival focusing of the Irish language begins with this introduction:

> In a world with continually growing levels of migration, globalisation, and commercialisation, it is inevitable that an increasing number of languages will come into contact with each other. The repercussions of these changes depend on "the kind and degree" of contact, as well as "the social and linguistic relationships of the languages" (Bell 49). As sociolinguist Allan Bell suggests, the consequences of language contact may include language stratification, code switching, language creation and endangerment (49). This paper focusses on the causes and consequences of language endangerment, as well as strategies to counteract its progress. In particular, we will observe this process in relation to the language status of Irish Gaelic, the indigenous Celtic language of Ireland. (Holborn, student paper)

Notice how Holborn sets up the global situation and the relevance of her research. She cites two quotes from the class textbook by Allan Bell. Why do you think she quoted these phrases instead of paraphrasing them while in the next sentence she paraphrased Bell? She introduces her topic with the phrase "This paper focusses on _____." This is a useful introductory phrase to add to the models in Figure 11.2. Look at the verbs she uses and the variety of tenses. Holborn's spelling reflects British conventions. Do your professors prefer American or British spelling conventions?

Sally Kim, in her paper on the use of Konglish, takes a different and more personal approach to the introduction. After setting the scene for her study in a church on "an ordinary Sunday afternoon," Kim ends with the line that sets up her research and she uses first person to do this:

> However, something major stood out to me that I would have missed had I not been introduced to the world of sociolinguistics, the entire conversation the moms were having with each other, their children, and the people around was not in English or Korean but in Konglish.

After giving a historical review of the use of tag questions in communications, Arianna Chinchilla introduces her study by contrasting earlier research on the subject with her own area of research:

> Other works, however, have studied the ways in which tag questions are used to exert power. When used with assertive illocutionary force, tag questions can suggest that giving a contrary response would be deemed unreasonable ("In a Different Register," 279). People in positions of power can even employ tag questions to "control the message recipient" or elicit information (Blankenship, 113). This applies particularly to lawyers, which will be the focus of this paper.

Defining terms and concepts

As we mentioned above, defining or explaining terms that are critical to understanding your research is an important but not required part of the Introduction to your paper. You need to decide which terms will be familiar to students in your class, such as *tag questions* in the Chinchilla paper, and will not need definition, and which, like Holborn's "Irish Gaelic" and Kim's "Konglish," do need an explanation.

We will look at some examples of how researchers in the papers we have been discussing defined terms and/or concepts. Here, in Deumart and Lexander (2013), notice the use of tenses and references to other researchers:

> Over the last ten to fifteen years, texting—the person-to-person transmission of typed messages via the "short message service" (SMS) available on mobile phones—has become a ubiquitous literacy practice across the world. (p. 523)

Here, in Sayer (2010), notice the use of colons to make the definition stand out from the sentence in the first sentence of the article.

> The modern urban landscape is covered with signs: naming stores and streets, adorning T-shirts and backpacks, giving directions, peddling products, and

promoting politicians. All these signs are written texts, or what Goodman (1986) calls "environmental print," and taken together they compose what Ben-Rafael, Shohamy, Amara, and Trumper-Hect (2006) and Shohamy and Gorter (2009) term our "linguistic landscape." (p. 144)

Sayer begins with examples and follows up with relevant research to define the term "linguistic landscape," which is central to his paper. In similar ways, Moore and Podesva (2009) and Becker (2009) also draw on outside references to help define key terms and place their study within existing literature:

> Adopting the definition proposed by the Half Moon Bay Style Collective, we treat style as a "socially meaningful clustering of features within and across linguistic levels and modalities." (Campbell-Kibler, Eckert, Mendoza-Denton & Moore, 2006; Moore & Podesva, p. 448)

> This acknowledgment that speakers agenticly authenticate their local identities through the use of regional features has been enriched by the concept of *enregisterment* (Agha, 2003), a process by which a linguistic repertoire becomes a socially recognized register or dialect. (Becker, 2009, pp. 636–37)

In the Moore and Podesva (2009) article, the authors reference the Half Moon Bay Style Collective by listing references in parentheses at the end of the sentence. In the Becker (2009) article, the author places the key work to be defined in italics to make it stand out and also refers to previous research relating to the term being defined, giving her use of the term credibility.

We can also examine examples of definitions from our student papers. Sally Kim in "I Can Speak Konglish" defines Konglish, a central term for her study, this way:

> Defined, Konglish is the combination of Korean and English and it is commonly spoken among first generation and second generation Korean-Americans. However, depending on how comfortable one is speaking either Korean or English, one's use of Konglish varies. Those who are more comfortable with Korean may mix a lot more Korean into their Konglish, whereas those who are more comfortable with English may mix more English. There are also certain words which have been labeled as "Konglish words," such as "fighting," which means "good luck" and "cider" which means "soda."

Rebecca Galpern in her paper "Hasidic Jews and *Klal* Yiddish" draws on the history of Yiddish in defining the language, as well as referencing two articles written by David Katz. As with the published paper examples, Galpern lends credibility to her definition by drawing on the two Katz articles:

> Yiddish is an approximately one thousand year old Germanic language with a large share of Semitic and Slavic components. Initially standardized in the 1920s as a

project of the YIVO Institute for Jewish Research, the resulting Yiddish *klal shprakh* (standard language) has been contentious since its very inception. (Katz, 1994, 1996)

Finally, Alessandra Rosen, in "Made for Yoga, Made for Manduka™: Recontextualizing Yoga in Terms of Brand Identity," defines indexicality in the following paragraph:

> In order for a commodity to be emblematic of a lifestyle, it must first achieve second order indexicality. At the second order of indexicality, the commodity is indexically linked to values, persons, and activities, with consumers purchasing it as a means of adopting and/or associating with those immaterial qualities (Johnstone, 164: 2009). The commodity can then take on third order indexicality, becoming an emblem of a certain person/social type and/or lifestyle, thereby becoming an object of overt comment and stereotype (164: 2009). As demonstrated above, this is the work at hand in an advertising campaign: to indexically link commodities to larger immaterial values and aspirational qualities, so that consumers may orient to the commodity in hopes of adopting those qualities.

Notice that Rosen defines *indexicality* with a paraphrase of Barbara Johnstone's 2009 research. When she refers to Johnstone's work a second time, she does not need to repeat the name since no other researcher has been mentioned.

Literature review

The literature review is an outgrowth of the notes and annotations you have been doing as you researched your topic. It includes the articles you have read that are relevant to your study, the media you have watched or read, as well as the earlier research that informed your project. Keeping careful notes with all the information about your sources will make the literature review much easier and will also help you construct your reference page.

In your literature review, you describe key concepts, discuss them, and cite previous research that is relevant to your own study as a result. In many sociolinguistics research papers, the literature review is contained in the introduction and is not a formal additional part of the paper. You should check with your professor about any formal expectations for your literature review. To summarize, the purpose of the literature review is as follows:

1. To set up a historical context for your work
2. To show the importance of your topic
3. To show how your work will fit in the larger picture—to enter the conversation, so to speak, of the scholarly work done in your area of interest

4. To make your research more credible because you have read and referred to earlier research

Regardless of its place in your paper, at some point in the opening sections of your paper, you will need to connect your current paper and study to preview work. Use Exercise 11.4 to further examine how other studies write literature reviews.

> **EXERCISE 11.4: Examining citations and literature review sections**
>
> Read through the introductions in at least three of the example articles discussed in this book, highlight the citations, and notice how they are cited. What section(s) have the most citations included: the introduction, methodology, data, conclusions, or elsewhere? Is there a Literature Review section, or is the survey of literature embedded in the introduction section? How does the author connect the study to previous research and open a new space for the current study? Check the reference page(s) at the end of the article to see how the articles are cited.

Methodology

This section of the research paper is often the first one that students write because in some ways it is the most clear-cut. In essence, the methods section describes the steps that you took to do your research and collect your data. In writing this section, you do have decisions to make in terms of how much information you will include, whether charts will be helpful in presenting your evidence, and whether to include any questionnaires, interview questions, and so forth in your appendix. Balance is important in describing your methods, as we have found that students often will not describe any details of their research methods or spend far too much space detailing every aspect of their data collection.

In general, the methods section should include the following:

1. An overview or short summary of the methods you used to collect data

2. A brief description of your research goals or aims

3. A description of the participants in your study as to gender, age, and ethnicity, if that is applicable for your study

4. A brief description of the processes you used to analyze the data

5. An acknowledgment of the limitations of your study (but this may come at the end of the paper instead).

It is usually acceptable to use the first person in this section to explain how you went about doing your research, but it is always good to check with your professor before doing this.

Similar to examining the introduction sections, it is useful to examine how the writers of the example papers we have been using describe their methods. For example, consider how Sayer (2010) describes his research process. Note that to make the methods stand out, we have underlined key terms.

> In order to find out about the use of English in the linguistic landscape of Oaxaca, I designed a modest research project I called "Environmental English" around a simple question: why do people in Oaxaca use English in public places? The procedure for carrying out the research was straightforward and can be easily replicated as a student project in almost any EFL setting. I <u>decided</u> to look at each sign as a text that I could collect as data. Armed with an inexpensive digital camera, I <u>collected 250 texts—photos of signs, billboards, posters, and banners in English</u>—in my daily comings and goings across the city over the course of a few months. The 250 signs became my <u>data set</u>.
>
> In order to make sense of my data set, I <u>did qualitative content analysis</u> (Silverman, 2006). Qualitative content analysis is a relatively simple process of <u>describing the data set and identifying connections and patterns</u> across parts of the data. (p. 145)

In the above paragraph, Sayers (2010) mentions that his study is "replicable," which means that as a student researcher, you could do a similar study and refer to Sayers's work as part of the relevant research that preceded your own as well as looking at his references for additional research on linguistic landscape.

Further, Sayer (2010) uses the first-person pronoun and active verbs such as *decided* and *collected* when describing how the data were collected and analyzed. This is similar to the research methods described in Negrón (2014), where she uses active verbs such as *interviewed*, *shadowed*, and *recorded*:

> Over the course of six months in 2005, I <u>interviewed</u>, <u>shadowed</u> and <u>audio recorded</u> eleven Latinas/Latinos (five women and six men) from Queens, NYC, as they went about their daily lives. My goal was to understand the process of situational ethnic identification among NYC Latinos. Hoping to capture naturally occurring instances of identification switching across different contexts, I <u>accompanied</u> the participants in a wide range of social settings, including work, school, church, family gatherings, and even dental appointments and dates. I used <u>short screening interviews</u> to select the eleven individuals from a pool of potential participants who responded to online and newspaper advertisements, flyers, and word of mouth. I sought individuals who represented a range of backgrounds and experiences and whose daily routines cut across at least three domains of social interaction (such as work, home, and social gatherings). Participants included first, 1.5, and second-generation immigrants. In the end, I <u>recorded</u> more than <u>500 hours of naturally occurring conversations</u>, many hours of which demonstrated the ways that Latinos in NYC negotiate multiple ethnic identities, including the panethnic Latino or Hispanic identity. (p. 93)

Further, we can see similarities between Sayer (2010) and Negrón (2014) in their listing of the type and number of data sources, including interviews, photos, and recorded conversations. Along with these descriptions, the authors also provide any additional information about the data, such as how the participants were found and chosen.

We can also see the way data were analyzed in the Sayer (2010) example through his reference to "qualitative content analysis." Note that he provides a short definition of the analysis method with a reference, but he does not describing his data analysis method in detail. Describing your data collection and analysis methods can be a lengthy process and may not be useful for the reader unless the collection and analysis techniques are unique or need to be justified for a particular reason. For this reason Sayer (2010) only briefly mentions his data analysis methods and provides the citation for the reader to learn more about them.

Turning to a student paper, Yan Zeng in her paper on code-switching in her family also uses the first person to describe her data collection methods and references common research methods terms such as *observation research*:

> Before exploring more possibilities about the social meaning of code-switching, my experience of doing research on this topic is quite rewarding. This research enables me to learn to look at one thing from different dimensions rather than a narrow, biased one. Since the participants are my cousin's family who are Cantonese and English speakers living in a bilingual community in Queens, and having been living with my participants for almost two years, I have gained easy access to the data that I expected. Using an observational research method, I spent a week with them, mixing in with them and observing their communicative interactions. After having a sense of their daily code-switching, I started to do research on the topic of code-switching. (Yan Zeng student paper).

In her Introduction earlier in the paper, Zeng described her methods as drawing from the previous code-switching studies and analysis of John Gumperz, Carol Myer-Scottons, and Peter Auer, and her research methods echo their work.

As a further example, consider again Rosen's discourse analysis paper on yoga brands. For her paper, she describes how she used YouTube as a resource and listened to the online interviews, transcribed them, and analyzed them in order to answer her research problem.

> I did a cross-comparison of two interviews conducted with Dana [Trixie Flynn] on Youtube, the first by AlignYo yoga channel uploaded on May 2, 2011, and the second by the yoga channel "Yogin' It", uploaded on April 5,

2012. My initial question in exploring these videos concerned authenticity: with the knowledge of Western yoga being a product of colonialism, and knowing that a genuine concern of many Western yogis is to remain authentic to ancient yogic philosophy, I assumed that authentication would be Dana's primary strategy in addressing any sense of ethnic difference. However, after <u>transcribing</u>, <u>analyzing</u>, and <u>identifying repeated themes</u> that occurred across both videos, I ultimately found that Dana's approach to addressing difference was through adequation: in this sense, all of the themes/recurring phrases that occurred throughout her speech worked to eliminate any sense of ethnic difference between her Western audience and "authentic" Hindu yogis. In this way, Dana's speech reflected an active attempt to de-ethnicize an ethnic practice.

I designed a research study in which I _____.

The research study on _____ is modeled on the research done by _____.

In order to answer my research question, I created a study in which I _____.

My goal was to understand the process of _____.

The goal of the research was to _____. To that end, the research entailed the following steps _____.

Participants included _____ and _____.

The participants were between _____ and ____ years of age. There were ____ females and ____ males.

I interviewed _____ of participants and recorded and transcribed the interviews (see interview questions in the Appendix).

_____ (number of) participants were interviewed, and the interviews were recorded and transcribed by the researcher.

The data for this study are drawn from _____.

I did a quantitative analysis in which I counted responses and analyzed them in the following way _____.

I did a qualitative analysis describing the data and looking for patterns such as _____.

FIGURE 11.3 WRITING EXAMPLE 2: VALUABLE PHRASES FOR DESCRIBING YOUR METHODS

Results, discussion, and conclusion sections

The results section includes the data that you have collected—demographics, numbers, findings that may be shown visually in charts and tables. In many instances, you can use any software package that you used to analyze the data to create charts and figures for your paper. We usually think of charts and tables for quantitative research that uses questionnaires, surveys, Likert scales, and so on. However, qualitative research that includes interviews, observational research, and/or recordings with transcripts can also benefit from creating charts, including transcripts or descriptions that can be interpreted with analytic categories to help sort out the data that was gathered and to look for patterns and themes. Many researchers agree that a variety of visual materials in addition to charts and tables such as maps, photos, drawings, and cartoons are helpful in presenting data, in helping to see patterns and to understand and interpret the findings.

Several of the example papers we have discussed throughout the book have used charts and tables that will be good examples when creating your own charts. For example, Moore and Podesva (2009) use charts throughout their paper in order to make sense of the enormous amount of data that was collected. We particularly like the chart they use as Figure 1 on page 457 to illustrate the use of tag questions used by their four focal groups of high school girls. This simple arrow graph allows the writers to include three dimensions of information: number of tag questions, number of participants in each group, and orientation to school (continuum between "anti-school" and "pro-school). Moore and Podesva (2009) include more complicated figures, graphs, and tables, but we recreate their Figure 1 in Figure 11.4 as a table showing the orientation of different communities of practice in their research toward schooling. This simple diagram is an example of something that students might be able to construct from their data. In addition, a wide variety of graphs and charts are available for presenting data, and many are included in the articles we have referenced in the preceding chapters, including bar charts (Becker, 2009), line charts (Yuasa, 2010), box plots (Morris, 2014), and scatterplots (Moore & Podesva, 2009).

Tables are another simple and effective way to present data and analysis in student papers. In her paper examining the use of tag questions by lawyers in cross-examinations, our student Arianna Chinchilla made a table of tag questions used in three trials that she was able to find on the internet: the murder trial of O. J. Simpson, the murder trial of Jodi Arias, and a mock trial investigating a traffic offense. She provides counts in her narrative analysis but also includes charts for each of the trials. Here is an example of one of her charts.

Anti-School			Pro-School
Communities of practice	Townie	Popular	Geek	Eden village
Number of members	3	9	10	5
Number of tag questions produced	142	321	232	83

FIGURE 11.4 DIAGRAM BASED ON DATA AND FIGURE FROM MOORE & PODESVA (2009)

Notice how looking at the table helps you to see that the lawyer used tag questions 72 times in his first 15 minutes of questioning the witness. Clearly, charts, tables, and other visual representations of your data make findings visually available as well as clarifying and supporting the findings.

In the discussion part of the paper, you synthesize and connect your findings to your research problem and methodology for answering it. Often

Correct?	6
Right?	53
Wasn't he?	1
Did you?	1
Could you?	1
Aren't you?	1
Was I?	1
Was he?	2
Didn't you?	1
Couldn't you?	4
Isn't it?	1
TOTAL:	72

TABLE 11.1 LAWYER'S USE OF TAG QUESTIONS IN FIRST 15 MINUTES OF JODI ARIAS TRIAL

words of comparison and contrast are used in this part of the paper—words like *more effective, less successful, higher numbers,* and *less responsive*. Take, for example, this following section from Morris (2014):

> The participants' opinions of Welsh were mostly positive, with no significant differences between the home language and area groups. The general consensus is that more should be done to promote bilingualism in Wales and that the Welsh language is beautiful, friendly, and perhaps more importantly, useful for their future job prospects. Questionnaire data of this nature should always be treated cautiously, but this result does suggest that the acquisition of Welsh is seen as being beneficial by students, as has been shown to be the case for parents (cf. Hodges, 2012), even if this belief does not necessarily stimulate use of the language. (p. 80)

Notice how Morris uses the phrases "mostly positive," "general consensus," "treated cautiously," "result does suggest." What does this kind of language suggest to you as a reader of this study? How would it read differently if Morris had written "positive," "consensus," "treated with confidence," "result tells us"? Why might a researcher exercise caution in the discussion section of a paper?

Finally, in the conclusion section, you goal is to provide an overview of your whole study, focusing in a general sense on what you found and how it helped you answer your initial research question or problem. However, the conclusion is shorter than the introduction and the discussion sections. It is a synthesizing or tying together of your work and your findings. Even though some researchers repeat their initial question, the focus is on summarizing what you did and what you found. Usually the conclusion, in addition to discussing what has been learned, acknowledges the limits of the research and the need for additional work on the subject. Some general principles for the conclusion are listed here:

- Keep it brief and to the point.
- Summarize and synthesize your findings focusing on how they helped answer your research question or problem.
- Acknowledge limitations of research and make suggestions for further research.

Let's look closely at a part of the conclusion section in Deumert and Lexander (2013):

> This paper considered the questions: what linguistic resources do African writers use when texting? And how do these resources allow writers to perform different personae, to write themselves "into being" as a particular kind of person (skillful, loving, sexy, etc.), and to negotiate their relationships with others? (p. 540)

> By drawing on data from five different African countries, we were able to go beyond local case studies ("the limits of the local"), and to show that there are important communalities which give texting in Africa its distinct shape. ... Texting has become popular in Africa, even among the populations with low literacy rates (cf. Kibora, 2009). For many African writers, text messages are the only place where they write in local languages, and even if this practice still is marginal—limited to particular purposes and contexts—texting has emerged as a new literacy domain for African language writing. (p. 540-41)

Notice how the authors reiterated their original questions and drew together their findings to form a general conclusion. If you read the article in its entirety, what else do you find in the conclusion?

Now consider the following excerpt from the conclusion in Becker (2009):

> In New York City, non-rhoticity persists as a socially imbued marker of localness—one that speakers access in their attempts to assert local authenticity. Continued study of non-rhoticity across time in NYCE [New York City English] will allow us to watch the progression of a locally-meaningful variable which individual speakers utilize to make place identity salient. (p. 654)

Notice that Becker concludes her paper in which she investigated the use of rhoticity (pronouncing the "r" in words like *floor*) and non-rhoticity in the Lower East Side of NYC suggesting that continued study of the variable she is studying will be valuable. This is a technique that researchers often use to support future research or replication of their work.

Turning again to the paper from our student Yan Zeng, we can notice how a question from the study is repeated in the conclusion along with a telling answer that helps to tie together the responses that the student got from her research. Here, Zeng ends her paper by acknowledging the complexity of the subject of code-switching and calls for additional observation and research:

> During the interview, they were asked the question "Why do you think you code-switch?" Ying commented, "Code-switching is almost a part of us, not separating from us. It's part of who we are." Code-switching is about identity searching, and cannot be interpreted by either one of those theories. The act of code-switching does not reflect their identities or the identities reflect it. It is part of our identity. Similar to the definition of sociolinguistics, even though those sociolinguists have their own strong arguments, one thing that should be addressed is that what sociolinguistics truly is. If the definition of sociolinguistics consists of both "socio" and "linguistics," we cannot separate them

and merely focus on one side of the equation (Cameron, 110). Likewise, the idea that Blommaert argues, labeling names for languages are only folk ideologies (391), and even the "code" in code-switching for those theorists stops at the language level. Code-switching is far more complex and cannot be explained by applying theories, rather its usage provides evidence of language shift and the act of bilingual heritage maintenance. Therefore, we should rethink about the meaning of code-switching, ask for more investigation and observation, and connect the idea of code-switching to the social context at large.

Finally, in this excerpt from Chinchilla's paper, notice how the writer synthesizes her three examples and analyzes them, referring back to the original question about whether tag questions were indicators of uncertainty or of solidarity. Her study suggests that tag questions may be used as tools of manipulation, especially in a cross-examination:

> Furthermore, not once did the low-power examinees use tag questions when addressing their examiner in the rare case that they did have a question to ask. If anything, the questions in these excerpts were mostly limited to requests for the examiner to repeat themselves. In most cases, the "power of questioning" is largely denied to the person on stand, particularly the defendant (Harris 15). For the individual on the stand, it would be highly inappropriate to have used tag questions since doing so would essentially challenge the authority of the conversation, i.e. the attorney (Cameron et al. 88). Thus tag questions, in this context, are more often than not used as manipulation tools rather than genuine indicators of uncertainty, let alone as a form of engagement or an establishment of solidarity.

Thus,

Therefore,

In conclusion,

Our findings suggest

Overall, _____

Additional study _____

Continued study about _____

FIGURE 11.5 WRITING EXAMPLE 3: USEFUL TERMS WHEN WRITING YOUR CONCLUSION

Appendix

The appendix is the section of the research paper in which you include your interview questions, questionnaires, surveys, Likert-scale questions, and transcripts of interviews and recordings that you have utilized to gather your data. You need to label each item in the appendix and include that item number when you refer to it in your paper. The pages in the appendix do not typically count toward the total pages of your research paper. For example, if your professor said that your paper should be between 8 and 12 pages, the appendix and reference pages will not count toward that page count.

References

Make sure to include all references and resources that you used in your reference page. Doing this is required by all academic institutions in order to avoid any suggestion of plagiarism. Your reference page includes any resources you used, including your textbook, materials distributed and discussed in class, articles you have read on your own, or any materials used from the internet in connection with your research. Most sociolinguistics professors prefer that you use APA citation style, although some accept MLA. Check with your professor first. You will find useful links to the requirements of either citation style on the internet. We have found that online resources and example papers at the Purdue Online Writing Lab to be particularly useful for our students: https://owl.english.purdue.edu/owl. Your university library will also have resources that you can find online and in person. You should get to know the university librarians. They will be of invaluable help as you do your research and when you have questions about sources for materials and for citing work correctly.

Further reading on research paper writing tips

Chapter 12 focuses on style issues as well as oral presentations. In terms of overall writing of academic research papers in sociolinguistics (including sentence level and overall organization tips), we recommend the following books and sources. Note that these books are pitched to a wide audience and cover academic writing in general.

Graff, G., Birkenstein, C., & Durst, R. (2014). *"They say/I say": The moves that matter in academic writing*, 3rd ed. New York, NY: Norton.
Swales, J., & Feak, C. (2012). *Academic writing for graduate students*, 3rd ed. Ann Arbor, MI: University of Michigan Press.
Williams, J., & Bizup, J. (2016). *Style: Lessons in clarity and grace*, 12th ed. New York, NY: Pearson.

12 Sounding like a sociolinguist

CHAPTER OVERVIEW

- Introduction
- Style Choices: How to Sound like a Sociolinguist
  - Word Choice and Vocabulary
  - Using References
  - Writing a Summary
  - Constructing Paraphrases
  - Using Quotations
  - Active or Passive Voice
  - First Person or Third Person
  - Plagiarism
- Final Thoughts on Thinking and Sounding like a Sociolinguist

---

Introduction

Students often ask what it means to sound academic, yet not stuffy and pretentious. In reading articles and textbooks, you have seen that academic writing utilizes a more formal vocabulary than the one that you use in expressive writing. For example, you generally use longer subordinated sentences to connect your ideas. In sociolinguistics, we talk about register, or about how we speak and write more formally or informally for different audiences. The way that we speak and write is determined by the audience, context, and purpose. The purpose of the research paper is to create a formal representation of the work you have been doing all semester on your project. The emphasis in the formal paper is a bit different from the in-class research presentation that some professors require, where you present your findings knowledgeably, but with perhaps more emphasis on your personal learning experience doing the research.

In this chapter, we continue our discussion about writing up and presenting your research project, with a focus on language and style questions such as whether first person is appropriate, whether to paraphrase or to quote, and whether to use active or passive voice. We also include a discussion of plagiarism and ways to avoid it. In the final section of Chapter 12, we offer some comments on the difference between research writing and speaking presentations.

Style choices: how to sound like a sociolinguist

Word choice and vocabulary

How you find a balance between stuffy and casual takes time and practice. Part of it relates to vocabulary. Every academic field has a vocabulary or jargon that is specific to it and that students learn over time. In your paper, you can assume that your readers (your professor and classmates) will know the meanings of words that you have discussed in class, like *bilingualism, tag questions, communities of practice*, or *discourse and conversation analysis*, but if your research is about a new concept, you need to define it, as we discussed previously. You also have to think about word choice and having an academic vocabulary that does not use overly long, complicated, or infrequently used words or concepts when short or clear ones will suffice (see Exercise 12.1).

EXERCISE 12.1: Academic word choice and vocabulary

Take the word *explicate*. It means "explain," "analyze," and "interpret." These words are all similar but are slightly different in meaning. When you are writing your paper, you will probably use *explain, analyze*, and *interpret* rather than *explicate*. Why do you think that is? What are the differences in the meanings of *explain, analyze*, and *interpret*? Which word describes best what you do in your paper?

A second example is *limpid*. It means "clear," "understandable," and "comprehensible." Again, these words are similar but have slightly different meanings. Which are you more likely to use in your papers? Which have you seen when you read academic papers?

Can you think of other examples of words and synonyms, some more likely to be used in academic papers than others? Can you find words in papers that you have read that obscure rather than reveal the meaning of the ideas?

Using references

Another way to demonstrate that you are a serious scholar is to show that you have read the important work relating to your topic and know how to apply it to your own research and analysis. Researchers do this through referencing other relevant research and showing how those references help to support their own findings. The fact that scholars do this helps you in your own project because when you look at the reference page of articles you have read, you will find lists of other studies that you should look at and annotate for future reference. Referencing others' work in your own paper serves several important functions:

- Establishes the relevance of your research topic
- Provides a brief history of the research and findings that have preceded your own
- Points out gaps in the research that your work will fill
- Describes the kinds of studies that your work is replicating or building on.

When you reference other writers in your paper, you do it in three main ways: summary writing, paraphrasing, and quotations. The next three sections look at all three ways of referencing the work of others.

Writing a summary

You have probably written summaries in other classes for a variety of purposes. If you look through the chapters in this book, you will see that we have included summaries of the important points of several of the articles. The length of summaries depends on their purpose, as you will see if you look through the ones we provided. As you have probably noticed, in a research paper, summaries are not very long, again depending on their purpose, but they are in your paper for a reason. You do not have to summarize the entire article; instead, you focus on the parts that are relevant to your own study. In some cases, you will see several names and dates along with a description of the research. Here is an example from Becker (2009) on rhoticity and identity in the Lower East Side of New York City:

> Of course, Labov (1966) is unique to New York City because the linguistic variables under analysis come from the repertoire of NYCE. One implicit consequence of place in sociolinguistics is that it often defines the linguistic variables we choose to investigate, particularly in sociophonetics. The recent interest in social practice (Bucholtz 1999; Coupland 2007; Eckert 1999, 2003b; Eckert and McConnell-Ginet 1992; Mendoza-Denton 2008; Podesva 2007; Schilling-Estes 2004; Zhang 2005, 2008), where speakers actively create and change social meaning through talk, recognizes that social agents do not normally have total linguistic freedom, but select features that are both available and meaningful to them. (p. 635)

Notice that Becker mentions 11 studies preceding her own, setting up both the history and the importance of her topic. The first mention refers to the linguistic variable she is studying. Becker's study is an outgrowth of Labov's 1966 work on the use of rhoticity in New York City speakers of different classes, so it is critical that she mention him. She summarizes the next group of studies that spans 1992–2008 in a much more general way. She describes them as having an "interest in social practice" that shows how "speakers actively create and change social meaning through talk" and that speakers do not have total freedom, but choose "features that are both available and meaningful to them." This is an example of the use of a very short summary connecting several studies and researchers to Becker's own work, thereby illustrating how she is part of a scholarly conversation on this topic. Observe that Becker lists the names of the researchers in alphabetical order, followed by the date of the study. You will find a reference to each of these studies in her References page.

When mentioning other research in your own paper:

- Include the name and date of the research and cite it in your References page.

- Focus on the points in the original article that relate specifically to your research problem.

- Write the summary, paraphrasing in your own words while maintaining the important and relevant points.

One place where we find brief summaries of salient research is in the introduction. Here are a few examples from papers we have discussed:

> As Eckert (2004) notes, descriptions of social variation within class-based, ethnic, or gendered categories are often disconnected from the places where they occur. We rarely investigate the linkages between speakers and places, knowing little about how speakers negotiate the places we use to define them. (Becker, 2009, pp. 634–35)

Notice how Becker uses Eckert's research to set up her own research interest, and how the second sentence with the phrase "rarely investigate" suggests the gap in the research that her research will attempt to fill.

See Exercise 12.2 for practice writing summaries.

EXERCISE 12.2: Writing a summary

Read an article that you read as part of your research for your paper. Turn the article over so you do not see it, and write a summary of its findings.

For extra practice, read a paragraph or short excerpt from your textbook or a relevant article in sociolinguistics. Turn the article over so you do not see it, and write a summary of what you have read.

Constructing paraphrases

When you summarize and refer to research or articles in your paper, as you have seen in the examples above, you usually will need to paraphrase, or put the ideas in your own words, rather than use quotations. Paraphrasing is a skill that needs to be practiced in order to do it well (see Exercises 12.3 and 12.4). When you paraphrase, you are not just looking for synonyms and substituting them, as in the following:

> The participants' opinions of Welsh were <u>mostly positive</u>, with <u>no significant differences</u> between the home language and area groups. The <u>general consensus</u> is that more should be done to promote bilingualism in Wales and that the Welsh language is beautiful, friendly, and perhaps more importantly, useful for their future job prospects. (Morris, 2014, p. 83)

Here is an example of how a student's paraphrase of the above Morris quote can be seen as plagiarism:

> Morris said that the people's ideas about Welsh were generally affirmative, with no big disparity between the first language and other groups. The finding is that learning both languages is important.

All the student did was find synonyms, but kept the sentence almost exactly the same and did not paraphrase it in his or her own words. Here is an example of a paraphrase that is acceptable:

> Morris found that most of the people he researched felt positively about the Welsh language and supported teaching it in schools. They were proud of the language and thought that knowing Welsh could be helpful in getting jobs in the future.

EXERCISE 12.3: Paraphrasing practice

Look at the summaries you wrote for Exercise 12.2. Turn those over and write a sentence or two paraphrasing them. Look at your summaries and paraphrases. What words did you use in both? Why? Did you ever use the author's original language? If so, would that need to be in quotations?

EXERCISE 12.4: More paraphrasing practice

> Indeed, the data presented here confirm that *dude* is an address term that is used mostly by young men to address other young men; however, its use has expanded so that it is now used as a general address form for a group (same or mixed gender and by and to women). *Dude* is developing into a

discourse marker that need not identify an addressee, and more generally encodes the speaker's stance to his or her current addressee(s). (Kiesling, 2004, p. 281)

1. Write a one-sentence paraphrase of the Kiesling paragraph above. Read the paragraph carefully, think about its meaning, turn it over so you do not see it, and write the paraphrase. You can share paraphrases with other students in your class to see the differences in what was emphasized and how the paraphrase was organized.
2. As extra practice, you might want to do this with any of the excerpted paragraphs in this chapter. Writing paraphrases that convey the important information but are in your own words is a skill that takes practice.

Using quotations

Although most professors prefer that students only use paraphrases rather than direct quotations, there are times when a quote is the best choice to present someone's ideas. The suggestion is that you use quotes sparingly—only for specific phrases or concepts that are important to your project or that define a concept and cannot be paraphrased without losing the meaning. Consider again the quoted terms in the following excerpt from Sayer (2010):

> The modern urban landscape is covered with signs: naming stores and streets, adorning T-shirts and backpacks, giving directions, peddling products, and promoting politicians. All these signs are written texts, or what Goodman (1986) calls "environmental print," and taken together they compose what Ben-Rafael, Shohamy, Amara, and Trumper-Hect (2006) and Shohamy and Gorter (2009) term our "linguistic landscape." (p. 144)

Notice that Sayer puts the phrases "environmental print" and "linguistic landscape" in quotes and cites the users of those phrases. Sayer's title refers to linguistic landscape, so it is important that he acknowledges the source of this term.

Now consider again the following excerpt from Reyes (2005):

> African Americans have contributed enormously to American English slang over the past several decades (Eble 1996). Many scholars argue that slang terms rooted in African American culture, such as *cool, hip*, and *gig*, are taken up by mainstream Americans because non-mainstream lifestyle and speech are seen as inventive, exciting and even alluringly dangerous (Chapman, 1986; Eble 1996). Yet that non-African Americans benefit from appropriating the verbal dress of a group that has been the target of much discrimination and racism in the United States is a complex subject that deserves more attention from scholars of language and ethnicity. Eble (2004) notes, "Adopting the vocabulary of a non-mainstream culture is a way of sharing vicariously in the plusses of that culture without having to experience the minuses associated with it." (p. 383)

Notice that Reyes begins with two paraphrases of Connie Eble's work on slang. However, in the last sentence of this paragraph, Reyes quotes an entire sentence from Eble's work. What is the effect of the quotation? How does it add credibility to Reyes' paper, and how does it help to focus Reyes' paper?

Now consider this excerpt from our student Rachael Holborn's paper:

> In a world with continually growing levels of migration, globalisation, and commercialisation, it is inevitable that an increasing number of languages will come into contact with each other. The repercussions of these changes depend on "the kind and degree" of contact, as well as "the social and linguistic relationships of the languages" (Bell 49). As sociolinguist Allan Bell suggests, the consequences of language contact may include language stratification, code switching, language creation and endangerment (49). This paper focusses on the causes and consequences of language endangerment, as well as strategies to counteract its progress. In particular, we will observe this process in relation to the language status of Irish Gaelic, the indigenous Celtic language of Ireland.

Notice how Holborn uses both paraphrases and quotations to set up the relevance of her research area. What seems to be the purpose of the quoted phrases Holborn uses?

Active or passive voice

Many professors and most word processing systems prefer that you use the active voice in your writing, although there are situations when passive voice is appropriate. In fact, at one time almost all scientific writing was done using the passive voice because it made the writing impersonal and formal. Recently, even authors doing scientific writing use the active voice more often. In active voice, the sentence subject does the action and is emphasized. In passive voice, the subject is acted upon. Consider the following examples:

- Harold speaks French at home with his family.—Active voice
  (Harold is doing something, and emphasis is on Harold.)
- French is spoken at home by Harold and his family.—Passive voice.
  (Emphasis is on French.)

Now consider the differences in an active versus passive construction from Morris (2014, p. 65):

- The majority of Welsh-English bilinguals now acquire Welsh through immersion education rather than via parental transmission. (Original active voice construction)

- Welsh is acquired through immersion education by the majority of Welsh-English bilinguals rather than parental transmission. (Revised quote to passive voice)

In Morris's sentence, the emphasis is on the Welsh-English bilinguals; in the revised sentence, the emphasis is on Welsh. Similarly, consider a sentence that was originally in the passive voice in Deumert and Lexander (2013, p. 522):

> Texting is frequently used in intimate interactions, especially for expressions of love, affection and attraction. (Original passive voice construction)
>
> People frequently use texting for intimate interactions like love, affection, and attraction. (Revised quote to active voice)

In the original Deumert and Lexander quote, the emphasis is on the texting; in the revised sentence, the emphasis on is on the people. In both of the above excerpts, the authors are writing about their findings. Did you prefer active or passive voice in the excerpts above? Why? Does one seem more academic than the other?

In situations when writers are citing research from other researchers, they may choose to use passive voice. For example, Reyes (2005) uses the passive voice extensively in her introduction. For example:

- While there has been some work examining the use of African American slang by European Americans, studies of its use by Asian Americans are extremely scarce. (p. 511)
- Similar to how the concept of "style" has been approached by many sociolinguists (e.g. Bell 1984; Coupland 1985, 2001; Eckert and Rickford 2001), slang should not be defined by its internal inventory, but by how principles of differentiation organize the relationships and distinctiveness between slang and its alternatives. (cf. Irvine, 2001).(p. 513)

In Morris (2014), however, he prefers to use the active voice and the present perfect tense when citing the work of others. For example:

> Further studies, based on smaller samples, have shown differences between the language practices of groups within a single bilingual school (e.g. Musk 2006, 2010). (p. 66)

This same sentence could have been written in the passive voice as follows:

> It has been found that differences exist between the language practices of groups within a single bilingual school (e.g., Musk 2006, 2010).

Which sentences do you prefer for citing previous research and why? Do the meanings of the sentences change? See Exercise 12.5 for additional practice examining passive and active voice.

> **EXERCISE 12.5: Examining passive and active voice**
>
> Choose any of the articles that we have focused on in this book and find an example of the author's use of passive or active voice. Change the sentence from one to the other. Which do you prefer? Why? How does the change affect the meaning or emphasis of the sentence?

First person or third person

When you use the first person, the subject is "I" or "we." When you use the third person, the subject is "the researcher," "he," "she," or "they." Many professors prefer that students not use the first person as it makes the research paper too personal and informal. In some cases, students are permitted to use the first person in the research question or problem and in the methodology section, even if the professor does not permit the first person in the other sections of the paper. You need to check this with your professor first.

In terms of our example articles, we do find some use of the first person (see Exercise 12.6). For example, in their introduction Deumert and Lexander (2013) use the first person "we" and "our" in the following sentence:

> In our discussion below we will focus on texts (what Brandt and Clinton [2002] call 'literacy-in-action'), and show how writers create meaning when texting. (p. 526)

In general, we recommend against using first person when you are the only author and writer, but in the above example, there are two writers, so the use of "we" is acceptable if you prefer to use first-person pronouns. In describing the sections of his paper, Kiesling (2004) illustrates a perhaps more controversial use of the first pronoun "I" in the following example:

> I first investigate the wider use of the term and then excerpt several uses in the fraternity to illustrate its discourse functions and how it is used in interaction. I also discuss the personalities of the men who use *dude* the most in the fraternity, then describe the most salient phonological characteristics of the term—a fronted /u/—and possible connections between this feature of dude and the ongoing fronting of this vowel across North America. Finally, I explain the rise and use of *dude* by exploring cultural discourses of masculinity and American identity more generally in the 1980s. (p. 283)

> **EXERCISE 12.6: First-person pronouns**
>
> Choose any of the articles that we have focused on in this book finding when and if the author(s) used first person or third person. In what sections of the paper did you find examples of each? Change one of the sentences from one to the other. Which do you prefer? Why? How does the change affect the meaning of the sentence?

Plagiarism

We have been looking at strategies for avoiding plagiarism throughout this chapter. Almost all universities have policies that inform students about how serious it is to plagiarize or use other people's writing, images, or ideas without giving credit to the creator or source of the information. This includes using materials from the internet, your textbook, articles, and even personal correspondence.

In general, you can avoid any problems with plagiarism by taking a few steps:

1. Scaffold your work. This means you do it piece by piece, so you are ready when it comes time to put together your final draft of the research paper.

2. Take careful notes and keep them in a safe place where you can find them when you put together your paper. You should have more than one copy of your notes. If you do this digitally, copy the material in more than one place. If you are writing notes, make duplicate copies and keep them in a safe place. It is not a good excuse that your computer lost your data or that your laptop isn't working. You must keep multiple copies of everything to be safe and to get your work in on time. It is sad when someone has worked hard but gets a lowered or failing grade because the work was not submitted on time.

3. If you copy a sentence or phrase from something that you have read, be careful to put it in quotes (you may want to mark the quotes in a different color so you know they are not your own words), and make notes on every source—name, publication, date, and page number(s) — so you can find it again.

4. Practice paraphrasing. Read articles or even paragraphs and rewrite them in your own words. As you do the paraphrase, turn the work over so you cannot see it. Check your paraphrase to see if you got the main idea. You can even make a game of this and paraphrase an article into a paragraph, then into two sentences, then one sentence; some people even paraphrase into a single phrase.

5. Start to make a References page from the very beginning, putting down information about your sources right away. Many professors ask students to annotate any articles they have read. An annotation includes the relevant name, publication, date, and so on, but it also contains a short summary of the article or source and how it applies to your research.

6. Once again, scaffold your work. This means that you do your work slowly, part by part. When it comes time to put together your first draft, you will have all the pieces so you can organize and put them together. You will not be lost trying to find notes, quotes, data, and paraphrases at the last minute when things can go very wrong.

7. If your professor allows you to do this, write drafts and get feedback on your work, so you will find problems early on and be able to correct them.

8. Write a final draft that you feel proud about and that shows the hard work you put into it.

Final thoughts on thinking and sounding like a sociolinguist

We have come to the end of our book introducing the basic topics and methods for completing a sociolinguistics research project in your classroom. As we have stressed throughout the book, there are many ways to do sociolinguistic research projects, and there are many ways to write them up and display information. The key in all classroom research projects is to pick something that you are passionate about and that connects in some way to your interests and background. If you cannot answer the "So what" question for yourself (i.e., "Why is this research topic important to you?"), then you should consider picking another project.

In concluding the book, we also wanted to point out that in addition to traditional written research papers, students may be asked to present their research projects as class presentations, poster presentations, blog posts, or other nontraditional presentation formats for communicating their findings. We enjoy having students present their projects at the end of the course as poster presentations. For this activity, we reserve the final two periods of the course for students to present their projects to the entire class in small groups of presenters (3–4 at a time). During the poster presentations, classmates can walk among the posters and ask the authors questions in an informal setting that encourages dialogue and discussion.

When presenting your data in a more informal context, you may rely more on visual images, bulleted lists, and graphs to get your points across than you would in a traditional written paper, and of course, you can take cues from the questions and body language of your audience to decide what needs to be explained in more detail. Even during a poster presentation or individual presentation, however, you should still be careful to cite and paraphrase previous work, present you findings in a similarly organized manner as in your research paper, and explain or define key terms for your audience.

From watching many student presentations over the years, we offer the following tips when preparing for a presentation, be it with overhead slides, PowerPoint slides, a poster, or any other visual aid.

- *Organization:* Be sure to offer an outline to your presentation on an overhead slide or abstract on your poster. Stick to the outline, and refer back to it as you progress through your presentation.

- *Speaking:* Sociolinguistics presentations are typically not read, but you may use notes to remind you of key points and keep you on track. If you are nervous speaking in front of groups, be sure to practice beforehand both on your own and in front of friends. Project your voice to fill up the room, and when possible and appropriate depending on the context, make eye contact with your audience and pause to check on their understanding.

- *Visual aids:* For overhead slides and text on posters, choose a standard font such as Times New Roman or Arial; use a large font (typically over 18 points); and use a color of font that contrasts with the background page or slide. Try to limit the amount of text needed, and instead use graphs, diagrams, pictures, or other visual aids as much as possible. Many do not allow students to play online videos during presentations, but you may need to play samples of your recorded data. Be sure these and any other samples that you wish to show are working before you present.

- *Questions:* Be sure to leave enough time at the end of your presentation for questions and discussion. You may want to suggest questions during your presentation or list questions on your final slide that you are prepared to speak about.

- *Class activity:* Some professors require students to include a short class activity in their presentations in order to allow the class to practice and participate in what they have learned in the presentation.

- *Formality:* Overall presentations use a less formal style. As evidenced in research done using MICASE (Michigan Corpus of Academic Spoken English), features of academic lectures that differ from written English include contractions, slang (even some limited swearing), filler words, hesitations, and many discourse fillers. A key difference between a conversation with a friend and an academic presentation is, however, the purpose of presenting information, and we recommend that students can present their projects in fun and formal ways but still remain focused on the job of presenting their findings and offering questions for further research.

We hope that the previous chapters and examples have been useful in getting you started on your projects. As we can attest from experience, similar to most academic pursuits, sociolinguistic research is a matter of trial and error, determining what did and did not work and then revising your research methods or analysis plan. As we often tell our students, the point of doing classroom research projects is not to complete a dissertation or come up with a completely new way of analyzing sociolinguistic data. Instead, you should focus on collecting data about an issue or problem in your community and drawing some limited but important generalizations from your data. In your next projects, you can pioneer a new branch of the sociolinguistic tree.

Glossary

axial codes A part of qualitative data analysis in which a researcher establishes links between different categories and concepts that were identified during the initial open coding of that data. Axial coding builds to the themes that the researcher will report in response to a study's research questions. (Chapter 7)

back-channeling The verbal and nonverbal responses listeners use to show attentiveness in a conversation and interviewers use to encourage participants to continue speaking. Examples include terms and phrases such as *yes, uh-huh, mmm, okay*, and *wow*. (Chapters 3, 4, and 8)

bilingualism (multilingualism) The ability of an individual to use two languages (bilingualism) or more than two languages (multilingualism). Sociolinguistics researchers are interested in aspects of bi- and multilingualism from education policy to cognitive benefits, to discourse analysis studies. (Chapter 1)

code or variety Both are general terms used by sociolinguists to refer to specific dialects, accents, or language. Sociolinguists often prefer to use *code* or *variety* instead of *language* or *dialect* in order to remain neutral and avoid ideological and political determinations of language and dialect definitions. (Chapter 1)

code-meshing Related to code-switching in that code-meshing involves use of more than one language or code in a conversation. Researchers have used *code-meshing* to describe uses of more than one language or semiotic system in speaking, writing, and other communication as part of one integrated system and not as a switch between two language systems. In this way, code-meshing emphasizes the idea that almost all language use involves mixing linguistic systems. For example, a student may insert particular nouns or ideas in his or her home language of Spanish into an essay that is otherwise written in English. See also *code-switching*. (Chapter 1)

code-mixing Use of elements of two or more languages within a single sentence, intrasententially. The distinction between code-mixing and code-switching is often blurred. See also *code-switching*. (Chapter 4)

code-switching Use of two or more languages, codes, or language varieties during an interaction or conversation. Sociolinguists research many aspects of code-switching, including the discourse and grammatical basis for particular changes in language use (both intrasententially and intersententially) and societal beliefs and attitudes toward code-switching. See also *code-meshing*. (Chapters 1, 2, 4, and 6)

communities of practice (COP) A term borrowed into sociolinguistics from educational theory and anthropology that describes a group of people defined by their joint participation in a task or common endeavor. Through participation in the group, members develop shared linguistic practices, values, and attitudes, with some members being considered more representative of the group's linguistic style and others more peripheral. For student projects, the term can be useful as a way to understand a variety of different groups' language practices from student-interest groups such as sports teams to groups organized around certain careers, such as a prelaw society. (Chapters 1, 2, and 5)

computer-mediated communication (CMC) Human communication via computer or digital media such as email, social media sites, mobile messaging platforms, or educational and professional workspaces. Synchronous CMC is when communication takes place in real time. Asynchronous CMC is when interlocutors and participants are not necessarily online or communicating at the same time, such as in emails or blogs. (Chapter 6)

concordance (or KWIC [key word in context]) A concordance in corpus linguistics reveals the linguistic context of a search term or terms. Corpus analysis tools typically display sets of concordance lines. The most common concordance format is the KWIC concordance (key word in context), in which the search word is in a central position, with all lines vertically aligned around the node. Concordance lines can be sorted to reveal different patterns of usage. (Chapter 10)

construct validity Typically considered as one of three types of validity that researchers need to define, along with content and criterion-related validity. Construct validity determines whether the research tools used in a study measure what they intend to measure. For example, do the questions on the survey accurately measure the participants' attitudes about a linguistic change? Many researchers now view construct, content, and criterion-related validity as all related in that they require researchers to clarify both empirically and theoretically the basis for making generalizations from the data collection methods. See also *validity*. (Chapter 9)

convenience sampling A common sampling method, used in qualitative research, in which a researcher chooses cases or participants based on their availability to the researcher and connection to the research questions. Convenience sampling may also be used in quantitative research studies: for example, students often only have time to survey their friends and family for class projects. The main drawback of this type of sampling is the limited ability of researchers to make generalizations from their findings. (Chapters 3 and 6)

conversation analysis (CA) One of the main methods of discourse analysis, in which researchers record, transcribe, and analyze spoken interactions as a way to investigate the structure, patterns, and turn-taking of conversations and how participants jointly construct meaning through their spoken interactions. Conversation analysts focus on the language and interactions within the conversation, unlike the wider political and ideological analysis of critical discourse analysis (CDA). (Chapters 1, 2, and 8)

corpus linguistics A type of sociolinguistic research that uses extant and real-world texts of spoken or written language use and organizes them into corpora (electronic collections) in order to perform analysis using a number of computational tools. (Chapters 2, 6, and 9)

correlation (correlational studies) In sociolinguistics, correlation is a commonly used measure in quantitative methods that reveals the relationship between sociolinguistic variables (such as use of the word *pop* for a carbonated beverage) with other demographic and social variables (such as regional and age differences). (Chapter 9)

creaky voice (vocal fry)   A register of speaking in which partial closure of the glottis while speaking produces a bubbling or rattling sound as air passes through the glottis. The speech style has been associated with young, urban women in the United States and around the world and has produced a wide range of opinions and attitudes, making it a good topic for undergraduate students to research. (Chapters 4 and 8)

critical discourse analysis (CDA)   A type of discourses analysis that studies language and discourses in order to analyze how power, inequalities, and identities, and dominant knowledges are constructed and reproduced in written and spoken interactions. See also *discourse analysis* and *conversation analysis*. (Chapter 8)

data (data sets)   Data and analysis of data sets are central to the research process in sociolinguistics. Data is the information that researchers collect through either quantitative or qualitative methods (or both) and from which they make inferences and generalization in response to their research questions. (Chapters 1 and 2)

data saturation   Occurs when enough data has been collected that no new patterns or findings in relation to the research questions emerge. (Chapters 6 and 7)

dependent variable   In sociolinguistics, a language unit or expression that is expected to change in relation to the independent variable (or social variable such as age, class, region, etc.). See also *sociolinguistic variable* and *independent variable*. (Chapter 9)

descriptive statistics   In quantitative research, numerical data such as measures of central tendency (mode, median, and mean) and measures of dispersion (range, variance, and standard deviation) that describe the basic features of a set of data and point to relationships between aspects of the collected data. See also *inferential statistics*. (Chapters 3 and 9)

dialect (dialectology)   Term used by both sociolinguists and the general public to refer to ways of speaking that indicate a distinctive region or social group and the study of those local and social dialects (dialectology). Many sociolinguists prefer to use the term *variety* or *code* to avoid the connotation that a dialect is less important than a language or standard variety of a language. See also *variety* and *code*. (Chapters 1 and 2)

diglossia   The use of two languages or varieties of a language that have different social value and prestige levels in a society. The varieties are stratified into H (high) and L (low) and may be used for different functions, with the low variety used for everyday conversations with family and friends, and the high variety used for more formal functions such as education, work, government, and media. (Chapter 1)

discourse   Sociolinguists analyze discourse as related stretches of language across spoken, written, and signed texts that index and are representative of social categories and identities. For example, academic discourse can be analyzed according to grammatical features such as the use of nominalizations and passive voice, and its use in writing can index a formal and professional register. (Chapters 7 and 8)

discourse analysis (DA)   A qualitative research method that describes a number of ways of collecting and analyzing spoken, written, and signed texts. See also *conversation analysis (CA)* and *critical discourse analysis (CDA)*. (Chapters 2, 7, and 8)

discourse markers Linking words and other lexical phrases, such as *well, so* and *however*, used in speaking and writing to organize segments of discourse. In writing, especially academic writing, discourse markers are more formal, but in speaking, for example, in interviews, they can be informal and are used to show empathy and connect to previous statements. (Chapters 5 and 8)

domain Social situations in which different varieties of language are used depending on the context and the relationships among participants, as well as the setting—the time and place—and the topic of the interaction. Domains include situations such as family, work, friends, school, religion, sports events, and courtrooms, for example. (Chapters 2 and 11)

ellipsis The omission of a word or phrase necessary to complete a syntactic structure, such as "Did you read the chapter for tomorrow's class?" "I did." Both participants understand that "read the chapter" has been left out, and so the communication is understood by both participants. (Chapter 8)

emic Research that is conducted within the social group or community. Participant observation research is done from the both the emic (insider) and etic (outsider) perspective, because the researcher is a part of the group but is also looking at it from a meta, or outsider, perspective. See also *etic*. (Chapters 1, 5, and 7)

ethnography (ethnographic research methods) A central qualitative research method in which researchers attempt to record and understand a culture, linguistic practice, institution, or space through an insider or emic perspective. Researchers collect a wide variety of data through participation in community events, interviews, and multiple observations of the natural setting in which the community lives, works, and interacts. See also *participant observation research*. (Chapters 1, 5, and 6)

etic Research that is conducted outside the group from the perspective of the observer. Participant observation research is done from both etic and emic perspectives, with the researcher being part of the group but also looking at it from the etic or outside perspective. See also *emic*. (Chapters 1 and 5)

fieldwork Associated with ethnographic and participant observation research methods, this refers to the collection of data in a naturally occurring setting. Researchers typically take extensive field notes and recordings while interacting with their participants. These notes become the basis of their analysis and findings. (Chapter 5)

focus group An interview of more than one participant, and typically between 5 and 10, in which the interviewer moderates a discussion on the research topic. Researchers may try to group participants who share an experience, background, or perspective in order to delve more deeply into a research topic, but focus group interviews may be limited if some participants fail to participate or feel uncomfortable in a group setting. (Chapter 3)

generalizability The extent to which researchers can draw conclusions from their findings to a wider population. See also *validity*. (Chapter 2)

grounded theory A qualitative approach to analysis that generates theory and explanations from collected data through systematic note taking, memoing, and theme building. (Chapter 6)

high rising terminal (uptalk) A speech feature also known as upspeak, uptalk, or rising inflection that is characterized by rising intonation in a declarative statement that makes the statement sound like a question. It has been associated with female speech and is a common topic for student research projects. (Chapters 8 and 10)

hypothesis The common starting point for experimental and statistical research projects. A hypothesis is a statement of prediction about the relationship between two or more variables. The research hypothesis is the researcher's expected relationship, and an inferential statistical test measures the extent the research hypothesis is true in relation to a null hypothesis, which states there is no relationship between the variables in a study. See also *null hypothesis*. (Chapter 9)

independent variables Variables that researchers change in order to see the effect on dependent variables. In sociolinguistics, the independent variables are often social variables, such as age, class, or region, that are studied in relation to a particular linguistic feature (i.e., a sociolinguistic variable such as /r/-less speech). See also *sociolinguistic variable* and *dependent variable*. (Chapter 9)

indexicality The way linguistic forms or codes can take on particular social meanings. Sociolinguists refer to first-order indexicality, in which there is a clear differentiation between the codes spoken by different social groups, and second-order indexicality, in which linguistic features of one group are appropriated by outsider members and become markers of the speech style of particular social groups. (Chapters 1, 3, 5, and 7)

inferential statistics Whereas descriptive statistical tests reveal the central tendencies of collected data, inferential statistical tests make inferences about participants and variables under investigation. Through hypothesis tests, inferential statistics tools such as a t-test and an analysis of variation (ANOVA) measure the statistical significance and estimate the degree to which variables are correlated; researchers can then make generalizations to the wider population. See also *descriptive statistics*. (Chapter 3 and 9)

language ideology The "commonsense" beliefs and understandings on which societal systems, values, and discourses rest. (Chapter 1)

language shift (language maintenance) Occurs when speakers stop using a language or variety in particular contexts (e.g., school, government, etc.) and adopt a dominant or outside language for these contexts of function. Language shift typically leads to language loss and language death, and is contrasted with language maintenance and heritage language learning policies that attempt to protect the use of minority languages in a community. (Chapter 1)

Likert rating scale A popular way to construct items on questionnaires. Likert items typically offer five to seven options for respondents to choose from in response to a question or statement. For example, a survey item may ask participants to choose from the following: 5—strongly agree, 4—agree, 3—no opinion, 2—disagree, 1—strongly disagree. (Chapters 3 and 9)

linguistic landscape (LL) Includes analysis of the languages and images displayed in public spaces, including commercial and government signs, advertisements, graffiti, and other public displays of language. (Chapters 2, 5, and 6)

longitudinal research   Studies that involve qualitative data collection over extended periods of time in order to analyze changes or developments over time. Most students are not able to complete data collection over a long period of time, but life history projects are longitudinal in nature and are doable as term-length projects. (Chapters 1 and 3)

mixed-methods research design   Studies that use both qualitative and quantitative data collection and analysis methods. Projects may collect data using both approaches at the same time or sequentially. For example, a researcher may first conduct a series of interviews that inform the creation of a questionnaire distributed to a larger group of participants. Alternatively, participant observation of a speech community may take place at the same time as a survey of community member speech samples is collected and analyzed. (Chapters 1, 2, 3, and 9)

null hypothesis   The alternative of the research hypothesis that states any correlation between variables is random and not predictive. Accepting or rejecting the null hypothesis is the basis for many statistical tests. See also *hypothesis* and *significance*. (Chapter 9)

participant observation research   Used most often as part of linguistic ethnography projects, participant observation methods involve the collection of data in which researchers participate in and join events and activities in research participants' everyday lives. Researchers take extensive field notes about their experiences and may collect other data from interviews, documents, or other artifacts related to their research questions and topics. See also *fieldwork*. (Chapters 1, 5, 6, and 8)

postvocalic /r/ (r-lessness)   The absence, or /r/, in post-vocalic position is a feature of many different English varieties around the world and was one of the earliest topics for sociolinguistic study by William Labov and others. Students may develop projects repeating some of the data collection methods used in previous studies and compare their results. (Chapters 1 and 3)

probability sampling (nonprobability sampling)   Requires that every member of a population studied has a chance to be selected for participation in the study. It differs from nonprobability sampling methods because participants are chosen at random in probability sampling methods. Probability sampling offers quantitative researchers the ability to make the widest generalization. See also *purposive sampling*, *systematic sampling*, and *stratified sampling* (Chapter 3)

purposive sampling   A data collection method such as snowball sampling in which participants are not chosen at random, but are selected based on criteria such as the relevance a participant has to the study's research questions or the availability of a participant to complete the interview, survey, or data collection tool. This type of sampling allows researchers to choose participants who fit well with the study's topic and goals. See also *convenience sampling* and *snowball sampling*. (Chapter 6)

qualitative research   A collection of data collection and analysis methods that broadly share the goals of conducting research projects in natural settings and through multiple perspectives before making any generalizations about or comparisons to larger populations or theories. Qualitative research methods emphasize the role of the researcher in the data collection and analysis process and use nonstatistical and textual data as primary data sources. See also *reflexivity*. (Chapters 1, 3, 5, and 7)

quantitative research A collection of research methods based on numerical measurements and statistical procedures. In sociolinguistics, researchers equate linguistic features with frequency and distribution numbers in order to compare and analyze variation across individuals and groups. Quantitative research is hypothesis driven in that researchers begin with a testable hypothesis that will be confirmed or rejected based on the significance of patterns and correlations in the statistical analysis. See also *descriptive statistics, null hypothesis*, and *inferential statistics*. (Chapters 1, 3, 5, 7, and 9)

reflexivity (reflexive stance) The notion that researchers must recognize their role in the research process and reflect on their biases. Reflexivity is typically associated with qualitative research methods in which researchers and their intuitions play a large role in determining findings and making generalizations. Often in qualitative research writing, authors will take a reflexive stance and mention their role in the research process as part of their report. (Chapters 1 and 7)

reliability In sociolinguistic research, the consistency of the study tools or instruments in measuring the topic or construct under examination. For example, the data will not be considered reliable if a participant takes the same test or questionnaire and has widely different scores. Another sense of reliability is the extent to which the entire research process is described and other researchers could replicate the study and receive the same data. Reliability tends to be associated mostly with quantitative research methods, with some qualitative researchers using the term *dependability* to indicate the extent to which the data collection methods are described and connected to the study's findings. (Chapters 2, 3 and 7)

sampling In both qualitative and quantitative research designs, researchers will have to make decisions about who to select as participants in their studies and how to select these people. Generally, they can choose probability sampling methods that choose participants randomly or purposive sampling that chooses participants based on specific characteristics or traits. See also *probability sampling, purposive sampling, snowball sampling*, and *convenience sampling*. (Chapters 3, 6, and 9)

significance Used in quantitative and statistical research designs, significance is an indication of the probability that the null hypothesis is true. For example, if the level of significance is 0.05, a researcher is 95 percent certain that the research hypothesis and findings are correct and not random. In sociolinguistic studies, the significance level is typically set at 0.05. (Chapter 9)

snowball sampling A type of purposive sampling in which researchers ask their initial participants to find other participants from the same target group to participate in the research study. In this way, researchers can quickly find participants who may be otherwise difficult to identify and reach. It is a common sampling strategy for student research projects. (Chapter 3)

social constructivism Associated with qualitative research, social constructivism is based on the idea that there is no universal truth or meaning that can be accessed through the research process. Instead, the world is constructed by social groups in their interactions, and it is the role of researchers to document and analyze the socially constructed beliefs, discourses, and ideologies of group members. (Chapter 7)

sociolinguistic variable A linguistic unit that researchers examine for variation based on linguistic and social factors such as the independent variables ethnicity, class, age, gender, or style. See also *independent variable* and *dependent variable*. (Chapters 1 and 9)

speech community Generally understood as a group of people who share linguistic features when communicating including pronunciation, lexical, discourse, and style patterns. (Chapters 1 and 5)

stratified sampling A type of purposeful sampling in which researchers organize collected data into different groups or strata and then randomly choose the needed number of participants from each group. This type of sampling is useful when a research project is collecting data from different levels within the target population, such as from first- through fourth-year students at a university. (Chapter 3)

style (style shifts) In sociolinguistics, style refers to the level of formality expected in different communication contexts, for example, academic writing, classroom discussions, and social media. Like code-switching, style shifts occur based on a variety of factors and can be a useful area of exploration for student projects. (Chapters 1, 5, and 8)

systemic-functional linguistics (SFL) Systemic-functional linguistics is a theory of language, initially developed by M.A.K. Halliday, that focuses on what language does and how it does it, instead of more structural and syntactic approaches to language theory. A foundational SFL insight is that language creates and is constrained by social context. Students may find the theoretical notions of SFL, such as the appraisal system, useful as frames or sources for research questions and data collection. (Chapters 7 and 8)

systematic sampling A probability sampling technique in which researchers assign numbers to each participant and then choose to include every participant in their data set according to a fixed internal. For example, every 10th participant will be included. See also *probability sampling*. (Chapter 3)

thick description Term used to describe the type of note taking and details involved in ethnographies and qualitative research. The goal of thick description is to provide rich descriptions of the context, events, participants, and actions observed in relation to the speech community or research topic. See also *emic, ethnography,* and *qualitative research*. (Chapters 1, 5, 6 and 7)

translanguaging (translingual approach) Broad term that denotes the use of multiple languages, varieties, registers, styles, and discourses as one integrated system. Related to code-meshing and code-switching, translanguaging and a translingual approach investigate how multilingual speakers consciously and strategically use language resources. (Chapters 1 and 5)

triangulation Refers to the collection of different perspectives and types of data in qualitative and mixed-methods research designs, with the goal of improving the overall understanding of the research topic and adding validity to the study's findings. See also *validity*. (Chapters 1, 5, and 8)

validity Refers to the extent that the research design, data collection, and findings have analyzed what was intended and to what degree the study's findings can be generalized to a larger population. In qualitative research, thick description and triangulation can add to a study's validity. In quantitative research, validity increases with the use of probability sampling techniques that reveal statistically significant results. See also *construct validity, reliability, thick description,* and *triangulation.* (Chapters 2, 3, 5, and 7)

variationist research One of the first objects of study in sociolinguistics. Variationist research has studied the linguistic features of speech communities and the correlations between sociolinguistic variables with class, race, and gender (first wave), but more recent studies have expanded to include ethnographic information (second wave) and looked at how language use indexes and constructs identity and group membership. (Chapters 1, 2, and 4)

References

Agha, A. (2003). The social life of cultural value. *Language and Communication, 23,* 231–73.

Alim, H. S. (2009). "Creating an empire within an empire": Critical hip-hop language pedagogies and the role of sociolinguistics. In H. S. Alim, A. Ibrahim, & A. Pennycook (eds.), *Global linguistic flows: Hip hop cultures, youth identities, and the politics of language* (pp. 213–30). New York: Routledge.

Alim, H. S., Rickford, J. R., & Ball, A. F. (eds.) (2016). *Raciolinguistics: How language shapes our ideas about race.* New York: Oxford University Press.

Alim, H. S., & Smitherman, G. (2012). *Articulate while black: Barack Obama, language and race in the U.S.* New York: Oxford University Press.

Androutsopoulos, J. (2014). Computer-mediated communication and linguistic landscapes. In J. Holmes & K. Hazen (eds.), *Research methods in sociolinguistics: A practical guide* (pp. 74–90). Malden, MA: Wiley-Blackwell.

Auer, P. (1998). Bilingual conversation revisited. In P. Auer (ed.), *Code-switching in conversation: Language, interaction, and identity* (pp. 1–25). London: Routledge.

Backhaus, P. (2007). *Linguistic landscapes: A comparative study of urban multilingualism in Tokyo.* Clevedon, UK: Multilingual Matters.

Bailey, B. (2000). The language of multiple identities among Dominican Americans. *Journal of Linguistic Anthropology, 10*(2), 190–223. Available at http://www.jstor.org/stable/43103242.

Baker, P. (2010). *Sociolinguistics and corpus linguistics.* Edinburgh: Edinburgh University Press.

Baker, P. (2014). Corpus linguistics in sociolinguistics. In J. Holmes & K. Hazen (eds.), *Research methods in sociolinguistics: A practical guide* (pp. 107–18). Malden, MA: Wiley-Blackwell.

Baker, P., Hardie, A., & McEnery, A. (2006). *A glossary of corpus linguistics.* Edinburgh: Edinburgh University Press.

Bakhtin, M. (1981). *The dialogic imagination: four essays.* Edited by Michael Holquist; trans. by Caryl Emerson & Michael Holquist. Austin: University of Texas Press.

Basso, K. (1970). "To give up on words": Silence in Western Apache culture. *Southwestern Journal of Anthropology, 26*(3), 213–30. Available at https://doi.org/10.1086/soutjanth.26.3.3629378.

Baugh, J. (2015). SWB (Speaking while black): Linguistic profiling and discrimination based on speech as a surrogate for race against speakers of African American vernacular English. In J. Bloomquist, L. J. Green, & S. L. Lanehart (eds.), *The Oxford handbook of African American Language.* Oxford: Oxford University Press. doi:10.1093/oxfordhb/9780199795390.013.68.

Becker, K. (2009). /r/ and the construction of place identity on New York City's Lower East Side. *Journal of Sociolinguistics, 13*(5), 634–58. Available at https://doi.org/10.1111/j.1467-9841.2009.00426.x.

Becker, K., Aden, A., Best, K., & Jacobsen, H. (2016). Variation in West Coast English: The case of Oregon. *Publication of the American Dialect Society, 101*(1), 107–34. Available at https://doi.org/10.1215/00031283-3772923.

Bell, A. (1984). Language style as audience design. *Language in Society, 13*(2), 145–204. Available at http://www.jstor.org/stable/4167516.

Bell, A. (2014). *The guidebook to sociolinguistics.* Oxford: Wiley-Blackwell.

Berg, B. (2009). *Qualitative research methods for the social sciences*, 7th ed. Boston, MA: Pearson.

Biber, D. (2006). *University language: A corpus-based study of spoken and written registers.* Amsterdam: John Benjamins.

Blom, J., & Gumperz, J. J. (1972). Social meaning in linguistic structure: Code-switching in Norway. In J. J. Gumperz & D. Hymes (eds.), *Directions in sociolinguistics: The ethnography of communication* (pp. 407–34). New York: Holt, Rinehart and Winston.

Blommaert, J. (2005). *Discourse: A critical introduction.* Cambridge: Cambridge University Press.

Blumer, H. (1986). *Symbolic interactionism: Perspective and method.* Berkeley, CA: University of California Press.

Bright. W. (1966). Language, social stratification, and cognitive orientation. *Sociological Inquiry, 36*(2), 313–18. Available at https://doi.org/10.1111/j.1475-682X.1966.tb00632.x.

Brown, P., & Levinson, S. (1987). *Politeness.* Cambridge: Cambridge University Press.

Bucholtz, M. (1999). "Why be normal?" Language and identity practice in a community of nerd girls. *Language in Society, 28*(2), 203–23. Available at http://www.jstor.org/stable/4168925.

Bucholtz, M., & Hall, K. (2005). Identity and intersections: A sociocultural linguistic approach. *Discourse Studies, 7*(4–5), 585–614. Available at https://doi.org/10.1177%2F1461445605054407.

Cameron, D. (2001). *Working with spoken discourse.* London: Sage.

Cameron, D. (2011). Performing gender identity: Young men's talk and the construction of heterosexual masculinity. In A. Mooney et al. (eds.), *The language, society and power reader* (pp. 179–90). London: Routledge.

Canagarajah, S. (ed.) (2013). *Literacy as translingual practice: Between communities and classrooms.* New York: Routledge.

Chand, V. (2011). Elite positionings towards Hindi: Language policies, political stances and language competence in India. *Journal of Sociolinguistics, 15*(1), 6–35. Available at https://doi.org/10.1111/j.1467-9841.2010.00465.x.

Charmaz, K. (2006). *Constructing grounded theory: A practical guide through qualitative analysis.* Thousand Oaks, CA: Sage.

Chun, C. (2014). Mobilities of a linguistic landscape at Los Angeles City Hall Park. *Journal of Language and Politics, 13*(4), 653–74. Available at https://doi.org/10.1075/jlp.13.4.04chu.

Clark, L., & Schleef, E. (2010). The acquisition of sociolinguistic evaluations among Polish-born adolescents learning English: Evidence from perception. *Language Awareness, 19*(4), 299–322. Available at https://doi.org/10.1080/09658416.2010.524301.

Connor, U., & Upton, T. (eds.) (2004). *Discourse in the professions: Perspectives from corpus linguistics.* Amsterdam: John Benjamins.

Coupland, N. (2003). Introduction: Sociolinguistics and globalization. *Journal of Sociolinguistics, 7*(4), 465–72. Available at https://doi.org/10.1111/j.1467-9841.2003.00237.x.

Coupland, N., & Jaworski, A. (eds.) (2009). *The new sociolinguistics reader.* Basingstoke: Palgrave Macmillan.

Creswell, J. W. (2013). *Qualitative inquiry and research design: Choosing among five approaches*, 3rd ed. Thousand Oaks, CA: Sage.

Croker, R. A. (2009). An introduction to qualitative research. In J. Heigham & R. A. Croker (eds.), *Qualitative research in applied linguistics: A practical introduction* (pp. 3–24). New York: Palgrave MacMillan.

Curzan, A., & Adams, M. (2012). *How English works: A linguistic introduction*, 3rd ed. New York: Pearson.

Cutler, C. A. (1999). Yorkville crossing: White teens, hip hop and African American English. *Journal of Sociolinguistics, 3*(4), 428–42. Available at https://doi.org/10.1111/1467-9481.00089.

Davies, M. (2008). *The corpus of contemporary American English (COCA): 560 million words, 1990–present.* Available at https://corpus.byu.edu/coca/.

Deumert, A., & Lexander, K. V. (2013). Texting Africa: Writing as performance. *Journal of Sociolinguistics, 17*(4), 522–46. Available at https://doi.org/10.1111/josl.12043.

DeWitt, K. M., & DeWitt, B. R. (2010). *Participant observation: A guide for fieldworkers*, 2nd ed. Lanham, MD: AltaMira Press.

Dillman, D. A. (1978). *Mail and telephone surveys: The total design method.* New York: Wiley.

Dörnyei. Z. (2007). *Research methods in applied linguistics.* Oxford, England: Oxford University Press.

Dörnyei, Z., & Csizér, K. (2012). How to design and analyze surveys in SLA research? In A. Mackey & S. Gass (eds.), *Research methods in second language acquisition: A practical guide* (pp. 74–94). Malden, MA: Wiley-Blackwell.

Drager, K. (2014). Experimental methods in sociolinguistics. In J. Holmes & K. Hazen (eds.), *Research methods in sociolinguistics: A practical guide* (pp. 58–73). Malden, MA: Wiley-Blackwell.

Eckert, P. (n.d.). *Third-wave variation studies.* Retrieved from https://web.stanford.edu/~eckert/third.html on June 27, 2018.

Eckert, P. (1989). *Jocks and burnouts: Social categories and identities in the high school.* New York: Teachers College Press.

Eckert, P. (2012). Three waves of variation study: The emergence of meaning in the study of sociolinguistic variation. *Annual Review of Anthropology, 41,* 87–100. doi:10.1146/annurev-anthro-092611-145828.

Edwards, R. (2006). What's in a name? Chinese learners and the practice of adopting "English" names. *Language, Culture, and Curriculum, 19*(1), 90–103. Available at https://doi.org/10.1080/07908310608668756.

Elrod, S., Kinzie, J., & Husic, D. (2010). Research and discovery across the curriculum. *Peer Review, 12*(2). Available at https://www.aacu.org/peerreview.

Fairclough, N. (2001). Critical discourse analysis as a method in social scientific research. In R. Wodak & M. Meyer (eds.), *Methods in critical discourse analysis* (pp. 121–38). London: Sage Publications.

Fairclough, N. (2006). *Language and globalization.* London: Routledge.

Feagin, C. (2002). Entering the community: Fieldwork. In J. K. Chamber, P. Trudgill, & N. Schilling-Estes (eds.), *The handbook of language variation and change* (pp. 20–39). Oxford, UK: Blackwell.

Ferguson, C. A. (1959). Diglossia. *Word, 15,* 325–40.

Fishman, J. (1966). *Language loyalty in the United States: The maintenance and perpetuation of non-English mother tongues by American ethnic and religious groups.* The Hague: Mouton de Gruyter.

Fishman, J. (1991). *Language and ethnicity.* Philadelphia, PA: John Benjamins.

Fishman, J. (2001). *Can threatened languages be saved?* Clevedon: Multilingual Matters.

Flowerdew, L. (2012). Corpus based discourse analysis. In J. P. Gee & M. Handford (eds.), *The Routledge handbook of discourse analysis* (pp. 174–87). New York: Routledge.

Fowler, F. J., Jr. (2013). *Survey research methods,* 5th ed. Thousand Oaks, CA: Sage.

Fuller, J. M. (2003). Use of the discourse marker *like* in interviews. *Journal of Sociolinguistics, 7*(3), 365–77. Available at https://doi.org/10.1111/1467-9481.00229.

Fuller, J. M. (2005). The uses and meanings of the female title Ms. *American Speech, 80*(2), 180–206. Available at https://doi.org/10.1215/00031283-80-2-180.

Gal, S. (1979). *Language shift. Social determinants of linguistic change in bilingual Austria.* New York: Academic Press.

Garvin, R. (2010). Postmodern walking tour. In E. Shohamy, E. Ben-Rafael, & M. Barni (eds.), *Linguistic landscape in the city* (pp. 254–76). Clevedon: Multilingual Matters.

Gee, J. P. (2011). *How to do discourse analysis: A toolkit.* New York: Routledge.

Gee, J. P. (2014). *An introduction to discourse analysis: Theory and method,* 4th ed. New York: Routledge.

Gee, J. P. (2015). *Social linguistics and literacies: Ideology in discourses,* 5th ed. New York: Routledge.

Gee, J. P. (2017). *Teaching, learning, literacy in our high-tech world: A framework for becoming human.* New York: Teachers College Press.

Giles, H. R., Bourhis, R., & Taylor, D. M. (1977). Towards a theory of language in ethnic group relations. In H. Giles (ed.), *Language, ethnicity, and intergroup relations* (pp. 307–48). London: Academic Press.

Glaser, B. G. (1992). *Basics of grounded theory analysis.* Mill Valley, CA: Sociology Press.

Glaser, B. G., & Strauss, A. L. (1967). *The discovery of grounded theory.* Chicago, IL: Aldine.

Glesne, C. (2015). *Becoming qualitative researchers: An introduction,* 5th ed. New York, NY: Pearson.

Goffman, E. (1981). *Forms of talk.* Philadelphia, PA: University of Pennsylvania Press.

Goodwin, M. H. (1990). *He-said she-said: talk as social organization among black children.* Indianapolis, IN: Indiana University Press.

Graff, G., Birkenstein, C., & Durst, R. (2014). *"They say/I say": The moves that matter in academic writing,* 3rd ed. New York: Norton.

Grundmann, R., & Krishnamurthy, R. (2010). The discourse of climate change: A corpus-based approach. *Critical Approaches to Discourse Analysis Across the Disciplines, 4*(2), 125–46. Available at http://www.lancaster.ac.uk/fass/journals/cadaad/.

Grundmann, R., & Scott, M. (2012). Disputed climate science in the media: Do countries matter? *Public Understanding of Science, 23*(2), 220–35. Available at https://doi.org/10.1177%2F0963662512467732.

Guest, G., Namey, E., & Mitchell, M. (2013). *Collecting qualitative data: A field guild for applied research*. Thousand Oaks, CA: Sage.

Guy, G. (2014). Words and numbers: Statistical analysis in sociolinguistics. In J. Holmes & K. Hazen (eds.), *Research methods in sociolinguistics: A practical guide* (pp. 194–210). Malden, MA: Wiley.

Hansen, A., & Machin, D. (2008). Visually branding the environment: Climate change as a marketing opportunity. *Discourse Studies, 10*(6), 777–94. Available at https://doi.org/10.1177%2F1461445608098200.

Hazen, K. (2014). A historical assessment of research questions in sociolinguistics. In J. Holmes & K. Hazen (eds.), *Research methods in sociolinguistics: A practical guide* (pp. 7–22). Malden, MA: Wiley-Blackwell.

Heath, S. B. (1983). *Ways with words: Language, life and work in communities and classrooms*. Cambridge: Cambridge University Press.

Heigham, J., & Croker, R. A. (2009). Glossary of qualitative research terms. In J. Heigham & R. A. Croker (eds.), *Qualitative research in applied linguistics: A practical introduction* (pp. 306–24). New York: Palgrave MacMillan.

Herring, S. C. (2004). Computer-mediated discourse analysis: An approach to researching online communities. In S. A. Barab, R. King, & J. H. Gray (eds.), *Designing for virtual communities in the service of learning* (pp. 338–76). New York: Cambridge University Press.

Hoffman, M. (2014). Sociolinguistic interviews. In J. Holmes & K. Hazen (eds.), *Research methods in sociolinguistics: A practical guide* (pp. 25–41). Malden, MA: Wiley.

Holmes, J. (1995). *Women, men, and politeness*. London: Longman.

Holmes, J. (2006). *Gendered talk at work*. Oxford: Wiley-Blackwell.

Holmes, J. (2015). Discourse in the workplace. In D. Tannen, H. Hamilton, & D. Schiffrin (eds.), *The handbook of discourse analysis*, 2nd ed. New York: Routledge.

Holmes, J., & Hazen, K. (eds.) (2014). *Research methods in sociolinguistics: A practical guide*. Malden, MA: Wiley-Blackwell.

Holmes, J., & Wilson, N. (2017). *An introduction to sociolinguistics*. New York, NY: Routledge.

Horvath, B. M. (1985). *Variation in Australian English: The sociolects of Sydney*. Cambridge: Cambridge University Press.

Hutchby, I., & Tanna, V. (2008). Aspects of sequential organization in text message exchange. *Discourse & Communication, 2*(2), 143–64. Available at https://doi.org/10.1177%2F1750481307088481.

Hymes, D. H. (1972). On communicative competence. In J. B. Pride, & J. Holmes (eds.), *Sociolinguistics: Selected readings* (pp. 269–93). Harmondsworth: Penguin Books.

Irvine, J. T., & Gal, S. (2000). Language ideology and linguistic differentiation. In P. Kroskrity (ed.), *Regimes of language: Ideologies, polities, and identities*. (pp. 35–84). Santa Fe, NM: School of American Research Press.

Jaeger, R. M. (1988). Survey research methods in education. In D. Nunan (ed.), *Research Methods in Language Learning* (p. 140). Cambridge: Cambridge University Press.

Jaffe, A. (1999). *Ideologies in action: Language politics in Corsica.* Berlin: Mouton de Gruyter.

Jaffe, A. (2007). Minority language movements. In M. Heller (ed.), *Bilingualism: A social approach* (pp. 50–70). Basingstoke: Palgrave Macmillan.

Jaffe, A. (2009). Stance in a Corsican school: Institutional and ideological orders. In A. Jaffe (ed.), *Stance: Sociolinguistic Perspectives* (pp. 119–45). Oxford: Oxford University Press.

Jaffe, A. (2014). Anthropological analysis in sociolinguistics. In J. Holmes & K. Hazen (eds.), *Research methods in sociolinguistics: A practical guide* (pp. 213–29). Malden, MA: Wiley-Blackwell.

Jaffe, A., Androutsopoulos, J., Sebba, M., & Johnson, S. (eds.) (2012). *Orthography as social action: Scripts, spelling, identity, and power.* Berlin: Mouton de Gruyter.

Johnstone, B. (2009a). Pittsburghese shirts: Commodification and the enregisterment of an urban dialect. *American Speech, 84*(2), 157–75. Available at https://doi.org/10.1215/00031283-2009-013.

Johnstone, B. (2009b). Stance, style, and the linguistic individual. In A. Jaffe (ed.), *Stance: Sociolinguistic perspectives* (pp. 29–52). New York: Oxford University Press.

Johnstone, B. (2013). *Speaking Pittsburghese: The story of a dialect.* New York: Oxford University Press.

Johnstone, B. (2018). *Discourse analysis,* 3rd ed. Oxford: Wiley-Blackwell.

Jones, R. H. (2012). *Discourse analysis: A resource book for students.* Oxford: Wiley-Blackwell.

Jongensen, D. (1989). *Participant observation.* Newbury Park, CA: Sage.

Journal of Sociolinguistics. (2018). Overview. Available at https://onlinelibrary.wiley.com/journal/14679841.

Kachru, B. B. (1986). The power and politics of English. *World Englishes, 5*(2–3), 120–40. Available at https://doi.org/10.1111/j.1467-971X.1986.tb00720.x.

Kachru, B. B. (1992). *The other tongue: English across cultures.* Urbana, IL: University of Illinois Press.

KhosraviNik, M. (2010). The representation of refugees, asylum seekers and immigrants in British newspapers: A critical discourse analysis. *Journal of Language and Politics, 9*(1), 1–28. Available at https://doi.org/10.1075/jlp.9.1.01kho.

Kiesling, S. F. (2004). Dude. *American Speech, 79*(3), 281–305. Available at https://doi.org/10.1215/00031283-79-3-281.

Kozinets, R. V. (2010). *Netnography: Doing ethnographic research online.* Thousand Oaks, CA: Sage Publications.

Kuh, G. D. (2008). *High-impact educational practices: What they are, who has access to them, and why they matter.* Washington DC: Association of American Colleges and Universities. Available at https://www.aacu.org/.

Kulkarni, D. (2014). Exploring Jakobson's "phatic function" in instant messaging interactions. *Discourse & Communication, 8*(2), 117–36. Available at https://doi.org/10.1177%2F1750481313507150.

Kurath, H., & McDavid, R. I. (1960). *The pronunciation of English in the Atlantic states.* Ann Arbor, MI: University of Michigan.

Labov, W. (1963). The social motivation of a sound change. *Word, 19,* 273–309. Available at https://doi.org/10.1080/00437956.1963.11659799.

Labov, W. (1966). *The social stratification of English in New York City.* Washington, DC: Center for Applied Linguistics.
Labov, W. (1972a). *Language in the inner city: Studies in the black English vernacular.* Philadelphia, PA: University of Pennsylvania Press.
Labov, W. (1972b). *Sociolinguistic patterns.* Philadelphia, PA: University of Pennsylvania Press.
Labov, W. (2005). *Atlas of North American English: Phonetics, phonology and sound change.* The Hague: Mouton de Gruyter.
Labov, W. (2010). *Principles of language change: Social factors.* Malden, MA: Wiley-Blackwell.
Landry, R., & Bourhis, R. (1997). Linguistic landscape and ethnolinguistic vitality: an empirical study. *Journal of Language and Social Psychology, 16*(1), 23–49. Available at https://doi.org/10.1177%2F0261927X970161002.
Langfitt, F. (2015, June 1). So long "Cinderella," website helps Chinese find better English names. *NPR.* Avaiable at https://www.npr.org/sections/parallels/2015/04/20/400399802/so-long-cinderella-website-helps-chinese-find-better-english-names.
Lawrence, C.B. (2012). The Korean linguistic landscape. *World Englishes, 31*(1), 70–92. Available at https://doi.org/10.1111/j.1467-971X.2011.01741.x.
Li, W., & Milroy, L. (1995). Conversational code-switching in a Chinese community in Britain: A sequential analysis. *Journal of Pragmatics, 23*(3), 281–99. Available at https://doi.org/10.1016/0378-2166(94)00026-B.
Liao, S. (2008). A perceptual dialect study of Taiwan Mandarin: Language attitudes in the era of political battle. In M.K.M. Chan & H. Kang (eds.), *Proceedings of the 20th North American conference on Chinese linguistics* (pp. 391–408). Columbus, Ohio: The Ohio State University. Available at https://naccl.osu.edu/sites/naccl.osu.edu/files/21_liao-s.pdf.
Lopatto, D. (2003). The essential features of undergraduate research. *CUR Quarterly 23*(3), 139–42. Available at https://www.cur.org/.
Lopatto, D. (2010). Undergraduate research as a high-impact student experience. *Peer Review, 12*(2). Available at https://www.aacu.org/peerreview.
Lowie, W., & Seton, B. (2013). *Essential statistics for applied linguistics.* London: Palgrave Macmillan.
Macaulay, R.K.S. (1997). *Language, social class, and education: A Glasgow study.* Edinburgh: Edinburgh University Press.
Macaulay, R. K. S. (2009). *Quantitative methods in sociolinguistics.* London, UK: Palgrave Macmillan.
Martin, J. R. (2000). Beyond exchange: APPRAISAL systems in English. In S. Hunston & G. Thompson (eds.), *Evaluation in text: Authorial stance and the construction of discourse* (pp. 142–75). Oxford: Oxford University Press.
Mautner, G. (2007). Mining large corpora for social information: The case of elderly. *Language in Society, 36*(1), 51–72. Available at https://doi.org/10.1017/S0047404507070030.
Maxwell, J. A. (2013). *Qualitative research design: An interactive approach,* 3rd ed. Thousand Oaks, CA: Sage
McEnery, T., & Hardie, A. (2012). *Corpus linguistics.* Cambridge, UK: Cambridge.
McEnery, T., & Wilson, A. (2001). *Corpus linguistics: An introduction,* 2nd ed. Edinburgh: Edinburgh University Press.

McEnery, T., Xiao, R., & Tono, Y. (2006). *Corpus-based language studies: An advanced resource book*. New York, NY: Routledge.

McPherron, P. (2009). "My name is Money": Name choices and global identifications at a South Chinese university. *Asia Pacific Journal of Education, 29*(4), 521–36. Available at https://doi.org/10.1080/02188790903312706.

McPherron, P. (2016). English in the professional lives of college graduates in China. *TESOL Quarterly, 50*(2), 494–507. Available at https://doi.org/10.1002/tesq.305.

McPherron, P. (2017). *Internationalizing teaching, localizing learning: An examination of English language teaching reforms and English use in China*. London: Palgrave Macmillan.

Menard, S. (2002). *Quantitative applications in the social sciences: Longitudinal research*. Thousand Oaks, CA: Sage.

Menard-Warwick, J. (2005). Transgression narratives, dialogic voicing and cultural change. *Journal of Sociolinguistics, 9*(4), 534–57. Available at https://doi.org/10.1111/j.1360-6441.2005.00305.x.

Menard-Warwick, J. (2008). Because she made the beds every day: Social positioning, classroom discourse, and language learning. *Applied Linguistics, 29*(2), 267–89. Available at https://doi.org/10.1093/applin/amm053.

Mesthrie, R., Swann, J., Deumert, A., & Leap, W. (2009). *Introducing sociolinguistics*, 2nd ed. Amsterdam: John Benjamins.

Meyerhoff, M., & Schleef, E. (eds.) (2010). *The Routledge sociolinguistics reader*. New York: Routledge.

Miles, M. B., & Huberman, A. M. (1994). *Qualitative data analysis: A sourcebook of new methods*, 2nd ed. Thousand Oaks, CA: Sage.

Milner, R. M. (2011). The study of cultures online: Some methodological and ethical tensions. *Graduate Journal of Social Science, 8*(3), 14–35. Available at http://gjss.org/sites/default/files/issues/chapters/papers/Journal-08-03--01-Milner.pdf.

Milroy, L. (1987). *Language and social networks*, 2nd ed. Oxford: Blackwell.

Moore, E., & Podesva, R. (2009). Style, indexicality, and the social meaning of tag questions. *Language in Society, 38*(4), 447–85. Available at https://doi.org/10.1017/S0047404509990224.

Morris, J. (2014). The influence of social factors on minority language engagement amongst young people: An investigation of Welsh-English bilinguals in North Wales. *International Journal of the Sociology of Language, 230*, 65–89. Available at https://doi.org/10.1515/ijsl-2014-0027.

Mühlhausler, P. (1991). Overview of the pidgin and creole languages of Australia. In S. Romaine (ed.), *Language in Australia* (pp. 159–73). Cambridge: Cambridge University Press. Available at https://doi.org/10.1017/CBO9780511620881.011.

Myers-Scotton, C. (1993). *Social motivation for code-switching*. Oxford: Clarendon.

Nardi, P. (2014). *Doing survey research*, 3rd ed. New York, NY: Routledge.

Negrón, R. (2011). *Ethnic identification among urban Latinos: Language and flexibility*. El Paso, TX: LFB Scholarly Publishers.

Negrón, R. (2014). New York City's Latino ethnolinguistic repertoire and the negotiation of latinidad in conversation. *Journal of Sociolinguistics, 18*(1), 87–118. Available at https://doi.org/10.1111/josl.12063.

Nunan, D. (1992). *Research methods in language learning*. Cambridge: Cambridge University Press.

Orton, H., & Wright, N. (1974). *A world geography of England.* New York: Seminar Press.
Phillipson, R. (1992). *Linguistic imperialism.* Cambridge: Cambridge University Press.
Phillipson, R. (2009). *Linguistic imperialism continued.* New York: Routledge.
Piller, I. (2016). *Linguistic diversity and social justice: An introduction to applied sociolinguistics.* New York: Oxford University Press.
Pope, J., Meyerhoff, M., & Ladd, D. R. (2007). Forty years of language change on Martha's Vineyard. *Language, 83*(3), 615–27. Available at http://www.jstor.org/stable/40070904.
Porcel, J. (2006). The paradox of Spanish among Miami Cubans. *Journal of Sociolinguistics, 10*(1), 93–110. Available at https://doi.org/10.1111/j.1360-6441.2006.00319.x.
Preston, D. (1996). Where the worst English is spoken. In E. Schneider (ed.), *Focus on the USA* (pp. 29–360). Amsterdam: John Benjamins.
Preston, D. (1998). They speak bad English in the South & New York City, don't they? In L. Bauer & P. Trudgill (eds.), *Language myths* (pp. 139–49). Harmondsworth: Penguin.
Rasinger, S. (2010). Quantitative methods: Concepts, frameworks, and issues. In L. Litosseliti (ed.), *Research methods in linguistics* (pp. 49–67). New York: Continuum.
Reyes, A. (2005). Appropriation of African American slang by Asian youth. *Journal of Sociolinguistics, 9*(4), 509–32. Available at https://doi.org/10.1111/j.1360-6441.2005.00304.x.
Reyes, A., & Lo, A. (eds.) (2009). *Beyond yellow English: Toward a linguistic anthropology of Asian Pacific America.* New York: Oxford University Press.
Riazi, A.M. (2016). *The Routledge encyclopedia of research methods in applied linguistics.* New York: Routledge.
Richards, K. (2003). *Qualitative inquiry in TESOL.* New York: Palgrave Macmillan.
Richards, K. (2009). Interview. In J. Heigham & R. A. Croker (eds.), *Qualitative research in applied linguistics: A practical introduction* (pp. 182–99). New York: Palgrave Macmillan.
Rickford, J. (1986). The need for new approaches to social class analysis in sociolinguistics. *Language and Communication, 6*(3), 215–21. https://doi.org/10.1016/0271-5309(86)90024-8.
Rickford, J. (1999). Ebonics controversy in my backyard: A sociolinguist's experiences and reflections. *Journal of Sociolinguistics, 3*(2), 267–75. Available at https://doi.org/10.1111/1467-9481.00076.
Rickford, J. R., & Rickford, R. J. (2000). *Spoken soul: The story of Black English.* New York: John Wiley & Sons.
Rose, H., & McKinley, J. (2017). Realities of doing research in applied linguistics. In J. McKinley & H. Rose (eds.), *Doing research in applied linguistics: Realities, dilemmas, and solutions* (pp. 1–18). New York: Routledge.
Roulston, K. (2012). Interviews in qualitative research. In C. A. Chapelle (ed.), *The encyclopedia of applied linguistics.* doi:10.1002/9781405198431.wbeal0572.
Rubin, D.L. (1992). Nonlanguage factors affecting undergraduates' judgments of nonnative English-speaking teaching assistants. *Research in Higher Education, 33*(4), 511–31. Available at https://doi.org/10.1007/BF00973770.
Sayer, P. (2010). Using the linguistic landscape as a pedagogical resource. *ELT Journal, 64*(2), 143–54. Available at https://doi.org/10.1093/elt/ccp051.

Schiffrin, D. (1994). *Approaches to discourse: Language as social interaction.* Hoboken, NJ: John Wiley & Sons.

Schleef, E. (2014). Written surveys and questionnaires in sociolinguistics. In J. Holmes & K. Hazen (eds.). *Research methods in sociolinguistics: A practical guide* (pp. 42–57). Malden, MA: Wiley-Blackwell.

Shin, H. (2012). From FOB to COOL: Transnational migrant students in Toronto and the styling of global linguistic capital. *Journal of Sociolinguistics, 16*(2), 184–200. Available at https://doi.org/10.1111/j.1467-9841.2011.00523.x.

Shohamy, E., & Gorter, D. (eds.) (2009). *Linguistic landscapes: Expanding the scenery.* Clevedon: Multilingual Matters.

Shohamy, E., Ben-Rafael, E., & Barni. E. (eds.) (2010). *Linguistic landscape in the city.* Bristol: Multilingual Matters.

Sierra, S. (2016). Playing out loud: Videogame references as resources in friend interaction for managing frames, epistemics, and group identity. *Language in Society, 45*(2), 217–45. Available at https://doi.org/10.1017/S0047404516000026.

Silverstein, M. (2003). Indexical order and the dialectics of sociolinguistic life. *Language & Communication, 23*(3–4), 193–229. Available at https://doi.org/10.1016/S0271-5309(03)00013-2.

Simons, F., & Fennig, C.D. (eds.) (2018). *Ethnologue: Languages of the world*, 21st ed. Dallas, TX: SIL International. Available at http://www.ethnologue.com.

Simpson, J. (2002). Computer-mediated communication. *ELT Journal, 56*(4), 414–15.

Skutnabb-Kangas, T. (2000). *Linguistic human rights.* Berlin: Mouton de Gruyter.

Smakman, D. (2018). *Discovering sociolinguistics: From theory to method.* London: Palgrave.

Sutherland, S. (2015). *A beginner's guide to discourse analysis.* London: Palgrave.

Tagliamonte, S. (2011). *Variationist sociolinguistics: Change, observation, interpretation.* Oxford, UK: Wiley-Blackewell

Tagliamonte, S. A., & D'Arcy, A. (2004). He's like, she's like: The quotative system in Canadian youth. *Journal of Sociolinguistics, 8*(4), 493–514. Available at https://doi.org/10.1111/j.1467-9841.2004.00271.x.

Tagliamonte, S. A., & D'Arcy, A. (2007). Frequency and variation in the community grammar: Tracking a new change through the generations. *Language Variation and Change, 19*(2), 199–217. Available at https://doi.org/10.1017/S095439450707007X.

Tagliamonte, S. A., & D'Arcy, A. (2009). Peaks beyond phonology: Adolescence, incrementation, and language change. *Language, 85*(1), 58–108. Available at https://doi.org/10.1353/lan.0.0084.

Tagliamonte, S., & Hudson, R. (1999). Be like et al. beyond America: The quotative system in British and Canadian youth. *Journal of Sociolinguistics, 3*(2), 147–72. Available at https://doi.org/10.1111/1467-9481.00070.

Tagliamonte, S., & Roberts, C. (2005). So weird; so cool; so innovative: The use of intensifiers in the television series *Friends. American Speech, 80*(3), 280–300. Available at https://doi.org/10.1215/00031283-80-3-280.

Tannen, D. (1994). *Gender and discourse.* New York: Oxford University Press.

Tannen, D. (2004). Talking the dog: Framing pets as interactional resources in family discourse. *Research on Language and Social Interaction, 37*(4), 399–420. Available at https://doi.org/10.1207/s15327973rlsi3704_1.

Tognini-Bonelli, E. (2001). *Corpus linguistics at work.* Amsterdam: John Benjamins.

Trudgill, P. (1974). *The social differentiation of English in Norwich.* Cambridge: Cambridge University Press.

VanderStoep, S. W., & Johnson, D. D. (2009) *Research methods for everyday life: Blending qualitative and quantitative approaches.* San Francisco, CA: John Wiley & Sons.

Wardhaugh, R., & Fuller, J. M. (2015). *An introduction to sociolinguistics*, 7th ed. Malden, MA: Wiley Blackwell.

Waring, H. Z. (2017). *Discourse analysis: The questions discourse analysts ask and how they answer them.* New York, NY: Routledge.

Wenger, E. (1999). *Communities of practice: Learning, meaning, and identity.* Cambridge: Cambridge University Press.

Wodak, R. E. (2018). Language and politics. In J. Culpeper, P. Kerswill, R. Wodak, T. McEnery, & F. Katamba (eds.), *English language: Description, variation, and context*, 2nd ed. Basingstoke: Palgrave Macmillan.

Wortham, S., & Reyes, A. (2015). *Discouse analysis: Beyond the speech event.* Abingdon, UK: Routledge.

Yuasa, I. P. (2010). Creaky voice: A new feminine voice quality for young urban-oriented upwardly mobile American women? *American Speech, 85*(3), 315–37. Available at https://doi.org/10.1215/00031283-2010-018.

Zhang, Q. (2008). Rhotacization and the "Beijing smooth operator": The meaning of a sociolinguistic variable. *Journal of Sociolinguistics, 12*(2), 210–22. Available at https://doi.org/10.1111/j.1467-9841.2008.00362.x.

Index

AAVE (African American Vernacular English) x, 9, 18, 48
Alim, H. Samy 8, 13, 18, 33, 69, 229
AntCone 170
ATLAS.ti 113
Axial codes 113, 220

Back-channeling 61–62, 71, 130, 131, 137, 220
Bailey, Benjamin 78, 229
Becker, Kara 10, 50, 64, 115, 146, 150–154, 157, 161–162, 189, 193, 195, 201, 204, 209–210, 229–230
Bell, Allan 3, 6, 193, 213–214, 230
Bilingual/bilingualism 15, 69, 73, 84, 126, 135, 138, 140, 143, 154, 187, 189, 199, 202, 205, 207, 210, 213–214, 220
British Academic Written English Corpus (BAWE) 169
British National Corpus (BNC) 165, 169
Bucholtz, Mary 10, 34, 120, 209, 230

Canagarajah, Suresh 12, 230
Cascade model of language change 92, 94,
Chain sampling 45–46
Chain-shifting of vowels and accents x
Chi-square test 150, 163
Chun, Christian W. 99, 100, 101
Class stratification 79
Closed questions 15, 47, 48
Cluster sampling 44, 45, 47
Code-meshing 14, 220

Code-mixing 65, 67, 220
Code-switching 4, 11–14, 32, 34, 65, 67, 73, 74, 76, 84, 93, 97, 127, 136, 138, 141–143, 194, 199, 204–205, 213, 220
Cohesion 133
Collocation 133, 171, 173, 175, 177, 181
Concordance (KWIC key word in context) 172, 221–222
Conversation Analysis (CA) 14, 34, 35, 127, 128, 208, 221
Communities of practice (COP) 4, 6, 29, 202, 208, 220
Computer-mediated Communication (CMC) 90–101, 102, 104–106, 221
Computer-mediated Data (CMD) 90–92, 100, 104
Construct validity 148, 221
Contact linguistics 33
Continuous variable 147
Convenience sampling 45–46, 97, 221
Conversation Analysis (CA) 11, 14, 35, 127, 128, 208, 221–222
Corpora xvi, 158–159, 165–176, 178–179, 181, 221
Corpus-based research 165–168, 176, 178, 181–182, 230, 232, 236
Corpus-driven research 165, 167–168, 181
Corpus linguistics 34–35, 133, 165, 166, 169, 171, 173, 182, 221, 229–230, 235, 239
Corpus of Contemporary American English (COCA) 165, 168, 169, 171–174, 231

Corpus of London Teenage Language
  (COLT) 176
Correlation 151
Correlation tests 164
Coupland, Nikolas 6, 12, 14, 209,
  214, 231
Creaky voice 68–70, 137, 222, 239
Creoles 7–8, 14, 69, 236
Critical Discourse Analysis
  (CDA) 127–128, 221–222
Cross-sectional research 20
Cross-sectional survey 43
Cutler, Cecilia 9, 79, 231

D'Arcy, Alex 9, 15, 48, 146, 238,
Data saturation 98, 109–110, 222
Data set 33, 78, 149–150, 198, 222, 227
Deductive Approach 15–18
Dependent variable 146
Description validity 123
Descriptive statistics xv, 41, 44, 145,
  146, 149–151, 156, 158, 161,163,
  222, 224, 226
Deumert, Ana 5, 35, 165, 178, 189,
  203, 214–215, 231
Dialect 4–5, 7, 8, 9, 10, 11, 23, 25,
  62, 76, 101, 134, 166, 179, 181,
  195, 220, 222, 234, 235, 238
Dialectology 7–8, 33, 222
Diglossia 6–8, 222–232
Discourse Analysis (DA) xv, 4, 11,
  34–36, 62, 65, 81, 109, 120, 122,
  124–137, 140–144, 168, 199,
  220–222, 231, 232–234, 238–239
Discourse markers 54–55, 73, 136,
  212, 223, 232
Dispersion 171, 222
Domain 32, 94, 140, 198, 204, 223
Dörnyei, Zoltan Q. 15, 19, 30, 41,
  49, 58, 155, 164, 231

Eckert, Penelope 8–10, 17, 29, 34,
  78, 149, 195, 210, 214, 231
Ellipsis 131, 133, 223

Emic 17, 72, 83, 109, 223
Enregisterment 195, 234
Epistemics 238
Ethicality 36
Ethnographic research/studies xv, 8,
  11, 17–18, 29, 72–73, 84, 92, 99,
  100–101, 106, 109, 129, 178,
  223, 228
Ethnography xv, 223, 225,
Ethnolinguistic 137–139
Ethnolinguistic Vitality 7
Ethnoracial 139
Etic 17, 72, 83, 223

Facebook Surveys 52
Factor analysis 163
Factor weights 151
Falsetto 137
Fieldwork 59, 71, 74, 84, 91, 223,
  225, 231–232
Filler words 62, 85, 219
First-order Indexicality 12, 224
Focus group 59–60, 224
Footing 139–140
Framework 15, 29, 125–126, 232,
  237
Frame/ framing 83–84, 93, 122, 135,
  177, 227, 238
Frequency 126–127, 170–172,
  175–180, 226, 238
Fuller, Janet 3, 5, 33, 232, 239
Functionalist 7
Functional-structuralist 7

Gatekeeper 74, 76
Gee, James Paul 11, 125, 126, 144,
  232
Generalizability 12, 16–17, 36,
  44, 45, 51, 56, 123, 148–150,
  162–164, 166, 181, 219,
  221–227
Genre 73, 134–166, 169, 190
Gravity model of linguistic change 94
Grounded theory 98, 223, 231–232

Heath, Shirley Brice 11, 17, 78, 233
Hedge 74, 127, 136
High Rising Terminal (HRT) or Uptalk 137, 179–181, 224
Holmes, Janet 36
Hymes, Dell 11, 230, 233
Hypercorrect 8
Hypothesis 148, 150, 151, 161, 162, 163, 164, 224, 225, 226
Hypothetico-deductive Approach 15

Independent variable 146
Indexical 29, 81, 145
Indexicality 12, 55, 84, 110, 196, 224, 236, 238
Indexing 23, 87, 140
Inductive Approach 18, 109
Inferential statistics xv, 41, 44, 145, 149, 150–151, 156, 163, 222, 224, 226
Interactional Sociolinguistics 128, 129
Interlocutor 6, 54, 75, 80, 91, 96, 102, 104, 124, 127, 136, 221
Intermode data 104
Interpretive validity 123
Intertextuality 82, 84–85
Interval variable 147
Interview xv, 9–12, 17, 19, 31–36, 42–45, 48, 51, 56–71, 72–73, 76–78, 80–81, 88, 95, 97–98, 104, 105, 109–111, 113–115, 118–119, 121–122, 129, 132, 139–140, 142, 145, 152–155, 166, 178–179, 181, 197–201, 204, 206, 220, 223, 225, 232–233, 237
Intramode data 104
Iterative process 98

Jaffe, Alexandra 17, 34, 72, 73, 78, 84
Johnstone, Barbara 34, 62, 135, 144, 196, 234
Journal of Sociolinguistics 3–4, 28, 68, 82, 189, 229–232, 234, 236–239

Keying 84
Keyword 174–175
Keyword in Context (KWIC) 171
Kiesling, Scott 9–10, 27, 54–55, 116, 149, 193, 212, 215, 235

Labov, William x, 5, 8, 10, 12, 29, 33, 60, 62, 64, 79, 81, 92, 94, 152, 209, 225, 234–235
Language Ideology 6, 11, 84, 224, 233
Language shift 7, 10, 14, 32, 78, 84, 166, 205, 224 227, 232
Language variation 6, 8–9, 23, 27, 29, 33–34, 46, 48, 54, 65, 68–69, 94, 115, 144–145, 151–152, 154, 162, 166
Latching 130–131, 137
Lexander, Kristin Vold 5, 165, 178, 189, 203, 214–215, 231
Liao, Silvie 11–12, 235
Likert rating scale 15, 47, 54–56, 147, 155, 175, 201, 206, 224,
Linguistic anthropology 33, 34, 138, 229, 237
Linguistic Inquiry and Word Count (LIWC) 170–171
Linguistic landscape (LL) 34, 90–97, 100–102, 104, 114–115, 195, 198, 212, 224
Linguistic repertoire 11, 137, 195, 209, 236
Linguistic variable 130, 134, 138, 146–148, 152, 154, 209, 221, 227–228, 239
Longitudinal research 11, 20, 37, 43–44, 73, 84, 136, 225, 236
Lowie, Wander 149, 162–164, 235

Malinowski, Bronislaw 96
Mann-Whitney U test 151
Matched Guise Technique 15
Maximum variation sampling 45
McPherron, Paul 19–20, 24–25, 27, 30, 114, 116–117, 236

Mean   149–151, 156, 222
Median   149, 151, 222
Member validation   123
Menard-Warwick, Julia   33, 118–120, 236
Michigan Corpus of Academic Spoken English (MICASE)   169
Milroy, Lesley   5, 9, 12, 235, 236,
Mixed-methods research design, qual/quan   19, 154
Mode   149–151, 222
Moore, Emma   17, 150, 193, 195, 201, 236
Morris, Jonathan   47, 51, 147, 149, 150–157, 161, 188–189, 192–193, 201, 203, 211–214, 236
Multilingualism   6, 8, 14, 95, 101, 136, 166, 179, 190, 220, 227
Multivariate analysis   150

Negrón, Rosalyn   11, 129, 132, 137–141, 144, 191, 192–193, 198–199, 236
Nominal variable   147
Non-probability sampling   44–45, 225
Non-rhotic/ity   5, 64, 152–154, 189, 204, 237
Null hypothesis   148, 150–151, 163, 224–226
Nunan, David   15–16, 42, 48, 148, 236

Open interview   63–66, 77
Open questions   47
Operationalization   162
Ordinal variable   147, 151
Orthography   84, 234
Overlap   83, 96, 99, 127, 131, 137, 154

Participant-designed research   8–9,
Participant-observation research   11, 34, 59, 72–89, 100, 104, 109, 138, 223, 227, 231, 234

Pennycook, Alistair   12
Phatic communication – interpersonal communication   92, 95–96, 235
Phoneme   68
Pidgins   7, 8, 14, 69, 179, 236
Podesva, Robert   10, 17, 150, 193, 195, 201–202, 209, 236
Postvocalic [r]   8, 225
Pragmatics   32, 34, 179,
Probability sampling   44, 225, 228
Purposeful sampling   45, 227
Purposive sampling   97–98, 225

QSR NVivo   113
Qualitative research
Qual/Quan Mixed Methods
Qualtrics   53
Quantitative research   15
Quotative   9, 48, 74, 126, 136

Random sampling   46, 154
Ratio   150
Reflexive Stance   17, 226
Reflexivity   119, 226
Register   24, 73, 82, 134–137, 165–166, 194–195, 207, 222, 228, 230
Register shifting   73
Reliability   20, 36, 44, 49, 50–51, 123, 226
Reyes, Angela   34, 78–81, 83, 116, 128–131, 140, 144, 192, 212–214, 237
Rhotic/Non-rhotic   5, 152–153, 154
Rhoticity   10, 65, 204, 209–210
Rickford, John R.   x, 8–9, 13, 69, 229

Sample survey   43
Sampling   45–46, 226
Sayer, Peter   34, 90, 98–100, 104–105, 114–115, 193–195, 198–199, 212, 237
Schema   134
Semi-structured interview   63–67, 77

Seton, Bregtje   149, 162, 163, 164, 235
Shohamy, Elana   34, 101, 106, 195, 212, 232
Sierra, Sylvia   78, 82–86, 238
Significance   99, 101, 151, 156, 163, 224, 225–226
Silverstein, Michael   12, 238
Simple random sampling   44, 46–47
Situated learning   11
Skutnabb-Kangas, Tove   8, 13, 238
Smoke, Trudy   60
Snowball sampling   45–46, 226
Social constructivism   110, 226
Sociolinguistic variable   64, 74, 146, 221, 227
Speech community   5
Stance   17, 37, 55, 134–135, 187, 212, 226, 230, 234–235, 1
Stance taking   135
Standard deviation   150
Stratified sampling   45, 46, 47, 227
Structured heterogeneity   8
Structured interview   63, 64, 65
Style shifts   129, 136, 227
Subjective Stance   17
Substitution   133
Survey Monkey   50, 52
Symbolic interactionism   16–17
Synchronic Research   20
Systemic-functional linguistics (SFL)   120, 227
Systemic sampling   44, 46, 97, 227

T-test   163
Tag questions   65
Tagliamonte, Sali   9, 15, 35, 48–49, 146, 165, 168, 176, 179, 180, 238
Tannen, Deborah   11, 12, 36, 238
The *Time* Magazine corpus   169
Theoretical sampling   98
Theoretical validity   123
Thick Description   17, 75, 81, 83, 84, 109, 227
Translanguaging   93, 227
Translingual Approach   12, 227
Transcribe/Transcription   84, 88, 99, 105, 112, 115, 117–118, 121–122, 124, 126 –132, 140–142, 144, 153, 154, 166–169, 176, 180, 199–201, 206, 222
Transcription conventions   130, 131
Triangulation   19, 117
Trudgill, Peter   8, 71, 94, 232, 237, 239
Turn taking   127–128, 137, 221

Uptalk (or HRT high rising terminal)   137, 179, 180, 181, 224

Validity   21, 36, 44, 50, 51, 117, 119, 122, 123, 149, 154, 157, 162, 172, 176, 227–228
Variationist discourse analysis   126–127
Variationist research   8, 228
Variety   xv, 4, 5, 10, 12, 15, 18, 25, 27, 55, 139, 181, 220, 221, 222, 225
Vernacular   x, 9, 229, 235
Vocal fry

Wardaugh, Ronald   3, 5, 239
Wave variation studies   8
Wodak, Ruth   178, 231, 239
WordSmith Tools   170, 177

Yuasa, Ikuko Patricia   33, 68–70, 137, 193, 201

Zero hypothesis   148
Zhang, Qing   9, 23

www.ingramcontent.com/pod-product-compliance
Lightning Source LLC
Chambersburg PA
CBHW080537300426
44111CB00017B/2760